RE-LIVING BRITAIN
IN THE
1940s

This book is dedicated to the memory of
Betty Wichard (née Willetts) – Auxiliary Territorial Service, and
Sergeant Frank Wichard – Dorsets and South Wales Borderers.

It is also dedicated to Trooper Charles Wichard,
43rd Division Reconnaissance, who died trying
to liberate Normandy, June 1944.

RE-LIVING BRITAIN
IN THE
1940s

ROBIN WICHARD

Pen & Sword
MILITARY

Published in Great Britain in 2022 by
PEN & SWORD MILITARY
An imprint of
Pen & Sword Books Ltd
Yorkshire - Philadelphia

© 2022 Robin Wichard

ISBN 978 1 39901 8 128

The right of Robin Wichard to be identified as Author of this work has been asserted by him in accordance with the Copyright, Designs and Patents Act 1988.

A CIP catalogue record for this book is available from the British Library

All rights reserved. No part of this book may be reproduced or transmitted in any form or by any means, electronic or mechanical including photocopying, recording or by any information storage and retrieval system, without permission from the Publisher in writing.

Book Design by Dominic Allen

Printed and bound by CPI Group (UK) Ltd, Croydon, CR0 4YY

Pen & Sword Books Limited incorporates the imprints of Atlas, Archaeology, Aviation, Discovery, Family History, Fiction, History, Maritime, Military, Military Classics, Politics, Select, Transport, True Crime, Air World, Frontline Publishing, Leo Cooper, Remember When, Seaforth Publishing, The Praetorian Press, Wharncliffe Local History, Wharncliffe Transport, Wharncliffe True Crime and White Owl.

For a complete list of Pen & Sword titles please contact:
PEN & SWORD BOOKS LIMITED
47 Church Street, Barnsley, South Yorkshire, S70 2AS, England
E-mail: enquiries@pen-and-sword.co.uk
Website: www.pen-and-sword.co.uk

Or
PEN AND SWORD BOOKS
1950 Lawrence Rd, Havertown, PA 19083, USA
E-mail: Uspen-and-sword@casematepublishers.com
Website: www.penandswordbooks.com

CONTENTS

Introduction 9

CHAPTER ONE: **Choosing an Impression** 15

CHAPTER TWO: **The Leaders** 25

- King George VI 26
- Winston Churchill 31
- Field Marshal Alan Brooke 36
- Field Marshal Bernard Montgomery 40
- Air Chief Marshal Arthur Harris 47

CHAPTER THREE: **The Armed Forces: The Army** 53

- Infantry 57
- Airborne 67
- Auxiliary Territorial Service (ATS) 76
- Royal Artillery 84
- Local Defence Volunteers/Home Guard 90
- Auxiliary Units (Scallywags) 99

CHAPTER FOUR: **The Armed Forces: The Royal Air Force and the Royal Navy**.. 103

- Royal Air Force 103
- Women's Auxiliary Air Force (WAAF)........................... 114
- Air Transport Auxiliary (ATA)... 120
- Observer Corps/Royal Observer Corps...................... 127
- Royal Navy.. 132
- Women's Royal Naval Service (WRNS) 137
- Royal Marines, Commandos and Royal Marine Commandos 143

CHAPTER FIVE: **Civil Defence & Emergency Services roles** 149

- Civil defence personnel 149
- Fire Services 164
- Police... 172

CHAPTER SIX: **WLA & uniformed Voluntary Service roles**........ 181

- Women's Land Army (includes Women's Timber Corps) 181
- Women's Voluntary Service (WVS)............................... 191

CHAPTER SEVEN: **Non-uniformed Voluntary Service & other roles**.. 201

- National Air Raid Precautions Animal Committee (NARPAC) and Peoples' Dispensary for Sick Animals (PDSA).................. 201
- Street Fire Party/Fire Guards....................................... 212
- Miners – 'Bevin Boys'... 216

CHAPTER EIGHT: **Civilians** 223
- Civilian Roles 223
- Spiv 244

CHAPTER NINE: **Roles for children** 249
- Evacuees 249
- Boy Scouts 257
- Girl Guides 264

CHAPTER TEN: **Music & Entertainment** 271
- The Big Bands 274
- Solo Artists 280
- Female Harmony Groups 287
- Radio 290
- Film 294
- Records and gramophones 299

CHAPTER ELEVEN: **Transport** 303
- Military Vehicles 303
- Civilian Vehicles 314
- Trains 323

CHAPTER TWELVE: **Living with the '40s style** 327

CHAPTER THIRTEEN: **Events** 339

APPENDIX: **Acronyms used in the text** 353

INTRODUCTION

The 1930s had been a decade of harsh struggle as the world reeled from the effects of the Great Depression caused by the Wall Street Crash of 29 October 1929. The Crash caused an immediate collapse in demand for British products. By the end of 1930 unemployment in Britain had increased from 1 million to 2.5 million, and the value of exports fell by 50 per cent, plunging industrial towns and cities into poverty. Although a slow recovery had begun by the end of 1931, poverty and unemployment continued to blight the decade.

Added to economic problems were the actions of the European dictators threatening another European, if not world, war. People who had lived through the horrors of the First World War contributed to a strong peace movement in Britain which, in turn, informed the government's policy of appeasement. This policy granted many of Hitler's demands instead of opposing them and, arguably, left Britain ill-prepared for another conflict. Only Churchill spoke out against Hitler and appeasement while advocating preparations for war, but he was a lone voice communicating a sentiment few wanted to hear.

However, Hitler's incessant demands, coupled with the images of death and destruction from the Spanish Civil War – particularly the bombing of Guernica on 26 April 1937 by the German Luftwaffe – increasingly convinced the British people that Churchill was right and fascism could only be overcome by armed force. The Nazi invasion of

Poland on 1 September 1939 was the final straw and Prime Minister Neville Chamberlain declared war on Germany on 3 September 1939, followed shortly afterwards by France.

Supported by soldiers from across the British Empire and beyond, our American and Russian allies and those who had escaped from Nazi-occupied Europe, the Allies emerged triumphant following victory over Japan on 15 August 1945. However, by the end of the Second World War approximately 383,600 British servicemen and women had lost their lives, alongside a further 67,100 civilians. Huge parts of the country's industrial heartlands were destroyed, along with many important towns and cities. The war also left Britain with a debt of £21 billion, including debts to the United States of America of $4.34 billion (a debt which was not finally paid off until 2006). The restoration of peace also saw the dawn of a new world balance of power, with America and Russia as the new super-powers and the British Empire crumbling.

The end of the war also left Britain changed socially. German bombing raids meant that the traditional distinction between the front line and the home front had become blurred, with women playing a key role in the war effort. Well in excess of 7 million British women were employed by 1943, both in civilian roles and in uniform. For example, 1,930,000 women were employed in metal and chemical industries alone, and 212,500 joined the Auxiliary Territorial Service (ATS). Sadly, by 1951 the number of working women had returned to almost pre-war levels, but their legacy fuelled the feminism movements of the 1960s and '70s.

Another impact on society came from wartime rationing. The rationing of food (starting in January 1940) changed the eating habits

INTRODUCTION

of the population for decades to come. Far from a starvation diet, the calorific value of daily rations for an adult was about 3,000 calories – up to 1,000 calories more than is recommended today! The balance of dairy, meat and vegetables was carefully calculated to provide a healthy balance and citizens were urged to do their bit and 'Dig for Victory'. The absence of some food products was even commemorated in song, with dance hall favourite Harry Roy singing 'When Can I Have a Banana Again?' and Arthur Askey announcing in song that 'I Wanna Banana' in 1942. Despite the war ending in 1945, food rationing would continue until midnight on 4 July 1954.

The demand for material for uniforms and parachutes led to the rationing of clothing, which was introduced on 1 June 1940. However, the government were keen to ensure that clothing remained fashionable, in the belief that this would keep up morale at home. With the introduction of the 'CC41' label in 1941 (claimed to stand for 'Clothing Control' or 'Commodity Control' and the year of introduction) the style of clothing was restricted but soon became known for its quality and durability. The government even commissioned top fashion designers to create a collection of thirty-two 'utility' outfits – a move which proved very popular and changed the relationship between fashion designers and High Street outlets for ever. The CC41 label was extended to cover everything from furniture to footwear and even crockery. Many other aspects of life were also subject to rationing or limitations, including paper. The rationing of fuel meant that few private cars were running and people had to use bicycles, public transport or walk.

The presence of American GIs in the build up to D-Day in 1944 also contributed to the changing face of British society. 'Over-paid,

RE-LIVING BRITAIN IN THE 1940S

over-sexed and over-here', the GIs brought with them a range of goods which had not been available in Britain for some years. They also brought new musical influences including R&B, blues and jazz. The jitterbug soon replaced the comparatively staid dances that had previously been popular. Such was the impact of the friendly invasion that some 70,000 British women became GI brides, and an estimated 9,000 children were born out of wedlock.

Few decades have influenced Britain and the British people as much as the 1940s. Many wartime expressions have entered the lexicon of the English language including 'taking flak', the 'Dunkirk Spirit' and the 'Blitz Spirit', and many people still see the wartime years, in Churchill's terms, as 'our finest hour'. Small wonder then that so

Done well living history can almost literally take you back in time. This photograph could represent almost any town high street during the war years.

– With permission David Purkiss

INTRODUCTION

many people choose to dedicate their spare time to recreating the look and atmosphere of that decade. In extending their knowledge and understanding, enthusiasts study their particular area of interest in great detail and try to recreate it as accurately as possible – this is why what they do is known as 'living history'!

This book is intended to help those interested in recreating any aspect of the period by providing a brief contextual history of each major topic, together with some guidance on how to start. It is not, and never could be, complete. There are as many opportunities for impressions as there were jobs during the war years. This book concentrates on the most popular, as well as one or two more interesting, niche roles. There is much that is not covered simply through lack of space – workmen, postmen and women, doctors and nurses, teachers as well as different military and uniformed civilian roles like the Red Cross – but there should be enough guidance here to help anyone begin their journey into living history. It is a journey that few who embark on it ever regret – or completely finish!

Please note, the hyperlink addresses used throughout this book were correct at the time of going to press but may change. Google should give updated contact information where necessary.

CHAPTER ONE

CHOOSING AN IMPRESSION

This guide is intended to help those already in the hobby, and those new to it, to decide on an impression to work up and then showcase examples of excellence as a standard for all to strive towards. In addition to historical context, each chapter will include guidance on where to look for the materials necessary to improve and perfect your impression. If your intention is simply to dress-up then this is not the book for you!

Whatever impression we choose, whether military or civilian, voluntary services or ARP, we owe it to those we represent to be as accurate as reasonably possible. With each year that passes there are fewer people left who survived those turbulent years, so it is left to living historians to continue their legacy and to do that we should strive to be as knowledgeable and accurate as possible. There is no shortcut to a good impression – it takes time, money and research, but the rewards more than justify the effort. Never be afraid to ask for advice – more seasoned campaigners are always willing to help – remember, everyone had to start somewhere. Be open to constructive criticism, but if you see someone inaccurately dressed, do not mock – instead think back to when you started!

In some ways the hardest part of Living History is choosing the impression you want to develop. This has to be tempered with a degree of realism – the average age of the British soldier in the Second World War was 26 and he would have been of slim build. While we might all like to think of ourselves as such, the truth is often far removed and while larger uniforms are available, it is worth questioning how

A collection of road repair equipment creates a dramatic and amusing display as part of the West Somerset Railway 40s Weekend 2019.

– With permission Tim Wetherell

CHOOSING AN IMPRESSION

appropriate that would be. Older men could join the Home Guard or serve as Wardens. Similarly, beards were not allowed in the Army (other than Pioneers) – if you are unwilling to shave, then perhaps a naval impression would be more appropriate. Most impressions are informed by a personal interest (for example owning a military vehicle or a love of the music of the period) but with such a huge range of impressions available to men, women and children, it is important to research the options prior to committing. Occasionally an impression is based on marked physical similarity to a known character.

As with most things, the key to a successful impression is in the details, and the simplest error can undermine all the good work you have done. A beautiful period suit can easily be spoiled by a modern wristwatch and there is nothing more anachronistic than someone in period clothing holding forth on their mobile phone. What living historians strive for are those 'magic moments' which occur when you look around and see nothing other than 'period' around you and it is only a short leap of imagination to believe that you have been transported back in time. Re-enacting is **NOT** dressing up!

There is a valid debate to be had over the merits of using original period clothing and accessories when perfectly acceptable, good quality, reproduction items are available. Ultimately this comes down to individual conscience. Many civilian items are still robust and hard-wearing today, and will not suffer greatly from being worn by 'promenaders' – living historians whose role is to support events by populating them with characters who walk around the event interacting with the general public. 'Promenaders' may represent civilians, or military personnel home on leave. However, for more active military impressions, original '37 and 40' pattern battledress and trousers are getting harder to find, and very good reproductions are available, therefore there is little reason to use original items.

Period accessories can be found in antique and flea markets, auctions and online sites such as eBay. Do your research – be clear about what you want and find out what sort of prices such items are selling for. Prices on eBay are often ridiculously over-inflated so shop around or make the seller an offer (if that facility is available).

Increasingly, a small but enterprising group of charlatans are faking objects, and often placing a 'rare' fake in among a group of more common, original items in order to drive up the prices. If in doubt then ask – there are many specialist sites on Facebook where you can ask for advice. These sites include one devoted to (and named) 'Military Fakes and Forgeries', which includes a list of dealers (and their aliases) who are recognised as traders who habitually – and knowingly – pass off fake items as real. This is well worth checking prior to making any purchase – especially if you are not sure about the authenticity of an item.

Although recreating the atmosphere of the 1940s can be great fun, there is also a responsibility to be objective in the way we do it. It is not the job of living historians to censor history or indeed to pass judgement on it – merely to represent it as accurately as we can in order to preserve the memory, and respect those

1941 Food Ration Card.

– Author's collection

who lived through those times. Everyone has their reasons for the impression they choose – we must respect those choices and learn from them. The wearing of any uniform should not be taken as an indication of a person's views or political affiliations – they are simply living historians enjoying a hobby in which they have invested hours of time and considerable sums of money.

Some living historians are content to wander among crowds individually as 'promenaders' adding valuable atmosphere to events, while others prefer to have a display around them as a focal point for their impression and as a way of engaging the general public. Displays can be of any size from a substantial exhibition of 1940s mining equipment, or of the uniforms and equipment of the Women's Land Army down to just a few items. One of the most imaginative displays seen was also one of the simplest, which also really caught the attention of the public. Dressed in the uniform of a British soldier (a paratrooper as it happened, but any uniform would have had the same effect) the individual was seated, polishing his boots to get a parade shine while listening to a variety of original 78 rpm shellac records on a period gramophone. Veterans of any age immediately connected with the act of polishing boots, while younger members of the public – used to getting their music streamed – were astonished to see the wind-up gramophone and watch the needle being regularly changed. This display attracted a huge amount of attention out of all proportion to its size.

Any serious participant in heritage events will relish the opportunity to meet like-minded enthusiasts and interact with the public. However, such involvement also carries responsibilities. If, while handing a weapon to someone to handle, it was to fall on someone's foot and cause injury then you – as the owner – would be liable. That is why all re-enactors are encouraged to have Third-Party Liability Insurance (PLI). As a member of a recognised group, you will be covered by the group's insurance, but individuals are generally expected to have their own, and many events now make it a requirement for participants. There are two relatively inexpensive ways to obtain this. You can join the 'All Fronts Re-enactment Association' (www.afra.org.uk). Membership of AFRA will mean that you are automatically covered by their group insurance. Alternatively, you may choose to take out insurance with 'Country Cover Club'

Displays do not have to be large in order to beg questions and truly engage the public. This 'Knitting for the Forces' display justifiably attracted a large amount of interest.
— With permission Asia and Tim Wetherell

CHOOSING AN IMPRESSION

(www.ccc3.co.uk/home). Their very modestly priced 'Country Sports Insurance' (which does include re-enactment) offers £12 million in public liability cover as well as £10,000 personal accident cover and £100,000 legal expenses cover.

The key message is that whatever impression you choose, research it and do it to the best of your ability. Simply putting on something which roughly 'looks the part' is insulting to those whose memory you commemorate and to those who invest the time, money and research to get it right. Perhaps this sentiment is best expressed in the words of Helen Ayer Patton, granddaughter of US General George Patton, who has written a charter for Second World War re-enactors:

TO ALL MILITARY WW2 RE-ENACTORS

Wear the Uniforms and Insignia with Respect,
Keeping homage as your main purpose for doing so.

Practice Wisdom, Sensitivity, and Taste
Especially when in the presence of any Veteran or active-duty soldier from any army and any generation.

Be Aware
That once the last living Veteran of the Second World War has departed this earth, your role as the bearer of history's living flame will no longer be scrutinised by the only persons who have earned the total right to judge your act. Therefore I charge you to hone your methods of keeping one another in check in a stringent

yet non-violent way so that those who witness **YOUR** *witness are transported as near to the truth of what really happened as is humanly possible to experience through re-enactment.*

Contemplate
Your passion for paying tribute through acting the part, and accept that once you make a procession bearing the relics and concrete evidence of conflict, you consider yourself seekers of an ultimate permanent peace for this war-weary-world and guardians of the memory of the future.

Work in Union
With those risking their lives to free others, no less deserving of life, love and the pursuit of happiness than those they liberate, defend, or oppose.

Helen Patton 2011
With kind permission.

While the charter refers explicitly to Second World War military re-enactors, the sentiments expressed, and the responsibilities enshrined in the charter, apply equally to civilian re-enactors and those re-enacting uniformed, non-military roles. Together we carry the burden of accurately representing the past and commemorating those who fought and lived through those turbulent times to give us the freedoms we take for granted today.

A veteran of the Second World War – Eddie Robins, then aged 93 - demonstrates ranging on the 25-pounder field gun, eagerly watched by the re-enactors who operate the gun today.

— With permission Garrison Artillery Volunteers 69th field

CHAPTER TWO
THE LEADERS

The vast majority of living historians choose to represent generic individuals of the period (uniformed or civilian), even if their impression was inspired by a specific person. However, a small number of people have chosen to represent well-known political and military figures of the period and heritage events are enriched, for participants and public alike, by their presence, enthusiasm and commitment.

King George VI (Paul Eastwood) and Field Marshal Alan Brooke, Chief of Imperial General Staff (Stefan Dicks) share a moment of pensive reflection. Watchet, 2019.
– With permission Liz Elmont

KING GEORGE VI

The future King George VI was born Prince Albert Frederick Arthur George Saxe-Coburg-Gotha on 14 December 1895. As a child he was referred to as Albert, but within the family he was known as 'Bertie'. As the second son of King George V and Mary of Teck, it was not anticipated that Albert would ever become king. Albert had a challenging childhood. Although he loved his mother, she could be rather distant and aloof, whereas his father was harsh and critical. Albert was a fragile child – often ill and prone to mood swings – and, at the age of eight he developed a stammer which would affect him for the rest of his life. Knock-kneed, young Albert was forced to suffer leg braces for extended periods in an attempt to straighten his legs. Albert was not a naturally gifted student and his challenges were compounded by his tutors forcing him to write with his right hand, despite being left-handed.

Albert entered the Royal Navy Academy (graduating bottom of his class) prior to entering the Royal Navy as a midshipman. During the First World War Albert served on HMS Collingwood and was present at the Battle of Jutland in May 1916. After the war ended, he joined the Royal Air Force and qualified as a pilot. He then went to university at Trinity College, Cambridge, but only completed one year before becoming Duke of York and beginning to undertake public duties on behalf of his father, King George V. Around this time Albert met the attractive 18-year-old Lady Elizabeth Bowes-Lyon, whom he had known as a child. After two rejections, Elizabeth accepted Albert's proposal and they were married on 26 April 1923 at Westminster Abbey. The couple went on to have two daughters – Elizabeth, born 1926 and Margaret, born 1930.

THE LEADERS

King George V died on 20 January 1936 and was succeeded by his eldest son Edward, who ruled as King Edward VIII. Edward was never comfortable in the role and soon became embroiled in a political and constitutional controversy through his close friendship with twice-divorced American, Wallis Simpson. Less than a year after becoming king, Edward abdicated in order to marry Wallis Simpson and Albert was crowned King George VI on 12 May 1937. Understanding the strong pacifist movement in Britain at the time, the new king became a strong supporter of Prime Minister Neville Chamberlain in the hope that another war, for which Britain was poorly prepared, could be averted. In June 1939 the royal couple visited the United States where they were well received by the American people, and began a strong working relationship with President Franklin D. Roosevelt.

When Chamberlain resigned as Prime Minister in May 1940, King George favoured the Foreign Secretary, Lord Halifax as successor. The king was somewhat distrustful of Churchill, who eventually became Prime Minister, but the

Paul Eastwood as King George VI. A great deal of research has been undertaken to ensure that the uniform and medal ribbons are as accurate as possible.

– With permission Paul Eastwood

two men soon put aside their differences and developed a deep mutual respect for each other. The royal couple decided to remain in London during the Blitz and endeared themselves to the people by regular visits to shelters, hospitals and bombed cities. As Queen Elizabeth wrote in a letter at the time, 'The children will not leave unless I do. I shall not leave unless their father does, and the King will not leave the country in any circumstances, whatever.' King George VI visited the British Expeditionary Force in France in 1939 and, in 1943 he visited North Africa, after the victory at El Alamein.

Only ten days after the D-Day landings the king paid a personal visit to the troops in Normandy. Despite the challenges of his upbringing, he became a powerful and well-loved symbol of courage at a time when public confidence in the monarchy was at an all-time low. King George VI died in his sleep on the morning of 6 February 1952.

Today King George VI is represented by Paul Eastwood who is widely recognised at heritage events and is renowned both for the accuracy of his portrayal and his professionalism. Naturally having the looks, poise and mannerisms of the king gave Paul a big advantage when taking on this very high-profile role. Paul is all too aware of the responsibility he bears in portraying King George VI, noting that 'it goes without saying that the responsibility is immense representing a member of the royal family in this way; but it also gives me great pride to have the honour to portray such a very iconic and influential person.' Such is Paul's commitment to the role that he remains 'in character' as the king whenever he is seen in uniform. Getting the impression right has taken Paul many years of research. King George VI suffered from a childhood stammer which affected his confidence throughout his life. Paul has had to investigate the stammer and learn

King George VI with Field Marshal Alan Brooke on a visit to Watchet 2019. — With permission Liz Elmont

to replicate the way that the king spoke in public. Paul explains that 'news clips on YouTube and Pathé News played a huge role in studying his speech but also his stature while addressing the nation'.

To accurately represent the king, Paul has had four different uniforms made, allowing him to present as Admiral of the Fleet (Royal Navy), Air Marshal (Royal Air Force), Field Marshal (Army) and Field Marshal Battle Dress. Such is the accuracy of the uniforms that one spectator once asked Paul, 'Is that the original king's uniform you're wearing? Because it does fit well.' Paul could only reply, 'If only!' The reaction of the public to Paul's performances is always humbling, as he notes:

> *"While giving speeches, especially the King's speech at the outbreak of war in September 1939, I have noticed members of the public actually crying, or at least having tears in their eyes, on many occasions. This has happened not only here in the United Kingdom but also in the Netherlands too. Many people have spoken to me afterwards saying the speech had touched their hearts. That is especially moving and powerful coming from someone who actually remembers King George VI himself addressing the nation on that September day in 1939."*

Paul is often in demand by the public as he explains: 'I have frequently been asked by families, "could you come over and speak with Mum and Dad because they were there during the war?" … I always do, and what pride it gives me to speak with them, and what stories they tell!' Perhaps the best testimony came from a member of the public who asked Paul: 'Do you know you actually look and sound like that king chap?' Must be getting something right!

WINSTON CHURCHILL

Born on 30 November 1874 at Blenheim Palace, Winston Churchill has become an iconic figure for his leadership during the Second World War. From a very young age, the principal influence in Churchill's life was a nurse named Elizabeth Everest, whom he regarded as his most intimate friend during childhood. Elizabeth Everest would remain Churchill's principal carer until he was sent off to boarding school. He had little contact with his father and later remarked on his mother 'I loved her dearly – but at a distance.' Churchill began boarding school aged seven, but his school record was one of poor academic performance and regular poor behaviour and in 1888 he only just passed the entrance examination for Harrow School, where his marks improved considerably – although he was noted to be careless and lacked punctuality. The last years at Harrow were spent preparing for a career in the military but, despite his improved academic performance, he performed poorly in most of his exams.

Churchill passed the entrance examination for the Royal Military Academy at Sandhurst in September 1893, at his third attempt. Military discipline appeared to suit him and he graduated twentieth in a class of 130 in December 1894, shortly before the death of his father. Churchill was commissioned a second lieutenant in the 4th Queen's Own Hussars and sent to India with the Hussars in October 1896. Considering himself poorly educated, he began to read extensively, and also developed an interest in politics. He felt himself to be a Liberal but, because of their support for Irish Home-Rule, he allied himself with the Conservatives. Keen to see action, Churchill accompanied Kitchener's campaign in the Sudan in 1898. Back in England, he continued to give speeches in support of the Conservatives before sailing to South Africa as a journalist to cover the Boer War. While in South Africa he was captured by the Boers and managed to escape – an adventure which had been widely reported back home in Britain.

At the end of the Boer War Churchill returned to Britain and was elected MP for Oldham in 1900, entering Parliament in February 1901. Outspoken and critical of some Conservative policies, he soon found himself on the periphery of the party and, fearing that this would limit further advancement, he defected to the Liberal Party in May 1904. In 1908 he married the Honourable Clementine Hozier, and by 1911 he had risen to First Lord of the Admiralty where he led important developments in submarine warfare and established the Royal Naval Air Service. His career was blighted, however, by the failure of his strategy in the Dardanelles during the First World War, which led to the disaster at Gallipoli and his removal from the Cabinet. Instead, he returned to the army and served on the Western Front before rejoining the Cabinet in mid–1917, serving as Minister of Munitions at the end of the war. Post-war divisions in the Liberal Party led to his defeat in the 1922 election and so he returned to the Conservative Party, serving as Chancellor of the Exchequer. The Conservative defeat in 1929 left Churchill out of government and rather isolated in his views, which many considered extreme. During the 1930s Churchill focused on writing and also found solace in painting. As he himself noted, 'painting came to my rescue in a most trying time'.

Although he was not initially alarmed by the developments in Europe during the 1930s, as the German leader Adolf Hitler continued his policy of expansion Churchill became increasingly outspoken, deploring the government's policy of appeasement and urging rearmament. When

THE LEADERS

Prime Minister Neville Chamberlain reluctantly declared war on 3 September 1939, Churchill returned to the role of First Lord of the Admiralty and member of the War Cabinet; by April 1940 Churchill had become Chairman of the Military Coordinating Committee. Weakened by cancer, and with his policy of appeasement now discredited, Neville Chamberlain resigned as Prime Minister on 10 May 1940 and King George appointed Churchill to the role. Churchill quickly assembled a coalition government to meet the growing threat. Exploiting his close friendship with American President Roosevelt, Churchill was able to secure vital war materials from the neutral US from March 1941, under the terms of the Lend Lease Act, which allowed goods to be bought on credit. America joined the war in December 1941 after the Japanese raid on Pearl Harbour.

Today Winston Churchill is regarded as the greatest statesman of the twentieth century because of his ability to inspire confidence, his relentless energy and his extraordinary leadership. He was also capable of great compassion. Although Chamberlain had resigned, Churchill retained him in

Stan Streather asnWinston Churchill.
— With permission Winstan

government and often consulted him. Churchill's ability to relate to the people of Britain has made him synonymous with victory and a truly iconic leader.

No commemoration of the '40s would be complete without Churchill's presence and several dedicated enthusiasts portray him. One of the best known in Stan Streather. As a frustrated actor and singer, Stan was amused to find that the fellow cast members of a production of 'The Merry Widow' in West London in 2011 had nicknamed him 'Churchill'.

Stan goes on to explain that in the same year, while working as a volunteer for the Mid-Hants Railway heritage line:

> "I was asked by the event organiser to come to the station in the morning and 'Inspect the troops'. A vintage car picked me up at the Swan Hotel and drove me into Alresford Station Yard where I was confronted with three ranks of troops and crowds of people. I must admit to a wobble at that point but the actor in me took over and I went for it! Thus, started my second career."

After a steep learning curve Stan felt able to capture the essence of Churchill and present him to a whole new audience. Stan has thoroughly enjoyed the reactions of veterans of the war years stating:

> "such is the reputation of the man that they have often held my hand and told me their story. They know that I am not the great man, but they want him to know what they did. I have been with relatives who have after said 'he/she has never spoken of that' or 'we didn't know'. It such a privilege to have met these wonderful people and we have a responsibility to pass those experiences on."

Stan Streather as Churchill examining the cut of the cloth on a newly tailored suit.

– With permission Winstan

Stan has also learned never to underestimate the public. He recalls a particular event:

> "Some parents asked me if I would meet their 8-year-old son who was autistic and very keen on Churchill. I said I was very happy to do so and he was brought forward. He began with a few of the expected questions then fixed me with a piercing stare and said 'Of course, your biggest mistake was the Dardanelles campaign!' Momentarily floored, I recovered well with something like 'it was indeed and that sent me into a depression which recurred all my life and I used painting to help with that depression.' We parted on good terms, honour restored but it taught me that I needed to be sharper and never underestimate people."

FIELD MARSHAL ALAN BROOKE
(CHIEF OF IMPERIAL GENERAL STAFF)

Alan Brooke was born on 23 July 1883 at Bagnères-de-Bigorre, France. Educated in France, Brooke finished his education at the Royal Military Academy (Woolwich) and was commissioned into the British Army in 1902 as a second lieutenant, serving in the Royal Artillery during the First World War. Between the wars Brooke was assigned staff duties and was in charge of military training at the War Office between 1936 and 1937. At the outbreak of war in 1939 he commanded II Army Corps in France and then assumed responsibility for covering the evacuation of troops following the retreat to Dunkirk – one of the few senior officers who distinguished themselves during that campaign. General Brian Horrocks later claimed in his autobiography that:

> "the man who really saved the BEF was our own corps commander, Lieutenant-General A.F. Brooke. I felt vaguely at the time that this alert, seemingly iron, man without a nerve in his body, whom I met from time to time at 3rd Division headquarters and who gave out his orders in short, clipped sentences, was a great soldier, but it is only now that I realise fully just how great he was."

Upon his return to Britain, Brooke was placed in command of Home Forces – a role that involved working closely with Prime Minister Winston Churchill. Brooke had great respect for Churchill but also had a number of major disagreements with him. On 30 November 1942 Brooke described Churchill as 'a hard taskmaster, and the most

THE LEADERS

Field Marshal Alan Brooke, as portrayed by Stefan Dicks.

— With permission Stefan Dicks

difficult man to serve that I have ever met, but it is worth all these difficulties to have the privilege to work with such a man'. Despite their differences, Churchill came to trust Brooke implicitly and, in December 1941, promoted him to Chief of Imperial General Staff (CIGS).

Brooke wanted another field command, but when offered command of British troops in the Middle East in August 1942 he declined. In his diaries, published after the war, he explained that he felt it more important to remain in Britain to keep Churchill in check. He wrote, 'we had to consider this morning one of Winston's worst minutes I have ever seen. I can only believe that he must have been quite tight when he dictated it. My God! How little the world at large knows what his failings and defects are!'

Churchill did promise Brooke command of the D-Day landings but President Roosevelt insisted that command went to American General Dwight Eisenhower; Brooke was promoted to Field Marshal in 1944 and as CIGS, he was still able to exercise considerable influence over Allied military strategy. As Field Marshal Bernard Montgomery stated, 'both as a commander and staff officer Brooke was by far the eatest soldier of the war.' In 1946 Brooke became 1st Viscount Alanbrooke of Brookeborough.

Sadly, today Field Marshal Alan Brooke's contribution to the war effort is largely unknown outside military history enthusiasts, but Stefan Dicks is working hard to redress the balance. Dressed impeccably as Brooke – and with rather more than a passing likeness – Stefan is dedicated to ensuring that Brooke's legacy is never forgotten, and with considerable success. As Stefan himself notes: 'the public who attend these events are starting to recognise the character and so I am achieving my aim of education. Re-enactors are now starting to know the CIGS and understand what he did.' There is tremendous responsibility in representing an actual figure from history which Stefan takes very seriously having undertaken hundreds of hours of research.

> "I feel enormous pressure and responsibility portraying Alan Brooke accurately. This also extends into how I (as Brooke) act around other iconic characters like Winston Churchill. Brookie was very respectful of Winnie but very firm with him. I will not allow pictures of me/him doing uncharacteristic activities or eating."

Stefan is also touched by the reaction of veterans to his portrayal:

> "at one event, a little old lady who had been an ATS corporal during the war, was hovering in the near distance watching the intercourse between Winnie and I in character. I had a feeling she wanted to talk to us and so I addressed her. She stood up tall (not quite sprang to attention) and proudly said 'Sir, you're the CIGS aren't you?' In character I said, 'Yes', to which she said, 'it's been a pleasure serving under you; God Bless you sir.' I returned her salute and she left."

FIELD MARSHAL BERNARD MONTGOMERY

Bernard Montgomery was born in London in 1887, the son of an Ulster clergyman and educated at St Paul's School. After graduating from the Royal Military Academy at Sandhurst, Montgomery was commissioned and joined the Royal Warwickshire Regiment. At Meteren, Belgium, he was shot through the lung by a German sniper during the First Battle of Ypres in 1914. Montgomery was not expected to live, and accounts suggest that a grave had already been dug for him, however he made a complete recovery and returned to the front as a staff officer serving at the Battles of the Somme (1916) and Passchendaele (also known as the Third Battle of Ypres, 1917). At the end of the war Montgomery was serving as Chief of Staff of the 47th Division. His service at the front gave him the opportunity to study the tactics of the leading generals and he quickly became disillusioned, noting in his memoirs (published 1958) that 'the frightful casualties appalled me. The so-called "good fighting generals" of the war appeared to me to be those who had a complete disregard for human life.'

Between the wars Montgomery held a number of command positions including commander of the 9th Infantry Brigade before becoming the General Officer Commanding (GOC) 8th Infantry Division. During the campaign in France at the beginning of the Second World War Montgomery led the 3rd Division and, following the evacuation from Dunkirk, he assumed command of the south-eastern section of Britain in readiness for the anticipated German invasion. Following the defeat in August 1942 of the 8th Army in North Africa by General Erwin Rommel's 'Afrikakorps', Churchill ordered Montgomery to take command. The troops were demoralised but Montgomery inspired

THE LEADERS

them, re-equipped them and restored their confidence over a two-month period. His vision for victory was clear and circulated to his troops – 'I want to impose on everyone that the bad times are over, they are finished! Our mandate from the Prime Minister is to destroy the Axis forces in North Africa…. It can be done, and it will be done!' Rommel was held and, after the Battle of El-Alamein (November 1942), forced to retreat until their final surrender in Tunisia in May 1943 – a series of events which allowed Churchill to announce 'the end of the beginning' of the war.

Following the D-Day landings, Montgomery commanded all Allied ground forces until 1 September 1944, when he took command of the 21st Army Group for the remainder of the campaign. Although criticised for not taking Caen earlier, Montgomery actually facilitated the American breakout by drawing German reinforcements in to defend Caen. Sadly, rather than explain this, Montgomery insisted on stating that everything was going to plan which was clearly untrue and contributed to his reputation as a vain and arrogant man. Montgomery's reputation suffered a further blow after the failure of his Operation Market Garden – a plan to invade the Low Countries and the Ruhr, which resulted in large losses of life. During the German offensive known as the Battle of the Bulge Montgomery restored his reputation by using 30 Corps to shore up the American defences and ultimately turning the tide of the battle. After crossing the Rhine in March 1945, Montgomery's troops advanced into Germany and he eventually accepted the surrender of all German forces in north-western Europe at Lüneburg Heath on 2 May 1945. In 1946 Montgomery took over as Chief of the Imperial General Staff (CIGS), and from 1948 to 1951 he was Chairman of the Commanders-in-Chief Committee of the Western Union.

Montgomery remains a divisive character to this day. His lack of tact and diplomacy are well documented. Even Field Marshal Alan Brooke, despite being greatly supportive of Montgomery, noted in his memoir that 'I had to haul him over the coals for his usual lack of tact and egotistical outlook which prevented him from appreciating other people's feelings.' Despite these failings, Montgomery was an inspirational leader. Perhaps the last word should go to US General Eisenhower, whose evaluation of Montgomery in 1943 stated:

> *"General Montgomery is a very able, dynamic type of army commander. I personally think that the only thing he needs is a strong immediate commander. He loves the limelight but in seeking it, it is possible that he does so only because of the effect upon his own soldiers, who are certainly devoted to him. I have great confidence in him as a combat commander. He is intelligent, a good talker, and has a flair for showmanship."*

At many commemorative events, Montgomery (played by Colin Brooks-Williams) can again be seen conversing with Churchill and Field Marshal Alan Brooke. Colin began playing Montgomery partly because of a chance comment by his brother, as Colin recalls:

> *"I had worn a post-war battledress and beret for a show back in 2006 and my brother happened to comment that 'I looked like Monty'. I didn't really take much notice of that until 2009 when I watched an episode of 'Heartbeat' that included a barn-find Second World War Jeep in the storyline. It turned out in the story that the Jeep had once belonged to 'Monty' and at the*

Colin Brookes-Williams as Montgomery in reflective mood.

– With permission Colin Brookes-Williams/Tim Lloyd

> end of the episode he returned to the village to inspect it. I was rather disappointed to see that the actor portraying 'Monty' had very little resemblance to him unfortunately and I felt that it could have been done better, and that got me thinking. So, I dug out that old beret and put two badges on it..."

The beret was the beginning of years of research into Montgomery in an attempt to accurately portray him. Simple things like reproducing Montgomery's medal ribbons were a challenge. Colin notes:

> "it took me two years to accurately research and recreate all of Monty's medal ribbons. I've seen so many instances of Monty being portrayed with an inaccurate set of internet-purchased medal ribbons pinned on upside down! There's no excuse for that, it's just sloppy research and a lack of care in my opinion."

He goes on to observe:

> "the joy of it is that the more you do, the more rewarding (and expensive) it gets and you can take it as far as you like. I've read all I can about Monty himself and his war-time double, M.E. Clifton James, and found them both fascinating characters.
>
> [...]
>
> I am, through my portrayal, representing a very real person who meant, and still means, a lot to a great many people, and as long as I am doing this then I at least owe it to his memory (and to his family, his

THE LEADERS

descendants) to do it with due respect and reverence, and with as much accuracy as I can bring to the role. As a result, I'm pleased to say that in the ten years I have been doing this I have never encountered anything other than encouragement and enthusiasm from the public. Monty, like Churchill, was, and still is, a popular figure in Second World War history, and that helps me a great deal. Monty had his critics of course and therefore I do occasionally come across some who are not great fans of Monty but they are still keen to discuss their opinions."

Sometimes the portrayal of Montgomery can be a little too real. Colin recalls that 'on one occasion I was standing by Monty's Humber Staff Car, "The Victory Car", at Coventry Transport Museum and a passing woman let out a scream when I moved – she had presumed that I was a wax-work of Monty!'

Colin's enthusiasm and commitment to accurately portraying Montgomery goes beyond the uniforms and

Colin Brooks-Williams has assembled an impressive collection of Montgomery related material which will be displayed in the replica campaign caravan.

– With permission
Colin Brooks-Williams

mannerisms. Colin is in the process of making a virtually full-size replica of Montgomery's war-time campaign caravan.

Built to be easily transported to shows, schools and museums, the caravan will serve as a mobile exhibition and educational piece of 'Touring Theatre', as well as being available for hire as a mobile 'film set' for documentaries and similar projects. At the time of writing the project is progressing well. Colin states:

> *"there is still a lot of sanding, staining and painting and other work to do on fitting out the interior and exterior as accurately as possible with great attention to detail. The objective is to have the project fully completed and ready for 'deployment' by the end of this year (2021). Once the windows have been specially made and fitted, the exterior of the caravan will be canvassed over and the sides 'planked' in order to look as much like the original caravan as possible.*
>
> *[…]*
>
> *once completed, the caravan will house a large collection of artefacts relating to Monty, including personal signed correspondence and papers, as well as many original documents and photographs. There will also be faithful and accurate replicas of his uniforms and medal ribbons. The caravan will be used as a focal point for the recreation of Monty's speeches and radio broadcasts but also by my colleagues Steve McTigue (who portrays Winston Churchill) and Stefan Dicks (as Field-Marshal Alan Brooke)."*

THE LEADERS

AIR CHIEF MARSHAL ARTHUR HARRIS

Born in Cheltenham, Gloucestershire in 1892, Arthur (Bomber) Harris remains to this day one of the most controversial figures of the Second World War. With his father working in India, Harris was raised with the family of a rector in Kent. At the age of 17 he decided to emigrate to Southern Rhodesia where he took up farming but, on the outbreak of the First World War he returned to Britain and joined the Royal Flying Corps (having served briefly with Rhodesian forces) on 6 November 1915. Harris served with distinction throughout the war and rose in rank to become Commanding Officer of 45 Squadron. He never forgot his deep feelings for Rhodesia and wore a 'Rhodesia' shoulder flash on his uniform jacket.

One thing that horrified Harris about the First World War was the horrendous loss of life sustained by the ground forces in attempting to seize enemy trenches. He became convinced that bombs dropped from planes would be the decisive weapon of the future. Between the wars he had the opportunity to test his ideas while commanding a squadron flying the Vickers Vernon aircraft in Mesopotamia. Intended as a cargo and troop transport plane, he adapted some of the planes to take bombs, explaining, 'we cut a hole in the nose and rigged up our own bomb racks and I turned those machines into the heaviest and best bombers in the command'.

He also developed delay action fuses for bombs, making area bombing more successful. In 1937 Harris was appointed Air Commodore AOC 4 Group. He continued to rise through the ranks until being appointed Air Vice Marshal in July 1939. With war looming, Harris campaigned for larger strategic bombers which would allow the RAF to bomb targets in

Air Chief Marshal Arthur (Bomber) Harris as portrayed by Denis Turner.

– With permission Denis Turner

THE LEADERS

Germany from bases in England. This campaign would ultimately lead to the construction of the Short Stirling, Halifax and Avro Lancaster heavy bombers.

A report produced in August 1941 shows that less than 35 per cent of bombers actually got with five miles of their targets. As part of the solution Harris was made Commander in Chief (CiC) of Bomber Command in February 1942. When Churchill advocated the bombing of German cities, Harris was instructed to make it happen. He justified the bombings by saying:

> *"the Nazis entered this war under the rather childish delusion that they were going to bomb everyone else, and nobody was going to bomb them. At Rotterdam, London, Warsaw and half a hundred other places, they put their rather naive theory into operation. They sowed the wind, and now they are going to reap the whirlwind."*

In March 1943 Harris was promoted to Air Chief Marshal. Limited numbers of aircraft meant that the initial impact of bombing was also limited but later, 1,000 bomber raids devastated cities including Hamburg and Cologne. Harris strongly felt that this was the way to bring Nazi Germany to its knees, but Churchill had qualms and distanced himself from the raids, informing the public that only specific military targets were being hit.

Given the strength of anti-aircraft defences around Berlin, Harris's tactics met with increasingly limited success and rising losses. Prior to D-Day he was ordered to begin targeting French railways but after the success of the Normandy landings Bomber Command reverted to area bombings. The devastating destruction of Dresden was widely condemned and turned public opinion against Harris and Bomber Command. Harris retired from the RAF on 15 September 1946 and moved to South Africa.

Today 'Bomber' Harris is brought to life again by Denis Turner who attends many events in the north of England. Having retired from a career in the forces Denis was advised to consider re-enacting as a hobby and has never looked back. The decision to portray Arthur Harris, however, was more serendipitous than calculated as Denis explains, 'my portrayal of Harris started not long after I started

Denis Turner as 'Bomber' Harris in front of preserved Lancaster bomber NX611 – 'Just Jane'. — With permission Denis Turner

re-enacting. People noted that, in my RAF uniform, I had a strong resemblance to him. As I had served in Bomber Command for a short time I felt it was entirely appropriate.' Denis is very clear how he personally feels about Harris noting that 'it is my opinion that after the Second World War Harris was harshly treated by Churchill, and the Church, over his bombing of German cities. Area bombing was not Harris's idea. He followed a plan already in operation. He just did it better!' – a view which many historians share and one even Albert Speer (Nazi German Minister of Armaments and War Production) appeared to endorse when he commented on the effectiveness of Bomber Command's night raids.

Denis is grateful for the opportunity to use his portrayal of Harris to correct the wrongs done by history. He notes that many members of the public are unaware of the debate and that fellow re-enactors are generally supportive of Harris. 'I try to portray Harris as accurately as possible, ensuring that my dress, looks and speeches are an accurate representation'. Denis remains convinced that 'both Harris and Bomber Command generally were treated badly at the war's end. No Knighthoods, no campaign medal and no Bomber Command tribute.' One thing at least is certain – Harris's legacy is in good hands!

CHAPTER THREE

THE ARMED FORCES
THE ARMY

In the years after the First World War there was a brief economic boom followed by increasing economic challenges which led to substantial cuts in public spending under what was known as 'The Geddes Axe' (after Sir Eric Geddes who chaired the Committee on National Expenditure). The armed forces were not spared these cuts which effectively reduced the role of the army to that of a police force, responding as needed to any minor crisis across the Empire. The army did help the 'Whites' in Russia against the increasing Communist threat and also maintained an occupation force in the defeated states including Germany (British Army of the Rhine) and Turkey. Further actions were in Iraq (1920), in Ireland (against the IRA), on the North-West frontier in India and in response to the revolt in Palestine (1936).

By the mid–1930s, Germany was under the control of the National Socialist German Workers' Party (NSDAP or Nazis) led by Adolf Hitler and, in violation of the Treaty of Versailles, was undergoing a programme of military expansion and re-armament. While the British Army had stagnated with no forward strategic planning, the German

Wehrmacht (armed forces) was enthusiastically embracing new technology and investing in a new style of mechanised warfare. Only the mechanisation of the cavalry was proposed in British planning, and this was not completed until 1941 when the Royal Scots Greys finally gave up their horses. For a long time, the British government failed to recognise the threat that Hitler posed (although Churchill and a few others spoke passionately about the dangers being faced by Britain) and followed a policy of 'appeasement' in the hope that by acceding to his demands, Hitler could be satisfied. Almost everyone accepted that the Treaty of Versailles, which ended the First World War with Germany, was seriously flawed and therefore many of Hitler's demands could be dismissed as 'reasonable' under the circumstances. Together with a strong pacifist movement there was little willingness to consider another major European conflict. As early as 1933, the Oxford University Student Debating Society voted by 257 votes to 153 that, 'this house will in no circumstances fight for King and Country' – a result that few would ever have predicted. This reluctance was reflected across the Empire. In 1938 Hitler demanded control of the Czech Sudeten region, which bordered Germany and contained most Czech defences and heavy industry, on the grounds that the majority of the population was German an event known as the Munich Crisis. Despite Hitler's demands making war a very real threat, only New Zealand gave a clear guarantee of support against Germany increasing the pressure on the government to avoid such a war if at all possible. Eventually Chamberlain agreed to Hitler's demands and heralded the Munich Agreement as 'peace with honour'. Churchill however retorted that, 'you were given the choice between war and dishonour. You chose dishonour and you will have war.' This proved prophetic when Hitler annexed the rest of Czechoslovakia in March 1939 and it

THE ARMED FORCES - THE ARMY

An infantry soldier of the 49th (West Riding) Division carrying a Mk.I Bren light machine gun. He is wearing the later 'austerity' battledress, a late war Mk.III steel helmet and '37 Pattern webbing.

– With permission Andrew Harrison

became clear that this had been his aim all along.

The realisation that Hitler could only be stopped by armed force led to a substantial expansion of the British Army which had, until that point, been a small volunteer army. David Fraser, historian of the British Army, notes that 'Britain spent the years between 1918 and 1939 with an army in India and an army at home, neither seriously designed, trained, equipped or organised for major war and neither in the least ready for it.' To release men for front-line duties, the Auxiliary Territorial Service (ATS) was formed for women in September 1939 and the Territorial Army was doubled in size. In May 1939 Britain introduced conscription with the Military Training Act, which required every man aged between 20 and 22 to do six months of military training. By mid–1939 there were 230,000 regulars in service and 453,000 territorials. By the end of the year over one million men had been conscripted as a result of the National Service (Armed Forces) Act 1939 which further required all men between 18 and 41 (subject to a medical) to register for training unless already in a reserved occupation.

Despite these measures, however, the army remained a force designed to deal with small insurrections around the Empire, but now expected to fight an extended war on several fronts. A number of early defeats soon revealed the deficiencies in planning and structure. However, mass conscription, coupled with better equipment and training, allowed the army to create larger units as well as specialist formations like the Special Air Service (SAS), Commandos, Long Range Desert Group (LRDG) and the Parachute Regiment.

By the time peace was restored in 1945, 2.9 million people had served in the British Army of which some 300,000 died and 376,239 were wounded.

INFANTRY

The First World War had created a generation of people angered by the perceived willingness of generals to sacrifice lives in attacks which achieved little. This manifested itself in a strong pacifist movement which, in turn, led the government to adopt a strategy of 'casualty avoidance'. This was coupled with a consideration of how new advances in technology might impact on the conduct of war. Sadly, these new initiatives were funded on the premise that Britain was unlikely to be involved in another major war for at least ten years – a premise which then rolled forward annually. The British Army was to be restructured, sacrificing manpower for mobility, in preparation for its role in putting down Imperial insurrections. This appeared to make sense since there was no identified threat and it also allowed the bulk of funding to go into the Royal Navy, regarded as the first line of defence. The imminent threat of war meant that boosting the numbers of infantry divisions was essential.

The British Army was organised by divisions. In 1939 a division officially had 13,863 men, but that figure had risen to 18,347 by 1944. Although the basic divisional structure remained the same, some of the specialist support units were increased in strength. Typically, a division would include three infantry brigades, a Medium Machine Gun battalion (MMG) armed with thirty-six Vickers .303 machine guns, a company of sixteen 4.2-inch mortars, a reconnaissance regiment, an artillery group with seventy-two 25-pound guns, an anti-tank regiment with forty-eight anti-tank guns and a light anti-aircraft regiment with fifty-four 40-mm Bofors guns. There would also be elements of the Royal Engineers (RE), Royal Army Service Corps (RASC); Royal Army

Medical Corps (RAMC), Royal Corps of Signals (RCS), Royal Electrical and Mechanical Engineers (REME) and the Corps of Military Police (CMP).

Upon joining the army, recruits were sent to a regiment and would usually remain a member of that regiment throughout their service. Many regiments had a long and illustrious history which is embodied in their colours. Each regiment has two colours – the King's (now Queens's) Colour with the Union flag with the regimental insignia at the centre, and the Regimental Colour showing the regimental insignia and the battle honours of that regiment. Most regiments had more than one battalion and different battalions of the same regiment rarely fought together. A brigade, commanded by a brigadier general, was a tactical grouping of three battalions (infantry or armoured), each under the command of a lieutenant colonel. Three brigades constituted a division commanded by a lieutenant general or a major general. Two or three divisions constituted a corps, and two or more corps made up an army (a structure retained to the present day).

This is not the place for a full history of the Second World War, suffice it to say that the British Army fought in almost every theatre of the war, except the Russian front, from the deserts of North Africa with Montgomery's 8th Army to the jungles of Burma with Slim's 14th Army, and throughout Europe. It is also important to recognise the role that the Empire had in the success of the army with troops from Australia, Canada, India, New Zealand, South Africa and other countries. Many soldiers who had escaped from occupied Europe also served in the British Army, as did over 110,000 Gurkhas (of whom almost 30,000 were killed or wounded and twelve Victoria Crosses were awarded to Gurkhas or their British officers).

UNIFORM

The uniform of the British soldier varied depending on the theatre of war. Given that this book deals with commemorative events in Britain it will focus on the uniform worn in the European theatre – particularly North-West Europe.

HEADWEAR

Introduced in 1938, the MkII helmet was the standard British Army helmet used throughout the war. The lining was fixed to the helmet with a bolt and screw to the top of the shell. The MkIII helmet went into production in November 1943 but its use was limited to assault units for the planned Operation Overlord – D-Day landings. The lining and fittings remained the same as for the MkII helmet.

When off-duty the Field Service Cap was worn with the battledress. Officially this was replaced with the General Service Cap in 1943 but continued in use with some units throughout the war. Scottish units wore the Tam O'Shanter bearing the regimental badge backed by tartan.

Field Service Caps in the regimental colours, made to the same pattern as the standard Field Service Cap, were allowed but unofficial and had to be purchased privately. Braiding and piping were of cotton for other ranks and gold or silver for officers.

CLOTHING

The British Army standard uniform was first introduced in the late 1930s and continued in use for over two decades. It is commonly referred to as 'battledress' or BD, and during the Second World War and throughout the 1940s it was worn for all activities (including formal ceremonies). The first pattern battledress is commonly referred to as '37 Pattern to distinguish it from the later 1940 or '40 Pattern battledress. Battledress consisted of short jacket and high-waisted trousers, both of wool serge with a mixture of green and brown threads. The jacket was intended to be buttoned to the trousers but because a gap often opened up, or buttons ripped off, braces were worn. The sleeves of the battledress jacket were designed with a forward curve to allow greater comfort when shouldering a rifle or

An infantry section moves forward in a Universal Carrier (sometimes called a Bren Gun Carrier since the vehicle was generally armed with a Bren light machine gun).

– With permission Andrew Harrison

driving. The trousers had a large pocket for maps at the left front, above the knee, and a further pocket for the First Field Dressing on the right upper hip. The jacket was copied by the US forces and named the 'Ike' Jacket and also inspired the German M44 jacket. A wool shirt was worn under the battledress jacket and webbing gaiters secured the bottom of the trouser leg and closed over the top of the boots.

A key characteristic of the '37 Pattern battledress was a fly-front, pleated pockets with concealed buttons and buttoned tabs to secure the bottoms of the trouser legs. Soldiers would also be issued with a greatcoat for cold and wet weather, referred to as the 1940 Pattern Dismounted Greatcoat. Officers wore the same uniform but were permitted to have the top jacket button undone and a tie worn underneath.

The introduction of the '40 Pattern variant saw a few minor changes to the battledress design – most notably to make the fit of the jacket and trousers a little tighter. By 1942, as the war progressed and shortages of material threatened uniform production, a further few relatively minor changes were made to the battledress pattern to produce the 'Austerity Pattern' (occasionally known as the '42 Pattern) battledress. The pocket pleats were removed; the fly, pocket and cuff buttons were exposed. Inside pockets were reduced to one and trousers lost the ankle tabs and belt-loops. A further version of the battledress was produced in khaki denim and intended for use as working dress and issued one size larger than the regular battledress in order to be worn over it. The denim battledress was also initially issued to Home Guard units until serge battledress became available.

The soldier would carry his equipment on a framework of webbing straps worn over the battledress. The '37 pattern webbing replaced the '08 Pattern used throughout the First World War. The webbing was produced in khaki colour and could be dyed using 'Blanco' to achieve the desired shade. A webbing set comprised a waist belt with a frog for either the 1907 or No. 4 Rifle bayonet, pair of shoulder straps, pair of universal pouches (for Bren gun magazines or even grenades), a pouch or harness for the water bottle, a small pack, a large pack and an entrenching tool (the latter two items unaltered from the '08 Pattern webbing). Officers used the same basic webbing but might include a holster for a revolver, pouch for ammunition, binoculars case and a map case.

WEAPONS

The standard weapon of the British soldier was the SMLE or Short Magazine Lee Enfield – a bolt action rifle using the standard British .303 ammunition. It takes its name from James Paris Lee, who designed the rifle's bolt system, and the Royal Small Arms Factory in Enfield. At the beginning of the war soldiers were using the No. 1 Mk. III model with the 1917 bayonet, but by 1942 this had largely been replaced by the Mk. IV version with a shorter 'pig sticker' bayonet. Whereas the equivalent German Mauser K98 held only five rounds in the magazine, the SMLE held ten and, coupled with its short bolt, allowed comparatively rapid firing.

Every ten-man infantry section would comprise the three men of the Bren Gun Group and a seven-man Rifle Group. The Bren gun was a light machine gun which was magazine fed using standard British .303 ammunition. Each magazine held thirty rounds (though only twenty-eight were usually loaded to prevent jamming). The Bren derived its name from the two places integral to its design – Brno, then in Czechoslovakia, and Enfield, in Britain. The gun had a quick-change barrel and was able to sustain a high rate of fire. Fired in semi-automatic mode the Bren gun was extremely accurate.

In addition to a rifle or Bren gun each soldier would also carry grenades, often referred to as Mills Bombs. This fragmentation grenade was first developed in 1915 during the First World War, and with subsequent modifications, continued in use until the 1960s. The Second World War model was classed as Mills No. 36 grenade. Its serrated shape meant that upon detonation it produced a large amount of shrapnel which could cause considerable damage and injury. Originally designed to have a seven-second fuse this was later reduced to four seconds which offered less opportunity for the grenade to be thrown back again.

Officers had a number of options. Early on some officers purchased the American M1911 Colt pistol, while others used the Webley revolver. The Webley was a .455 calibre weapon with a six-round cylinder. It was first introduced in May 1915 and, although partly replaced by the .38 calibre Enfield No.2 revolver (introduced in 1938), it remained in common usage.

Other weapons used by the British infantry soldier included the 2-inch mortar, larger mortars and the Sten sub-machine gun (see under **Airborne Troops**).

OBTAINING UNIFORM & EQUIPMENT

While original battledress jackets and trousers are becoming very scarce and expensive, there are a number of companies that offer reproduction uniforms. '**Soldier of Fortune**' offer a number of options from individual garments and webbing sections to complete sets of uniform and webbing. Details can be found at www.sofmilitary.co.uk. The '**History Bunker**' also offers both jackets and trousers at thehistorybunker.co.uk. '**Epic Militaria**' offer individual items or a 'bundle' and they also offer reproduction footwear as well – further details from www.epicmilitaria.com. A good source of original uniform and equipment is '**Militaria Zone**' (www.militariazone.com).

Acquiring weapons can be a challenging affair depending on what you are looking for. Blank firing and replica weapons are legal to own in the UK but purchase will require an age verification and usually proof of membership of a re-enactment society or intent to use in a film or theatre production. Membership of the Military Vehicle trust will also count. This is because of the 2006 Violent Crime Reduction Act (VCRA). Blank firing weapons can fire blanks but not be adapted to fire live ammunition – all such weapons must vent through the side and not the front to be legal. '**Soldier of Fortune**' sell a range of blank firing weapons (www.sofmilitary.co.uk). The group you join will be able to help with acquiring a suitable weapon. Many re-enactors now use Denix replica weapons which are reasonable quality replicas but which cannot be made to fire. Denix weapons can be ordered direct from the 'Denix' company at www.denix.co.uk. Deactivated weapons are original period pieces that have been altered by a gunsmith to ensure that they cannot fire live ammunition (usually by blocking the barrel and welding moving parts). Such snags then have to be approved by either the London or Birmingham arsenals. Such purchases should be made through a registered gun dealer and you must ensure that the weapon has a Certificate of Deactivation proving that it has been deactivated to current standards.

THE ARMED FORCES - THE ARMY

LIVING HISTORY GROUPS & LINKS

There are many groups across the length and breadth of the country portraying different units of the British Army. It is impossible to list them all but a few of the leading groups will serve as examples:

'**2nd Devons (reenactment)**' is a group portraying the typical Tommie in the 2nd Battalion Devonshire Regiment from the beaches of Normandy to the fall of Nazi Germany. See www.facebook.com/groups/23103658477

'**Suffolk Regiment Living History Society**' is a unit which attempts to accurately recreate the life of a British infantryman c. mid–1944 by living as they did, practicing their drill and infantry tactics through focused displays and battle re-enactments. Further details www.facebook.com/SuffolkRegimentLivingHistorySociety

'**The 39-45 Glosters Re-enactment Group**' portrays the 2nd Battalion the Gloucestershire Regiment (the Glorious Gloucesters). Supported by a 25-pounder field gun and a number of period vehicles, the group engages in authentic living history as well as raising money for veterans' charities. Further details www.facebook.com/groups/631609723947578

'**East Yorkshire Regiment Living History Group**' is a long-established group with an excellent reputation. Focusing on the war in north-west Europe 1944–45, the group is always looking for new recruits. There are also ATS members in the group whose displays are enhanced by period tentage, field and cooking equipment and vehicles. Further details www.facebook.com/eastyorkshireregimentlivinghistory

There are further groups which focus on more unusual aspects of the soldiers' life and these excellent groups also deserve attention. People interested in the Military police might wish to get involved with the '**21st Army Group Provost (Living History Society)**' (www.facebook.com/groups/1074421402617939). Those interested in photography will be fascinated by the work of the '**Army film and Photographic Unit Living History Group**' which uses period cameras to recreate photographs and bring to life the skills and courage of the photographers who chronicled the Second World War (www.afpu44.co.uk/home/4562984873).

FURTHER RESEARCH

The British Soldier in Europe 1939–1945; Peter Doyle and Paul Evans; The Crowood Press Ltd; 2009; ISBN: 1-8479-7102-9. A detailed and very well-illustrated account of the history of the British Army during the war, including detailed images of uniforms and personal effects. An excellent introduction for anyone trying to build up an accurate British military impression.

The Second World War Tommy: British Army Uniforms European Theatre 1939–45 In Colour Photographs; Martyn Brayley and Richard Ingram; The Crowood Press Ltd; 2007; ISBN: 1-8612-6914-5. A superbly illustrated guide to the uniforms and equipment of the British army during the war years. The book does not try to offer a history of the war but stays true to its title and, in doing so, provides an invaluable source.

From D-Day to VE Day; The British Soldier: Volume 1; Jean Bouchery; Histoire and Collections; 2001; ISBN: 2-9081-8244-0. Not always the easiest book to navigate but compensates for this with excellent photos of uniform and equipment. Sections on insignia, wings and proficiency badges, medal ribbons and other valuable information.

AIRBORNE

At the start of the Second World War Britain did not have any airborne troops but, impressed by the use of German parachute troops during the invasion of France, Prime Minister Winston Churchill instructed the War Office to look into setting up a 5,000-strong airborne force. On 22 June 1940, 2 Commando was chosen to retrain as an airborne unit. On 21 November 1940 2 Commando became the 11th Special Air Service Battalion. After service in Italy (Operation Colossus) the unit was again redesignated as 1st Parachute Battalion in November 1941. A further three Parachute Battalions were then raised from volunteers to form the 1st Parachute Brigade. After some early successes, for example the capture of a Würzburg transmitter on the French coast at Bruneval, the existing parachute battalions became the Parachute Regiment on 1 August 1942. Further infantry battalions were converted to airborne battalions and the Parachute Regiment boasted seventeen battalions by June 1944 in five Parachute Brigades.

Training for the 'Paras' involved a twelve-day course held at the Parachute Training School at RAF Ringway, Cheshire. Recruits began training with jumps from a converted barrage balloon and concluded with five jumps from an aircraft. Failure to jump would result in the

A paratrooper of the 1st Airborne Reconnaissance Squadron wearing the Dennison smock and maroon beret. Note the Reconnaissance badge instead of the Paratrooper wings on the beret.

– With permission Andrew Harrison

THE ARMED FORCES - THE ARMY

recruit being sent back to their previous posting. Upon completion of training the new Para was awarded the maroon beret and parachute wings insignia.

The now famous maroon beret has since become the symbol of airborne forces worldwide. The parachute wings arm patch was chosen

A group of Paratroopers accompanied by a WAAF medic prepare to board their aircraft, already marked up with the Allied 'zebra stripes' identification.

– With permission Megan Scott / 11 Group RAF Re-enactment

by Lieutenant General Frederick Browning and designed by Major Seago. It was the maroon beret that led German troops to first refer to the Paras as 'Red Devils'. Airborne troops were expected to be extremely mobile and able to show initiative, training was therefore tailored to promote self-discipline, self-reliance and aggression. Assault courses and route marches played an important part in building up fitness, and mock exercises encouraged resilience and initiative. An airborne battalion was expected to be able to move thirty-two miles in twenty-four hours. A smaller platoon should be able to cover fifty miles.

After actions in Italy and Greece, the Paras prepared for their toughest mission – destroying the German gun battery at Merville and capturing key bridges over the River Orne and the Caen Canal to prevent German forces reaching the beaches ahead of the D-Day landings. Despite many men unaccounted for because they missed the drop zones (only 150 men were available for the assault on the Merville battery) all objectives were met and the success of the landings owes much to the efforts of the Paras.

Between June and September 1944, the 6th Parachute Division suffered 821 killed, 2,709 wounded and 927 missing. The Paras next major action was as part of Operation Market Garden – the mission to capture the bridges that would allow the Allies to cross the Rhine and enter Germany. The Paras were tasked with capturing the key bridges at Arnhem, Holland. Although they did land successfully, only 2nd Battalion made it to the bridges and were able to capture the northern end of the Arnhem Road bridge (both the railway bridge and pontoon bridges having already been destroyed). They were cut off by the 9th SS Panzer Division which successfully prevented attempts to break through to relieve the Paras. Reinforcements did arrive, in the form of the 4th Parachute Brigade, but defeat was inevitable. After nine days the decision was made to try and withdraw as many men as possible. The two Parachute Brigades mustered 3,082 men at the start of the campaign. By the end, 2,656 were killed or reported missing and only 426 returned safely. The action at Arnhem has come to epitomise the courage and fighting character of the Paras. 6th Airborne Division was then sent to Belgium on 22 December 1944 to help stop Hitler's offensive through the Ardennes in the Battle of the Bulge. Their last major action was as part of Operation Varsity (the largest ever airborne assault) to cross the Rhine and enter Germany.

Although this section deals primarily with the parachute troops, the term 'airborne' also includes infantry landed behind enemy lines by glider and referred to as 'airborne infantry'. A glider force of 5,000 gliders was set up on Churchill's instructions in 1940 using either the British 'Horsa' or, later, the American 'Waco CG-4A' gliders. Despite the risks inherent in navigating a glider at night, locating a landing zone and avoiding other gliders and static objects on landing, actions immediately before and after D-Day showed that losses sustained were actually comparable to the losses sustained in parachute units. The advantage of glider-borne troops was that the gliders could carry heavier equipment including artillery pieces and even vehicles. Troops delivered by glider would arrive at the same spot whereas paratroops often found themselves dispersed and needed time to regroup. Furthermore, much less training was needed for glider infantry and units were often converted from regular infantry to glider infantry with the minimum of training.

UNIFORM

HEADWEAR

Rather than the standard army 'Brodie' helmet, airborne troops wore a specially designed steel helmet officially designated the 'Helmet Steel Airborne Troops' (HSAT). The shape was similar to that worn by despatch riders but the chinstrap was the most obvious difference, with a leather cup section for the chin. Paratroopers also wore the maroon beret with the instantly recognised winged badge displayed above the left eye.

CLOTHING

Paratroopers wore the same battledress jacket as ordinary infantry. The trousers were similar but had an extended map pocket, large enough to carry three grenades and lined with chamois leather. The trousers also had two additional first aid dressing pockets at the rear. Glider infantry wore the standard infantry trousers. All airborne troops wore the standard infantry boots and gaiters. The most notable item, after the maroon beret, was the Denison smock which was worn over the battledress. Made of a camouflaged heavy cotton drill, the smock had a half zip at the front and was pulled on over the head. A wide crutch strap allowed the garment to be secured during jumps. The webbing was the standard '37 pattern webbing usually augmented by a toggle rope.

WEAPONS

Airborne troops used the same weapons as their infantry counterparts. They carried the extremely reliable bolt-action Lee-Enfield rifle and either a Webley or Enfield revolver. Some carried the Colt 1911 pistol. In North-west Europe airborne troops generally used the Sten sub-machine gun but the American Thompson sub-machine gun was used in North Africa and the Mediterranean. Additional weapons included the Bren light machine gun and the 2-inch mortar.

The Sten gun was designed by Major Reginald V. Shepherd and Harold J. Turpin. The 'S' and 'T' initials from their last names were combined with 'EN' from the Royal Small Arms factory at Enfield to make the name STEN. Initially the weapon had two serious faults – it jammed, and would also fire uncontrollably in full-auto mode if knocked. This earned it a variety of nick-names including 'Stench Gun' and 'The Woolworth Special'. It was quickly made and showed it, looking more like something created from a box of spare parts and scrap metal, but it cost only a fraction of that needed to make the American Thompson submachine gun.

More than 4 million Sten guns were produced and, weighing only 7 pounds empty, it was light to carry. A magazine would hold twenty-eight to thirty rounds of 9mm ammunition, which meant that finding extra was relatively easy since the Germans widely used 9mm ammunition. As the production issues were overcome, soldiers soon began to trust the Sten, which could provide devastating fire if kept clean and well-oiled. In a ten-man section in the Paras, the sergeant and corporal would carry a Sten, as would most of the officers.

CHOOSING AN AIRBORNE IMPRESSION

By their nature Paratroopers were (and remain) an elite fighting force requiring a high level of fitness. It is important that enthusiasts wishing to portray Airborne troops reflect on this. All too often at events we see someone of rather generous build squeezed into a Denison smock and evidently likely to struggle to board a plane fully equipped, let alone leave one attached to a parachute. Sometimes we need to be honest about what we see in the mirror and consider what impressions are best suited. Like all military personnel, paratroopers were part of a unit and so joining a group is by far the best way to enjoy the role. If you plan on attending heritage events at civilian locations, consider what a fully equipped paratrooper might be doing there. If on leave, then a soldier would not have all of their equipment with them, nor be dressed in a Denison smock.

OBTAINING UNIFORM & EQUIPMENT

'**The History Bunker**' provides a basic Paratrooper uniform package which can be found at thehistorybunker.co.uk/WW2-British-Paratrooper-Battle-Dress-Uniform. 'Soldier of Fortune' offer several packages including the 'basic uniform set', but also the 'full uniform set'. In addition, they provide a comprehensive range of individual items from badges and insignia to the 1942 Pattern Bergen which was used by some glider infantry. Both the Mk1 and Mk2 helmets are available, as is the correct design scrim scarf. They also stock the British Airborne Body Armour, although this was not extensively used because it was felt to restrict movement. These items can be viewed in the Soldier of Fortune online shop at www.sofmilitary.co.uk/shop-re-enactment/british-ww2/british-airborne.html. Some items are carried by '**Epic Militaria**' at www.epicmilitaria.com/british-ww2/uniforms.html. '**Khaki on Campaign**' are highly regarded by re-enactors. Their products can be viewed at khaki-on-campaign.webs.com. See section above on 'Infantry' for information regarding the purchase of weapons.

LIVING HISTORY GROUPS & LINKS

'**NWW2A British 6th Airborne**' Is a friendly group representing a mixed 'drop' from the 6th Airborne during the Second World War and based in the North of England. Further details: nww2a6thairborne.weebly.com

'**Men of Arnhem Living History Group**' is a small living history group dedicated to commemorating the role of the 'Paras' and related events at Arnhem. Further details www.facebook.com/Men-of-Arnhem-living-history-group–192140281674949

FURTHER RESEARCH

The Day the Red Devils Dropped In: The 9th Parachute Battalion in Normandy D-Day to D+6: Merville Battery to the Chateau St Come; Neil Barber; Leo Cooper Ltd; 2003; ISBN: 1-8441-5045-3. The period covered by this book was key to preventing German reinforcements from reaching the Allied landing beaches. Meticulous research, supported by survivor testimony, reveals the full story of that heroic action.

First In: The Airborne Pathfinders: A History of the 21st Independent Parachute Company, 1932–1946; Ron Kent; Frontline Books; 2020; ISBN: 1-5267-8186-7. This is the story of the airborne troops who, as Pathfinders, were the first to drop into enemy territory to locate drop zones and then defend them. The author was a sergeant in that force which makes his writing even more personal. The unit served in Sicily, Italy, Norway, France and as part of Operation Market Garden.

The Devil's Own Luck: Pegasus Bridge to the Baltic 1944–45; Dennis Edwards; 2001; Pen & Sword Books Ltd; ISBN: 0-8505-2869-0. Unusually, and in defiance of orders, the author was able to keep a record of his experiences in Europe between 1944 and 1945. Edwards writes with humour, yet the brutal nature of warfare is never far away. An excellent account of one man's experience.

AUXILIARY TERRITORIAL SERVICE (ATS)

The origins of the Auxiliary Territorial Service lie in the frightening casualty figures of the First World War. In order to maintain front-line units, the government was forced to accept that women would have to take over some non-combatant roles. That led in 1917 to the formation of the Women's Army Auxiliary Corps (WAAC). Helen Gwynne-Vaughan was appointed as Chief Controller WAAC (Overseas) and was the logical choice (later Dame Helen) to become the first director of the ATS when it was formed in September 1938, as the threat of war increased. Princess Mary, the Princess Royal, became the Controller Commandant of the ATS and Queen Elizabeth served as Commandant-in-Chief of the ATS from 1940 until 1949. Even Princess Elizabeth (later Queen Elizabeth II) served in the ATS as an honorary Second Subaltern with the service number 230873, under the name Elizabeth Alexandra Mary Windsor, but not until 1945.

Even Dame Helen Gwynne-Vaughn has to admit 'that the ATS got off to a bad start!', initially having no uniforms and receiving little training. Furthermore, the ATS was set up as part of the Territorial Army, and therefore organised on a county basis. Communication

An ATS private takes a well-earned break.

— With permission John Wickham

was poor at best and many women wishing to join the ATS arrived as instructed at their local Territorial Army HQ only to find that they were not expected, and that no one knew what they were supposed to do. Some received a little training but many got bored and left. The early recruits were employed as cooks and in clerical roles. Experience in civilian life before recruitment generally determined the role given in the early ATS; so, a typist would almost certainly be allocated to clerical duties following a 'trade test' to determine her skills. Approximately 300 ATS members accompanied the British Expeditionary Force across to France, and a group of ATS telephonists were among the last to leave from Dunkirk.

Things improved when the ATS received full military status in April 1941, and in December 1941 conscription was extended to include women (who had formerly been volunteers); all women conscripted to the army joined the ATS between the ages of 17 and 43 (except nurses, who joined Queen Alexandra's Imperial Military Nursing Service or QAIMNS). Women could also serve in the Women's Royal Naval Service (WRNS), the Women's Auxiliary Air Force (WAAF) or the Women's Transport Service (FANY).

By September 1941 the ATS numbered some 65,000, with the range of their duties similarly expanded to include drivers, ammunition inspectors and other roles. By 1943 almost 75 per cent of the Anti-Aircraft Command's Heavy Anti-Aircraft (HAA) batteries were mixed-sex, with approximately 56,000 ATS women serving with anti-aircraft units around the country (although they were not allowed to actually fire the guns). Women also operated the heavy searchlight equipment, having shown that they could easily withstand the conditions of often isolated searchlight locations. Their integration into searchlight and anti-aircraft units freed up many men to join front-line units. The ATS retained a rank structure different to that of the army, however, when members were seconded to Royal Artillery batteries, they were given the Artillery ranks of gunner, lance-bombardier and bombardier, and also wore a white lanyard on the right shoulder.

As the war progressed women came from all over the British Empire to support the war effort. Some 300 women from the West Indies served in the West Indies Auxiliary Territorial Service, with around 100 of them serving in Britain. At first these women were rejected on the grounds of their colour but the on-going demand for more men at the front led to a new recruitment policy. From 1943, women of colour were allowed to join the ATS. The women of the ATS played an important part in the defence of the British Isles, but

An ATS Officer prepares for the day ahead by checking paperwork left by the previous shift.
– With permission John Wickham

also served in most theatres of war. Some 5,000 ATS women, for example, served in the Middle East (80 per cent of whom were locally recruited), while others served in the American capital, Washington DC. At its peak, 210,308 women served in the ATS and 335 lost their lives while in service. In 1949 the ATS was absorbed into the new Woman's Royal Army Corps (WRAC).

UNIFORM

HEADWEAR

The ATS cap shared its shape with the WAAF hat, which basically copied the ATS model. The cap has a khaki peak and chinstrap. The sides of the cap are internally supported with a soft crown. The brass ATS badge is fixed to a khaki band of coarse-woven material around the cap. The second pattern cap is similar to the first, but the visible stitching on the peak and curtain no longer showed and the khaki chin strap is replaced by a brown leather strap with brass slider.

Coloured field service caps were available through private purchase. These could be in brown with blue piping and the ATS badge, or reflect the colours of a unit to which the woman was attached – e.g. Royal Artillery – although still sporting the ATS badge. Mk.II steel helmets were issued to some ATS personnel e.g. those attached to anti-aircraft batteries.

CLOTHING

The ATS uniform was closely modelled on that worn by the First Aid Nursing Yeomanry (FANY). The jacket was of lightweight khaki serge and of mid-thigh length. It was tailored open at the neck and worn with a khaki shirt and collar and khaki tie. The jacket had two pleated breast pockets and two larger pockets on the tunic skirt. The pockets were secured with small, brass 'General Service' buttons, and four large 'General Service' buttons secured the front. The jacket had epaulettes on which were worn the brass ATS titles (mirroring the regimental titles still worn by male soldiers at this time). The skirt was of the same material and designed as a simple two-panel garment falling to mid-calf length. Stockings and plain brown leather shoes completed the uniform. ATS members who had transferred into the ATS before September 1941 were entitled to wear the 'Women's Transport Service F.A.N.Y.' shoulder title. ATS personnel were issued with the '39 Pattern men's greatcoat.

The '41 Pattern ATS Service Dress was basically an austerity version of the original design. The key changes were the addition of a waist belt with brass buckle, unpleated breast pockets and simplified pocket flaps. The late-war variant saw the brass 'General Service' buttons replaced by green plastic economy buttons and the removal of all buttons from the lower pocket flaps. The '41 Pattern skirt was of similar design to before, but made up of four panels instead of two. The '41 Pattern uniform did now come with a specific greatcoat differing from the men's by the lack of the short adjustment belt at the back, which gave the greatcoat a more fitted appearance. ATS personnel seconded to other units wore the badge of that unit on the breast above the left pocket.

There were some tasks for which the uniform was unsuited and therefore ATS personnel were issued with a battledress uniform. Similar to the men's battledress the ATS version was tailored to the female figure and it had a faced collar which allowed the blouse to be worn open at the neck with a shirt and tie. The trousers had a four-button fastening on the left side of the waist and an elasticated waistband. This uniform was worn with brown ankle boots and brown leather gaiters. As with the men's battledress, the ATS version also saw changes due to austerity, with the button coverings being removed along with the pleats on the breast pockets. The trouser fixing was reduced from four buttons to three. There was also an ATS leather jerkin which could be worn when the greatcoat was too restrictive.

The ATS officer's uniform at the beginning of the war was very similar to that worn by FANY personnel and styled after the male officer's uniform, even buttoning on the man's side. The jacket and skirt were similar to those worn by other ranks. The jacket had a leather Sam Browne belt instead of the cloth belt, but without the shoulder strap. The greatcoat was very similar to the male officer's equivalent, but lacked the 'sword slit' above the left pocket. The coat was fastened by two rows of four 'General Service' brass buttons. An austerity version of the uniform was introduced in 1942 which lost the breast pocket pleats and completely removed the skirt pockets, replacing them with internal pockets. The earlier cuff sleeves were also removed.

CHOOSING AN ATS IMPRESSION

By the end of the war ATS auxiliaries served in over 100 different roles from anti-aircraft batteries to drivers and cooks. This offers many opportunities to create a detailed and specific impression reflecting the diverse work of these women. As an individual you might portray an auxiliary on leave, or join a group to add greater depth and realism to your impression and enjoy the opportunity to share your interest with others.

OBTAINING UNIFORM & EQUIPMENT

Original uniform items are becoming scarce and expensive, but thankfully there are companies now providing very serviceable reproductions. '**Soldier of Fortune**' carry an impressive range of individual items through to complete uniform sets – see www.sofmilitary.co.uk . '**The History Bunker**' offers a reproduction service dress uniform and also offers the 'Suit Working, Serge' uniform. These can be ordered from their website at thehistorybunker.co.uk

LIVING HISTORY GROUPS & LINKS

'**ATS (Auxiliary Territorial Service) Section: Garrison Artillery Volunteers**' is the ATS section of this impressive Royal Artillery group who are known for their authenticity and professionalism. Their website also includes useful information on uniforms and related accessories to enhance an impression. For further details see www.thegarrison.website/ats-auxilliary-territorial-service

'**Auxiliary Territorial Service Reenactors**' is a group which celebrates the women of the ATS and undertakes research to learn more about their uniform and service history. Further details: www.facebook.com/ATSAuxiliaryTerritorialService

FURTHER RESEARCH

World War II British Women's Uniforms in Colour Photographs; Martin Brayley and Richard Ingram; The Crowood Press Ltd; 2001; ISBN: 1-8612-6475-5. Over 220 colour photographs record in detail the uniforms and insignia worn by the women's services in all theatres of the war. Close-ups of details and thorough text commentaries make this an invaluable source and a must-have book for the serious re-enactor.

'Dressed for Service! (Second World War Women's Military Uniforms of the British Empire)' is dedicated to providing a reference point for all serious researchers and re-enactors studying the uniforms of women in WWII British Empire uniforms. There are some good examples of ATS uniforms and insignia recorded. Further details: www.facebook.com/groups/636201423100487

Girls in Khaki: A History of the ATS in the Second World War; Barbara Green; Spellmount, Illustrated Edition; 2012; ISBN: 0-7524-6350-0. This book describes how members of the ATS assumed a wide range of roles from working at Bletchley Park to serving in Eisenhower's HQ in Reims. It shows their courage but also the role that the ATS had in reforming society after the war.

Woman at the Front: Memoirs of an ATS Girl; Sylvia Wild; Amberley Publishing; 2012; ISBN: 1-4456-0369-1. The author had volunteered to serve abroad and joined HQ as a shorthand typist working with senior Royal Engineer officers planning the D-Day landings. This book recounts those experience and her service in France and Germany after the landings. Sylvia's account of life in France immediately after the German retreat is very moving.

ROYAL ARTILLERY

The Royal Artillery (properly referred to as the Royal Regiment of Artillery) is the artillery arm of the British Army and often known simply as 'the Gunners'.

Despite the preparations for war which began in earnest in 1938, the Royal Artillery remained woefully ill-prepared for a new conflict. No real planning had gone into modernising the Royal Artillery to meet the technological and tactical demands placed on it over the previous twenty years. Most of the guns available were adapted artillery pieces from the First World War and 60 per cent of these were lost in the evacuation from France in May 1940.

Once the war began, pre-war plans were quickly completed and production started on a new light gun which was classed as the QF (Quick Firing) 25-pounder Mark II gun. By 1943 approximately 10,000 of these guns had been produced. The situation with medium and heavy guns was even worse, with only First World War models available, and no plans in place for a replacement. Acting with impressive speed, the first new 4.5 inch and 5.5-inch guns were available for use by late 1941, first seeing action in North Africa in 1942. No new heavy guns were produced and adapted First World War guns remained in use until American weapons replaced them towards the end of the war.

Gun production continued to increase and the Royal Artillery became a powerful resource by 1943, with more than 200 field and medium regiments in service. They also organised anti-aircraft regiments, anti-tank regiments and coastal artillery, employing around 700,000 men and women. Production of guns went hand in hand with training to ensure that all aspects of the artillery role – including

RE-LIVING BRITAIN IN THE 1940S

Men of the Royal Artillery prepare to reload.

– With permission Frank Brown, 69th Field Regiment Display

THE ARMED FORCES - THE ARMY

surveying, target acquisition, communications and fire observation – were perfected.

Two men were chiefly responsible for the development of modern gunnery tactical and deployment methods. Brigadier Sidner Kirkman introduced new procedures to allow all available artillery pieces to fire on a specific target, irrespective of units and formations. Brigadier Jack Parham implemented new approaches in fire support by which a fire observation officer could call on a few guns, the twenty-four guns of a regiment, the guns of several regiments or even the hundreds of guns in a Corps, to provide a measured response to a perceived target or threat.

The key to the successful use of artillery lay in the ability to accurately locate and range targets. Divisional artillery had six observation parties per regiment travelling in Bren Gun (Universal) Carriers or tanks.

Members of the Garrison Artillery Volunteers fire a 25-pounder field gun. The picture shows the muzzle flash as the gun is fired.

– With permission Frank Brown, 69th Field Regiment Display

Vision behind enemy lines was achieved using Light Auster aircraft or specialist squadrons of the Royal Air Force. The artillery also had the ability to screen movements using smoke. Historian Stig Moberg's assessment of the Royal Artillery was that 'British artillery, by the end of the war, was state-of-the-art and became a real battle-winner. It was a thoroughly efficient arm, able to deliver concentrations of the heaviest fire in support of the infantry and armour, both day and night.' Lieutenant General Brian Horrocks goes further stating that 'Although I am an infantryman, and proud of it, I have many times said that the Royal Regiment of Artillery, in my opinion, did more to win the last war than any other Arm of the Service'.

CHOOSING A ROYAL ARTILLERY IMPRESSION

A Royal Artillery impression is really only effective as part of a group like the 'Garrison Artillery Volunteers', unless commemorating an individual family member who actually served and intending to attend events as a 'promenader'.

OBTAINING RELEVANT ACCESSORIES

The uniform of the Royal Artillery is essentially the same as the infantry uniform above except with the Royal Artillery insignia. Full webbing was not generally worn when operating guns but a wool-lined leather jerkin was commonly worn over the battledress.

LIVING HISTORY GROUPS AND LINKS

'69th Field Regiment Display' is part of the Garrison Artillery Volunteers (see below) and based near Wigan. The group

Two 25-pounder field guns of the '69th Field Regiment Display' prepare to open fire.
– With permission Frank Brown, 69th Field Regiment Display

meets regularly and attends a wide range of events involving both static and firing displays. They are always keen to welcome new recruits. Further details: www.facebook.com/69Field.

'**Garrison Artillery Volunteers**' is a volunteer hobby group with a main group located near Salisbury and other affiliated groups across the country and even on the Continent! The group is divided into several sections by interest:

o **Gunnery** – portraying 489 Battery; 124th (Northumbrian) Field Regiment RA (TA) and 822 Battery 25th Light Anti-Aircraft Regiment RA.

- o **Anti-Aircraft** – a 3.7-inch Anti-Aircraft gun is used in combination with a 150 cm searchlight and other equipment to portray a typical 'Ack-Ack' unit;

- o **Auxiliary Territorial Service (ATS)** – portraying 301 Battery, 93rd (Mixed) Searchlight Regiment RA – the only predominantly female regiment. The group uses a fully restored searchlight which is the only 150 cm carbon arc projector in Britain restored and with an original Lister generator to power it.

- o **Operations Room** – complete with a full-size plotting table this section covers the roles of the Royal Navy, Royal Air Force and Royal Artillery in defending Britain against air raids.

The aim is to rediscover and learn all aspects of the technical side of Second World War Royal Artillery; to preserve and demonstrate the equipment and to keep the memories and skills alive for future generations. Further details from: www.thegarrison.website

FURTHER RESEARCH

Gunfire!: British Artillery in the Second World War; Stig K. Moberg; Pen and Sword Frontline; 2017; ISBN: 1-4738-9560-7. A very useful overview of the Royal Artillery at the outbreak of war and its development throughout the war. Moberg looks at the weapons used and considers key battles of the war to evaluate the use and effectiveness of artillery with the help of veteran interviews, maps and photographs.

THE ARMED FORCES - THE ARMY

LOCAL DEFENCE VOLUNTEERS / HOME GUARD

The Local Defence Volunteer organisation began on 14 May 1940 after the German invasion of France, with an appeal to the nation by the Secretary of War, Anthony Eden. The appeal asked all men aged between 17 and 65 to enrol in the newly formed Local Defence Volunteers (LDV). Before this date, the government had been reluctant to make use of volunteer organisations to undertake duties which should be the responsibility of the police and/or army. However, as the threat of invasion increased, militia units were spontaneously forming, for example the 'Legion of Frontiersmen' in Essex, forcing the government to react. In the first twenty-four hours

Men of the LDV and women of the WHD (Women's Home Defence) drill together until women were banned from any military involvement with the then Home Guard in November 1941.
— With permission Andrew Harrison

a quarter of a million men had volunteered, and that number had risen to a million by the end of July 1940. The initial LDV was a poorly organised body launched without any support structure, funding or even an administrative address. New recruits were told to report to their nearest police station but there were no further instructions after that. With no weapons or uniforms the LDV were forced to improvise, using everything from knives and pitchforks to shotguns and pistols brought back as souvenirs from the First World War. For identification recruits wore an armband bearing the letters 'LDV'.

Although the age range for recruits was supposed to be 17 to 65 this was not strictly enforced, leading to many older veterans also joining. Given their average age, the impression they gave with their mismatched weapons and motley appearance was far from martial, leading to the suggestion that LDV actually stood for 'Look, Duck and Vanish'. Women joined the LDV under the banner of the 'Women's Home Defence' (WHD), but were forbidden to have any military involvement in November 1941.

At Churchill's insistence, the LDV was renamed the Home Guard in July 1940, despite protestations from Anthony Eden and others in the Cabinet. Giving his support for the Home Guard in a BBC broadcast on 14 July 1940, Churchill stated:

> "these officers and men, a large proportion of whom have been through the last war, have the strongest desire to attack and come to close quarters with the enemy wherever he may appear. Should the invader come to Britain, there will be no placid lying down of the people in submission before him, as we have seen, alas, in other countries. We shall defend every village, every town, and every city."

Members of a Home Guard platoon prepare for parade shortly after receiving their serge battledress, replacing the earlier denim version.

– With permission Stuart Wilby

Following an appeal to the British people, some 20,000 weapons were supplied to the Home Guard, along with denim uniforms. The weapons shortfall was then made up with imports of weapons from America and Canada under Lend-Lease, and the hastily produced Sten guns. However, the priority remained to re-equip the regular army following the catastrophic loss of weapons and materiel arising from the evacuation from Dunkirk.

Churchill continued to support the Home Guard and ensured that equipment and appropriate military training were provided, although the War Office still viewed them as an unwanted burden throughout the war. As their training improved, and the older recruits left, the Home Guard became a formidable fighting force of 1.7 million men. They were tasked with guarding factories, beaches and ammunition stores. They also regularly patrolled areas where a night-time airborne landing might be expected. As the threat of a German invasion receded, so the need for the Home Guard diminished until the force was officially stood down on 3 December 1944. The Home Guard certainly had moments of drama, although many did not develop as anticipated. As Norman Longmate recounts in his book *The Real Dad's Army*:

> "the routine of patrols — usually involving two men on duty for two hours, before and after which they slept — soon became monotonous, but was varied by occasional thrills…. A solitary patroller, armed with a shotgun, having 'spied a stranger standing well out in a large field' challenged and finally shot him, only

Members of the Home Guard carry out a patrol on bicycles.

— With permission John Purkiss

> to discover that 'the enemy' was a scarecrow keeping guard over the farmer's potatoes. Other 'parachutists' carefully stalked at this time include sheep, cows and … a stationary hedgehog mistaken in the dim light for the head of a prostrate and cunningly camouflaged soldier."

It should never be forgotten that despite its comic reputation at times, 1,206 members of the Home Guard lost their lives while on duty. Despite his initial reservations about the Home Guard, Anthony Eden stated during a debate in Parliament in November 1940 that:

> "no one will claim for the Home Guard that it is a miracle of organisation … but many would claim that it is a miracle of improvisation, and in that way it does express the particular genius of our people. If it has succeeded, as I think it has, it has been due to the spirit of the land and of the men in the Home Guard."

Today, many people's perception of the Home Guard is based on the TV Series *Dad's Army*, which followed the comic adventures of a somewhat mismatched group of Home Guard

Tony Horton as Captain Mainwaring.

– With permission Sue Horton

volunteers. Led by the pompous Captain Mainwaring (played by Arthur Lowe) they defend the fictitious seaside town of Walmington-On-Sea from Nazi threat. Its humour and longevity come from the fact that the writers actually experienced life in either the Home Guard (Jimmy Perry) or as an ARP Warden (David Croft).

Perry is supposed to have based the character of Private Pike on himself. Many people believe that the iconic theme tune was a wartime hit song (performed as it was by popular wartime artist Bud Flanagan) but it was actually written for the series by Jimmy Perry and Derek Taverner. Today, Tony Horton is often seen at commemorative events, bearing an uncanny resemblance to the late Arthur Lowe, as Captain Mainwaring.

CHOOSING A HOME GUARD IMPRESSION

Recreating the Home Guard has the advantage that you can 'act your age' and still be historically accurate, unlike any other branch of the military. You can also be of more generous stature and still not look out of place while educating the public about the real contribution of those who served. The process by which this initially ramshackle organisation became an efficient and skilled force prepared to act as a last line of defence in the event of invasion is a story which deserves to be told. The public are always fascinated by 'Home Guard' groups and interested to see how they differ from the common 'Dad's Army' image.

UNIFORM

When first set up, the 'Local Defence Volunteers' wore no uniform and were identified only by a khaki cloth armband bearing the letters

'LDV'. Even when renamed the Home Guard, uniforms were slow to appear and so armbands with 'HG' replaced the earlier 'LDV' ones. By late 1940 denim uniforms had been issued and later these were replaced with normal army serge uniforms. For the earliest HG impression, civilian clothing and an armband are sufficient.

HEADWEAR

Home Guard members were issued with the Army Field Service Cap and also a Mk.II steel helmet.

CLOTHING & WEBBING

At first the Home Guard were issued with denim versions of the battledress, originally intended to be used as work dress. Gradually, as production improved, these uniforms were replaced with the standard British Army serge battledress (see under Army: Infantry, above). The battledress blouse upper sleeve would also have the 'Home Guard' shoulder title, district title and battalion number on khaki patches.

The main difference between army equipment and that of the Home Guard was the webbing. As the war started the government approached leather companies and asked them to design a version of the '37 Pattern webbing in leather. A million sets of this '39 Pattern equipment were ordered, but never issued to front-line troops. In the end they were issued to the Home Guard and the bulk to free Belgians and the Dutch, and also to Russia. Home Guard would typically receive either a '39 Pattern or pre-WWI '03 Pattern leather belt. The '39 Pattern belt featured a pair of short straps with buckles, to which the shoulder straps would be attached, but these were missing from the '03 pattern belt and so a webbing sleeve with the straps and buckles attached which the belt was slotted through. The shoulder straps were standard '37 pattern webbing but the pouches differed from those issued to the army, being designated 'Pouches, Web, Ammunition (Home Guard Pattern)'.

WEAPONS

In addition to the Lee-Enfield No 1 Mk.3 rifle (see under 'Infantry' above), many Home Guard units were issued the with First World War Enfield Pattern '14 (or P14) rifle, itself derived from the P13. The P13 was based on the German K98 Mauser and intended to provide increased accuracy. The P13 was to use a smaller bullet than the Short Magazine Lee-Enfield, which used the standard British .303. Some elements of the P13 design very closely followed the Mauser, others were adapted to meet British expectations – for example the angle of the bolt handle. The start of the war meant that plans to use a new type of ammunition were abandoned and the guns were rechambered to .303 as the demand for weapons increased. This rechambering led to the redesignation as the P14.

More than a million P14 rifles were produced by the American manufacturers Remington and Winchester on behalf of the British government. The overall design was highly successful with a rapid rate of fire and good accuracy. A number of the P14's design features would later be incorporated into the Lee-Enfield No.4.

OBTAINING UNIFORM & EQUIPMENT

The uniforms for these groups can be bought from various sources such as '**Epic Militaria**' (www.epicmilitaria.com), based in Aberystwyth in Wales, which has recently added Home Guard uniform to its stock list. Another supplier of reproduction Home Guard uniform is '**Soldier of Fortune**' (www.sofmilitary.co.uk/shop-military.html) including arm bands, shoulder titles, webbing equipment and anklets (gaiters) for a complete turnout. '**Combat Service Support**' also has some items of Home Guard kit in stock and it is worth calling them on 01673 858001. For weapons – see under 'Armed Forces: Infantry and Airborne' above.

LIVING HISTORY GROUPS & LINKS

'**Home Guard Re-enactment/Living History Groups**' is a website dedicated to the many groups around the country which represent the Home Guard. It lists the various groups by area and includes links to their individual website and social media pages. The list is not complete but offers an excellent starting point for further research for the potential recruit. The address is: www.staffshomeguard.co.uk/ J10GeneralInformationReenactmentGroups.html

FURTHER RESEARCH

In Search of the Real Dad's Army: The Home Guard and the Defence of the United Kingdom 1940-44; Stephen Cullen; Pen & Sword Military; 2016; ISBN: 1-4738-7822-5. This book attempts to strip away the humour and misunderstanding which have served to create a false image of the HG. In doing so the author traces the changing role of the HG as it developed in order to meet the changing demands of the war.

The Real Dad's Army: The Story of the Home Guard; Norman Longmate; Amberley, 2016; ISBN: 1-4456-5403-2. The author is a veteran of the Home Guard and has written a popular history of the HG punctuated with a wealth of humourous anecdotes. An easy introduction to the topic.

Britain's Final defence: Arming the Home Guard, 1940–1944; Dale Clarke; The History Press; 2016; ISBN: 0-7509-6731-5. This book chronicles the challenges faced in creating and then arming the 16 million unpaid and largely untrained volunteers of the Home Guard. A very useful consideration of the full range of weaponry used by the real 'Dad's Army'.

AUXILIARY UNITS (SCALLYWAGS)

One of the most secret final lines of defence in the event of a German invasion were the Auxiliary Units – a secret network of highly trained volunteers operating in cells from hidden underground bases. Having seen the speed with which the Germans were able to overrun countries they invaded, Churchill clearly recognised the need to use irregular warfare to slow any German landings and advance, and initiated the Auxiliary Units in the summer of 1940. Although the Auxiliary Units were responsible to GHQ Home Forces, they were officially a part of the Home Guard organisation. Colonel Colin Gubbins was appointed to set up the Units using experience he gained in Norway leading the Independent Companies (predecessors of the Commandos). Gubbins later moved to the Special Operations Executive (SOE).

THE ARMED FORCES - THE ARMY

The Auxiliary Units were organised on County lines and distributed around the coastal areas most at risk of invasion. The Units were divided in to Operational Patrols of between four and eight men recruited from local farmers, gamekeepers and poachers. These men knew the land around them intimately and also had the ability to live off the land. The men would wear Home Guard uniform and operate within a radius of up to fifteen miles from their base. Approximately 3,500 men were trained in assassination skills, unarmed combat and demolition in weekend courses at Coleshill House, Oxfordshire. Recruits arriving at Coleshill Station were directed to the village Post Office where they were required to give a password to the postmistress (Mabel Stranks). She would then contact Coleshill and a car would be sent to collect the recruits. Once trained, they were equipped with silenced pistols, Sten sub-machine guns, knives and plastic explosive. Auxiliary Units would fight behind the enemy lines, attacking fuel dumps and railways as well as assassinating senior German officers and local collaborators; their anticipated life expectancy was twelve days. They were not expected to be taken alive. Sworn to secrecy, many of the men recruited to the Auxiliary Units went to their deaths without ever divulging what their involvement.

The Auxiliary Units worked from underground Operational Bases (OBs) and above ground they would have Observation Posts (OPs) from which enemy movements could be observed. Although exact figures do not exist, there are estimated to have been between 500 and 1,000 Operational Bases by the time the Auxiliary Units were stood down in November 1944. Many of their underground bases remain clouded in secrecy, having collapsed and been long forgotten, although a few have been located. Excavation of the Operational Bases was undertaken either by the patrol members themselves or by the Royal Engineers, usually in woodland, with a camouflaged entrance and emergency escape tunnel.

Other OBs utilised disused mine shafts, cellars, caves and even 2,000-year-old Pictish dwellings in Scotland!

CHOOSING A 'SCALLYWAG' IMPRESSION

Although an attractive option in many ways it must be remembered that the Auxiliary Units were totally secret and we are still learning of their activities and membership today. Because of this a 'Scallywag' impression would only work as part of a display of equipment and information detailing the activities of these men.

OBTAINING RELEVANT EQUIPMENT & ACCESSORIES

The Auxiliary Units wore Home Guard uniforms (see above for details of the uniform and places to purchase). Much of the equipment they used – like sticky bombs and Molotov cocktails – were home-made so facsimiles can be reproduced after a study of original items. The best source for study is the 'Museum of the British resistance Organisation' in Suffolk – see 'Further Research' (below) for details.

LIVING HISTORY GROUPS & LINKS

'**The Scallywags Mons 202**' aim to research the stories of the men and equipment of the Auxiliary Units and to educate the public through displays of the equipment. Further details: www.facebook.com/The-Scallywags-Mon-202-677898632303394

See under 'Home Guard' above.

FURTHER RESEARCH

'**British Resistance Archive**'; run by the Coleshill Auxiliary research Team (CART), this site is a wealth of information about the duties of this secret organisation including a list of all known personnel and their patrol areas and Operational Bases. The address is: www.staybehinds.com.

'**Museum of the British Resistance Organisation**'; the only museum dedicated to the work of the Auxiliary Units is based adjacent to the 390th Bombardment Group Memorial Air Museum Control Tower at Parham Airfield, Suffolk. Complete with a reconstructed Operational Base, the museum houses a fascinating collection of original material. The museum's website can be found at: www.parhamairfieldmuseum.co.uk/british-resistance-organisation.

Fighting Nazi Occupation: British resistance 1939–1945; Malcolm Atkin; Pen & Sword Military; 2015; ISBN: 1-4738-3377-9. A useful evaluation of the role of the Secret Intelligence Services (SIS) – now MI6 – in establishing a secret resistance movement which remained operational for most of the war. Some conclusions which challenge conventional thinking. Well worth reading.

Churchill's Underground Army: A History of the Auxiliary Units in the Second World War; John Warwicker; Frontline Books; 2008; ISBN: 1-8483-2515-0. A well written and accessible account of the Auxiliary Units. Some additional information has come to light since the book was published but it remains a valuable contribution to understanding the work of this secret organisation.

CHAPTER FOUR

THE ARMED FORCES
THE ROYAL AIR FORCE & THE ROYAL NAVY

The Royal Navy has always been regarded as the 'Senior Service' and Britain's defence and supply during the Second World War owes much to the courage and resilience of the naval personnel. However, fewer people choose to re-enact the Royal Navy than the Royal Air Force and therefore the chapter will begin with 'per ardua ad astra' ('through adversity to the stars' – the official motto of the Royal Air Force).

ROYAL AIR FORCE

The Royal Flying Corps (RFC) was formed on 13 May 1912 with a flying school at Upavon, Wiltshire. On 1 July 1914 the naval element of the RFC broke away to become the Royal Naval Air Service

(RNAS). At the start of the First World War the RFC had 179 aircraft and 1,244 officers and men. The initial function of the RFC was for artillery spotting and reconnaissance; however, experience soon led to the development of aircraft designed for specific functions including bombing and fighting. These developments were accompanied by increases in speed and engine power. The increasingly important role of the air force during the First World War proved it was becoming an essential tool of war. In April 1918 both the RFC and RNAS were combined to form the new Royal Air Force (RAF). By the end of the war the RAF was flying bombing raids in specially designed aircraft – part of a fleet of 22,647 aircraft in all, spread across 200 operational squadrons and a further 200 training squadrons.

With peace restored and no prospect of another European war, the RAF was reduced to thirty-three squadrons, of which twenty-one were to be based overseas to maintain peace across the Empire. Successful actions by the RAF against insurgents in India, Aden and Somaliland appeared to confirm this strategy. The opening of a cadet college at Cranwell, Lincolnshire, a staff college at Andover, Hampshire, and a School of Technical Training at Halton, Buckinghamshire, ensured a supply of properly trained pilots and ground crew. In 1925, the Air Defence of Great Britain Command (ADGB) was established to take control of Britain's air defence with a plan to increase the RAF's operational strength. In 1936 this command became RAF Fighter Command, and a separate Bomber Command and Coastal Command were also established. Hitler's assumption of power in 1933 heralded a rapid deterioration in the prospects for European peace and aircraft production was dramatically increased to meet this new threat. When the Second World War began the RAF had approximately 2,000 aircraft.

The aircrew of Handley Page Halifax bomber 'Friday the 13th' relax after a successful mission. — With permission Andrew Harrison

To meet the needs of another major conflict, training programmes were established throughout the Empire and British aircrew were even trained at civilian training schools in the United States until the US formally entered the war. New methods were tested in partnership with the army to assist in the deployment of troops by air using parachutes and gliders. Finally, the RAF Regiment was formed to defend aerodromes. The Regiment followed similar training to that given to Commandos and, while under the authority of the local Air Force Commander, the RAF Regiment could easily be subsumed into the army command structure should the need arise.

Having conquered France it was inevitable that Hitler would soon begin the invasion of Britain, codenamed Operation Sealion.

However, to ensure the success of a landing by sea, the threat of the RAF had to be neutralised first. In March 1940 the RAF began to bomb strategic targets in Germany as part of a campaign that would continue throughout the war. On the 8 August 1940 the German Luftwaffe began to attack fighter airfields across Southern Britain destroying aircraft on the ground and making it difficult for those in the air to land. After a German bomber accidentally bombed London, the RAF carried out a raid on Berlin. Incensed, the head of the Luftwaffe, Hermann Göring, turned his attention to the bombing of London with the intention of breaking the morale of the citizens. By the end of September all hope for a German invasion had ended and the Battle of Britain had been won.

With the threat of invasion gone, the RAF could turn its attention to supplying the armed forces. Transport planes played an essential role in transporting food and ammunition to the troops at the front and even vehicles and artillery. Such transports were essential in the Burma campaign where the terrain made resupply by land almost impossible. Fighter Command remained operational in all theatres and also in the protection of Britain from ongoing German raids. The role of the RAF was crucial

A pilot leaves the cockpit of a Spitfire.
— Author's Photograph

THE ARMED FORCES - THE ROYAL AIR FORCE & THE ROYAL NAVY

in keeping the Luftwaffe away from the D-Day landing beaches and in destroying key railway installations and other infrastructure ahead of the landings. Meanwhile, Bomber Command maintained its strategic bombing campaign against German targets. As more aircraft were produced, so bombing raids became increasingly destructive under the command of Air Chief Marshal 'Bomber' Harris. Very controlled raids of specific targets were also undertaken, for example against the Möhne, Eder and Sorpe dams by 617 Squadron and to release prisoners from the Amiens prison. By the time the war ended there were 936,000 people serving in the RAF of whom 153,000 were women.

The ethnic composition of the RAF was very diverse following the removal of the 'colour bar' in 1939. During the Battle of Britain 20 per cent of Fighter Command aircrew came from overseas and represented sixteen nations. Many of these were from Nazi-occupied countries, but others came from America, Rhodesia, Jamaica and Barbados. The RAF trained almost 500 black Caribbean aircrew and 6,000 ground crew during the war – all of whom had joined voluntarily. Indians also made an important contribution to the RAF with eighteen qualified pilots joining in 1940. One of those, Squadron Leader Mohinder Singh Pujji, is saddened by the general ignorance of their contribution. Today there are very few re-enactors from ethnic minority backgrounds, but those we have are trying their best to commemorate the contribution of those who served.

Rishi Askoolum is passionate about history and the part that Indian people played in the war. He feels tremendous 'responsibility to get my portrayal and character right ... put a face behind the uniform, become personable and engage the public and be confident – like our forefathers ... they too, were proud wearers of the uniform and just as patriotic'.

As Richi says:

"I am most grateful for the freedom we have, thanks to those that made the ultimate sacrifice and those that survived the horrors of war. My decision to represent people from ethnic minorities who fought for Britain during the war, was largely based on having a connection that would enable me to give a truer representation e.g. colour, culture and heritage."

Richi's portrayal of an RAF pilot certainly gets attention. 'At some events you get noticed a lot, which spurs many conversations, whereas others you don't much. I am very personable and I willingly engage many people, this helps a lot – along with a sense of humour!' Richi would love to see more re-enactors from ethnic minority backgrounds but feels that many potential recruits do not pursue the hobby 'probably because of a genuine lack of interest, and recognition on the public stage – therefore we need more books, movies, national media articles and documentaries that explain our role and ignite our interest

Richi Askoolum in full RAF flight kit.

– With permission Mike Grierson

Mick Sinclair in RAF uniform.

– With permission Mick Sinclair

into a hobby.' When asked what advice he might offer to those potentially interested in taking up the hobby, Richi suggests:

"be confident, pick someone that you can represent and connect with, then study up on them. Pick out the important attributes that make the uniform, the character and the portrayal. And then of course – enjoy it! It's about who we are/were back in those days – wanting a way out from poverty, being noticed, getting recognized, being equal, proud and willing to fight for what's right....actions change history, words set the stage!"

Mick Sinclair feels that his portrayal of an RAF pilot is a 'tribute to the soldiers and airmen from the British Commonwealth who, up till a few years ago, were barely mentioned, let alone recognised, for their work and contribution in the Second World War.'

Like Richi, Mick would also like to see more re-enactors from ethnic minority background and offers the following advice 'go for it, and BE PROUD OF IT. Don't allow the ignorance of a small number of people to diminish your pride in what you are doing – celebrate those who embrace your enthusiasm and commitment.'

UNIFORM

HEADWEAR

The Field Service Cap was popular with aircrew because it could be folded flat during the flight. Officers would wear the peaked Service Dress (SD) cap. All RAF personnel were required to carry their gas mask and Mk.II steel helmet at all times when on duty during the early years of the war, although this did relax a little later on.

CLOTHING

The standard uniform for RAF personnel was the Service Dress which had remained fundamentally unaltered since 1919. The jacket was made of blue-grey serge, single-breasted with four brass 'RAF' buttons at the front. There were two pleated pockets with flaps on the chest and two further pockets with flaps on the tunic skirt and a waist belt of matching fabric secured with a brass buckle. Officers' jackets were of similar design but made from finer barathea cloth. Officers wore sleeve braid on the cuffs; other ranks wore sleeve eagles at the top of the sleeve, while officers did not. The trousers were button-fronted, high-waisted and of the same material as the jacket. Officers were responsible for having their uniforms tailored and so the high waist was sometimes lost in favour of a more fashionable cut. All ranks wore a light blue-grey shirt and black wool tie beneath the jacket. Black leather shoes completed the uniform.

In 1940 the RAF adopted the army-style battledress uniform for aircrew and, in 1943, for all ranks. This was officially designated 'Suit Flying, Blue Grey Aircrews', and was basically a copy of the '37 Pattern army battledress blouse with pleated breast pockets and concealed buttons. The trousers, however, differed from the army version, lacking the deep map pocket and smaller shell dressing pocket. Instead, there was a small, flapped first aid pocket on the left hip. After 1943 this was replaced with the standard army pleated dressing pocket.

There is insufficient room here to address all of the equipment that aircrew would have needed while in the plane. Much is available today as reproduction but the best guide for this is *The RAF Battle of Britain Fighter Pilot's Kitbag: The Ultimate Guide to the Uniforms, Arms and Equipment from the Summer of 1940* by Mark Hillier. See below for further details.

CHOOSING AN RAF IMPRESSION

Between operations flight crews would often go to the nearest town for a beer and some relaxation, so someone in RAF Service Dress or battledress would not be out of place at any event. If you are choosing an RAF portrayal however, it is important to consider whether you might represent Fighter Command or Bomber Command, where you might be stationed and what aircraft you might have connection with. Know something about them, and be aware of dates. Be prepared to argue the case for Bomber Command when challenged about the Allied policy of bombing cities like Dresden. Membership of a group allows for much more depth since there are so many more roles that can be developed from working in an Ops Room to re-enacting an aircraft crew.

OBTAINING UNIFORM & ACCESSORIES

One of the best ranges of RAF clothing and accessories is available from '**Soldier of Fortune**' (www.sofmilitary.co.uk) who carry all of the variants described above, including the officers' uniform. A very useful article on buying reproduction officer's clothing (but applicable to other ranks as well) can be found at www.wadhamsfamilyhistory.co.uk/FortiesRAFuniform.htm

LIVING HISTORY GROUPS & LINKS

'**11 Group RAF Re-enactment**' commemorates the role of the RAF during the Second World War including the WAAF, Based predominantly in the South-East. Further details: www.facebook.com/groups/743678496049340

'**Tail End Charlies**' – the nick name given to the rear gunners on wartime bombers – is a living History Society dedicated to representing the history of the RAF. Further details: www.facebook.com/rafreenactment

'**Field Squadron RAF Regiment Living History**' group is part of the wider 'Tail End Charlies RAF Living History' group (see above) and preserves the memory of the RAF Regiment. Further details: www.facebook.com/FieldSquadronTEC

'**WWII RAF Group – Ops room display**' is a living history group dedicated to preserving the memory of those airmen and women who served this country during the Second World War, particularly those who played such a crucial role in the Operations Rooms, Further details: www.facebook.com/ww2rafgroup

FURTHER RESEARCH

Bomber Command's War Against Germany: An Official History; Air World; 2020; ISBN: 1-5267-9087-4. While there are many books on individual raids this is a detailed overview of Bomber Command throughout the war and a dispassionate and objective interpretation of the effectiveness of the bombing campaign and its contribution to the overall victory.

The RAF in the Battle of France and the Battle of Britain; Greg Baughen; Fonthill Media: 2016: ISBN: 1-7815-5525-7. The result of extensive and thorough research, this book covers RAF strategy and operations as the war develops. There is also a useful evaluation of Dowding's leadership of Fighter Command and a comparison of the tactics of Luftwaffe and RAF fighter pilots.

Air Force Blue: The RAF in World War Two: Patrick Bishop: William Collins: 2018: ISBN: 0-0074-3315-8. Although the RAF started the war with second-rate planes and no clear role, the Battle of Britain cemented their reputation and the RAF went on to play a vital role in the Allied victory. Using letters and interviews this is a very personal account of the RAF in every theatre of the war.

The RAF Battle of Britain Fighter Pilot's Kitbag: The Ultimate Guide to the Uniforms, Arms and Equipment from the Summer of 1940; Mark Hillier; Frontline Books; 2018; ISBN: 1-4738-4999-3. A very well-illustrated guide to the equipment used by the RAF in the Battle of Britain and the uses of each item. Essential reading for re-enactors and military modellers.

WOMEN'S AUXILIARY AIR FORCE (WAAF)

Originally founded at the same time as the RAF in April 1918, the Woman's Royal Air Force (WRAF) was disbanded in 1920 but reformed as the Women's Auxiliary Air Force (WAAF) in June 1939, as the threat of a new war loomed ever closer, by taking over the forty-eight RAF companies of the ATS which were established in 1938. Unlike the ATS, the WAAF was under direct RAF control and its members served alongside men as individual members of RAF Commands. The first Director of the WAAF was Jane Trefusis Forbes who had also served in the First World War. The first members of the WAAF were recruited to roles such as clerks, kitchen staff and drivers in order to free men up for active service. However, as the war progressed the opportunities available to WAAF recruits increased dramatically. Clerical roles expanded into communications roles as telephone and telegraph operators. Others became mechanics or electricians, helping to maintain the aircraft essential for Britain's defence. A small number worked on the interception and identification of codes, including working at the Government Code and Cypher School at Bletchley Park. Another crucial role was working in the Operations Rooms plotting the movements of Allied and enemy aircraft. These women played a vital role in bringing victory in the Battle of Britain. Providing weather reports, interpreting aerial photographs of potential targets and evaluating the effect of bombing were further roles WAAF recruits could undertake.

Probably the most physically demanding job undertaken by the WAAF was the operation of barrage balloon site. The barrage balloons were massive static balloons – three times the size of a cricket pitch

THE ARMED FORCES - THE ROYAL AIR FORCE & THE ROYAL NAVY

– filled with hydrogen gas which were held in place by steel cables, presenting a serious collision risk to low flying aircraft (and later V1 flying bombs).

The balloons were held at heights up to 5,000ft and raised or lowered by winches. Although there was some doubt about whether women would have the physical strength required, they proved so successful that the WAAF were soon responsible for more than 1,000 barrage balloon sites across Britain. Despite this success, WAAF members were not permitted to actually pilot aircraft and were only paid two-thirds the pay of a male airman. WAAF personnel served in Britain, America, Egypt and Europe after the D-Day landings, and were recruited from Canada, Australia, New Zealand, South Africa, and also the Middle East. In 1949 the WAAF was reformed and resumed its original name – WRAF.

WAAF plotters together with RAF and Army liaison colleagues in a plotting room.
– With permission Megan Scott / 11 Group RAF Re-enactment

A small number of WAAF personnel with very specific skills joined the Special Operations Executive (SOE) where they were trained in espionage and sent into enemy occupied Europe. This was an extremely dangerous task and many were captured, tortured, then executed by the Gestapo. Assistant Station Officer Noor Inayat Khan (codenamed 'Madeleine') was a wireless operator but was betrayed and subsequently executed at Dachau concentration camp. Section Officer Cecily Lefort (codenamed 'Alice') was a courier until arrested by the Gestapo in 1943 and executed at Ravensbrück concentration camp in 1945. Section Officer Yolande Beekman (codenamed 'Mariette' and 'Kilt') was a wireless operator until arrested by the Gestapo and executed at Dachau concentration camp. Their work, along with that of other WAAF recruits to the SOE, did much to coordinate French resistance and hamper attempts by the Germans to bring up reinforcements to challenge the Normandy landings. Adam and Charles Black, in their book *The WAAF in Action*, record the comments of an RAF group captain who in 1939 was, at best, highly critical of the idea of women in the RAF. After the war, however, he noted that 'I have cause to thank goodness that this country can produce such a race of women as the WAAF of my station.' – a sentiment widely echoed!

UNIFORM

HEADWEAR

The WAAF cap shared its basic design with that of the ATS. It has a black, patent leather peak and chinstrap. The sides of the cap are internally supported with a soft crown. The RAF badge is fixed to a black band of material around the cap. A Mk.II steel helmet in RAF dark blue was also available to those engaged in outside work.

CLOTHING

Like the cap, the main WAAF uniform also took inspiration from the ATS equivalent and saw few design changes throughout the war. The uniform was made from barathea cloth. The jacket had two pleated breast pockets and two further, larger pockets on the tunic skirt and was completed with a belt in the same material. The pockets were closed with small brass RAF buttons and the jacket had four large buttons closing it. The skirt fastened with snap fasteners and a single button on the waistband. A cloth badge showing the RAF albatross symbol was worn at the top of each sleeve. Trade qualification patches were worn between the shoulder and elbow on the right sleeve. A blue-grey collared shirt was worn beneath the jacket with a black tie. Shoes were of black pebbled leather with an 'apron front' which was both fashionable and also allowed for the use of smaller pieces of leather in manufacture. There were five sets of eyelets for the laces. Apart from the lack of epaulettes, the WAAF greatcoat was almost identical to its ATS equivalent in design, being double-breasted and with five pairs of RAF brass buttons. The greatcoat was in RAF blue and also had the RAF albatross patch on each shoulder.

For some tasks the standard WAAF uniform was not well suited and so the WAAF 'Suit Working, Serge' was introduced which was based very closely on the '37 pattern army battledress uniform but in RAF blue. A major difference was the trousers, which buttoned up on the left hip. A black beret was issued with this uniform which – unusually – was worn with the beret pulled down over the back of the head. The RAF badge was affixed to the front of the beret. As the army later adopted the Austerity uniform with exposed buttons and no pocket pleats, the 'Suit Working, Serge' underwent similar changes. By the end of the war, it was not uncommon to see the serge working blouse being worn with the skirt.

Officer's dress was very similar to that worn by male RAF officers but tailored for women. There were two pleated breast pockets and two large concertina pockets on the tunic skirt and a belt of the same material finished the garment. Rank lace worn on the sleeve cuffs was the same as worn on male uniforms. The skirt was similar to that worn by other ranks but of superior quality. Shirts and stockings were usually privately purchased. Shoes were as per other ranks.

CHOOSING A WAAF IMPRESSION

As with most service impressions, unless you are thinking of providing a display related to the WAAF it is probably better to represent either a WAAF on leave or join a larger group where there will be greater opportunity to truly represent the work of the WAAF and their male counterparts.

OBTAINING UNIFORM & ACCESSORIES

Original uniform items are becoming scarce and – as with any items over seventy-five years old – there continues to be a valid debate as to whether they should be worn, especially when reproduction items are readily available. A useful guide to buying WAAF uniform can be found at www.wadhamsfamilyhistory.co.uk/FortiesWAAFuniform.htm, which is well worth reading before making any decisions. '**The History Bunker**' offers a reproduction service dress uniform and also the 'Suit Working, Serge' uniform thehistorybunker.co.uk/index.php?route=product/search&search=WAAF. '**Soldier of Fortune**' also offer a range of complete WAAF uniforms including the officer's uniform or individual items to complete an impression. Details at www.sofmilitary.co.uk/catalogsearch/result/?q=WAAF

LIVING HISTORY GROUPS & LINKS

'**Tail End Charlies**' – the nick-name given to the rear gunners on wartime bombers – is a living history group dedicated to representing the history of the RAF. Further details: www.facebook.com/rafreenactment

'**WWII RAF Group – Ops room display**' is a living history group dedicated to preserving the memory of those airmen and women who served this country during the Second World War, particularly those who played such a crucial role in the Operations Rooms. Further details: www.facebook.com/ww2rafgroup

FURTHER RESEARCH

World War II British Women's Uniforms in Colour Photographs; Martin Brayley and Richard Ingram; Crowood Press Ltd; 1998; ISBN: 1-8591-5032-2. With almost 200 colour photos this is a must-have book for anyone researching any aspect of British women's wartime uniforms. With detailed explanatory text this book documents many rare examples of uniforms from private collections.

The WAAF at War; John Frayn Turner; Pen & Sword Aviation; 2011; ISBN: 1-8488-4539-1. A well-written and moving account of the various roles undertaken by the women of the WAAF, including those seconded to SOE, many of whom never returned. This useful account also includes those women seconded to the Air Transport Auxiliary to actually fly aircraft to front-line units.

Our Wartime Days: The WAAF; Squadron Leader Beryl Escott; The History Press: 2009; ISBN: 0-7524-5029-8. With plentiful accounts from those who actually served, this book covers everything from recruitment to demobilisation. Poignant accounts of life away from home under the pressures of war and the relationships which formed between the WAAF members and the men they served alongside.

We All Wore Blue: Experiences in the WAAF; Muriel Gane Pushman; Tempus: 2006; ISBN: 0-7524-4130-2. A very personal account of the transition one woman made from an 18-year-old, inexperienced girl obsessed with the fit of the uniform, to a hard-working and dedicated professional with a successful career in the Women's Auxiliary Air Force.

AIR TRANSPORT AUXILIARY (ATA)

Those who served in the Air Transport Auxiliary would tell you that the letters 'ATA' actually stood for 'Anything to Anywhere'! Unlike the WAAF, the ATA was a civilian organisation originally intended to ferry mail, medical supplies and personnel from place to place. However, by August 1941 they had taken on the vital role of transporting new and repaired planes from factories and maintenance depots to active front-line squadrons, which freed up many male pilots

Pilots of the Air Transport Auxiliary pose in front of a Spitfire – one of the many types of aircraft they were called upon to fly.

– With permission 1940s Vintage Photography

for combat duty. In many ways the ATA was ahead of its time as a fully inclusive and equal opportunity organisation. Both male and female pilots were employed – and on equal pay from 1943. The ATA boasted pilots from twenty-eight different countries (including neutral countries) and even included some pilots with disabilities which would have precluded them from combat roles. Many of the pilots would have failed the fitness examinations for the RAF but as long as they could fly, the ATA would take them – leading to the irreverent suggestion that ATA actually stood for 'Ancient and Tattered Airmen'. Pilots Charles Dutton and Stewart Keith-Jopp both had lost an arm but could still fly.

The order to set up a women's section of the ATA was given in November 1939 under the leadership of Commander Pauline Gower. The first eight women were formally accepted into the ATA in 1 January 1940, but only permitted to fly the outdated Tiger Moth aircraft. On 19 July 1941 Winnie Crossley had the distinction of being the first woman to be cleared to fly a Hurricane fighter. Once cleared for a class of aircraft, pilots could be asked to ferry any plane in that class, whether they had trained on it or not.

Pilots were issued with a ring binder containing the key information and statistics necessary to operate each plane. If a pilot was cleared on more than one class of aircraft, it was possible to fly in with a Spitfire and fly out piloting a four-engine Lancaster heavy bomber. A pilot could be cleared on any number of classes as follows:

Class 1 Light single-engine

Class 2 Advanced single-engine

Class 3 Light twin-engine

Class 4 Advanced twin-engine

Class 5 Four-engine

Class 6 Flying Boats

No matter how skilled a pilot was, there were clear restrictions imposed – they were to ferry planes only, no blind-flying or aerial stunts – because the need to safely transport aircraft took priority. Since the aim was for the ATA pilots to simply move the planes between production factories or maintenance depots and front-line squadrons there was felt to be no need for the planes to be armed,

THE ARMED FORCES - THE ROYAL AIR FORCE & THE ROYAL NAVY

An ATA pilot in battledress uniform and Field Service cap.

– With permission Helen Murdoch

but after a number of encounters with enemy aircraft some planes were transported fully armed.

By the end of the war 173 ATA aircrew had died in service. The ATA had flown 415,000 hours and delivered over 309,000 aircraft. When the ATA was disbanded in 1945 the wartime Minister for Aircraft production paid tribute to their work saying:

> *"without the ATA the days and nights of the Battle of Britain would have been conducted under conditions quite different from the actual events. They carried out the delivery of aircraft from the factories to the RAF, thus relieving countless numbers of RAF pilots for duty in the battle. Just as the Battle of Britain is the accomplishment and achievement of the RAF, likewise it can be declared that the ATA sustained and supported them in the battle. They were soldiers fighting in the struggle just as completely as if they had been engaged on the battlefront."*

UNIFORM

HEADWEAR

The standard RAF pattern Field Service Cap was issued to both men and women but in an extremely dark blue shade (almost black). Males could also wear the standard male RAF peaked cap, again in the extremely dark blue colour but this was not allowed for ceremonial duties. Similarly, a peaked ski-cap was available for female ATA personnel, but again not for ceremonial duties. When the ATA began, all caps carried a gold metal badge of the ATA insignia but these were later replaced with woven examples. The ATA badge bore the letters 'ATA'. Of these, the letter 'T' was taller and surrounded by a wreath with an eagle on top.

CLOTHING

As with the peaked hat and Field Service cap, the ATA uniform for both male and female personnel was identical to that worn by RAF and WAAF equivalents, except in the extremely dark blue colour of the ATA. Instead of the brass RAF buttons the uniform had black buttons (sometimes plain and sometimes bearing the ATA letters surmounted by a coronet). Standard RAF light blue shirts and black ties completed the uniform. An RAF pattern greatcoat in ATA extreme dark blue was also available, the only difference being that the women's greatcoat fastened on the female side. Instead of the RAF pilots' winged insignia the ATA uniform bore a set of wings in gold thread with the letters 'ATA' in a central oval. Gold colour rank markings were also worn on the jacket epaulettes.

CHOOSING AN ATA IMPRESSION

Today many people have not heard of the ATA and are subsequently unaware of the huge contribution these pilots made to the war effort. Nor are they aware of the skills exhibited by ATA personnel – many of them women – in piloting a huge range of aircraft from single-engine fighters to four-engine heavy bombers. It is a story that needs to be told and an ATA portrayal allows the opportunity to do just that.

OBTAINING UNIFORM & ACCESSORIES

Being less well-known than the RAF and WAAF there are fewer companies offering reproduction uniforms however, '**The History Bunker**' offers a range of reproduction ATA uniforms and insignia (thehistorybunker.co.uk). '**Khaki on Campaign**' also offer an excellent reproduction uniform (khaki-on-campaign.webs.com).

LIVING HISTORY GROUPS & LINKS

'**Anything to Anywhere: ATA Living History Group**' is a re-enactment group which represents the work of the Air Transport Auxiliary and those who served in it. Further details: www.facebook.com/Anythingtoanywhere

'**Air Transport Auxiliary Re-enactment Group – ATA**' is a living history group which aims to raise public awareness of the Air Transport Auxiliary through re-enactment and education. Many WAAFs were seconded to the ATA so a linked area of interest. Further details: www.facebook.com/ATAReEnactmentGroup

'**Tail End Charlies**' – the nickname given to the rear gunners on wartime bombers – is a living History Society dedicated to representing the history of the RAF but includes the ATA. Further details: www.facebook.com/rafreenactment

THE ARMED FORCES - THE ROYAL AIR FORCE & THE ROYAL NAVY

FURTHER RESEARCH

Air Transport Auxiliary at War: 80th Anniversary of its Formation; Stephen Wynn; Pen & Sword Aviation; 2021; ISBN: 1-5267-2604-1. This book offers an introduction to the ATA and an insight into the lives of some of the pilots. It also pays tribute to those who died. An easy read and useful starting point for further research.

The Female Few: Spitfire Heroines; Jacky Hyams; Spellmount; 2016; ISBN: 0-7509-6818-4. This is the story of the women ATA pilots told through the experiences of five former pilots who talk about their work but set against the backdrop of their everyday lives. A well-written and moving book.

Spitfire Women of World War II; Giles Whittell; Harper Perennial; 2008; ISBN: 0-0072-3536-4. Although the title refers to Spitfires, this book looks at the work of the women ATA pilots flying all types of aircraft. The book looks at their wider lives as well as their work. An interesting contribution to social and aviation history.

OBSERVER CORPS/ ROYAL OBSERVER CORPS

Although not extensively bombed from the air in the First World War, raids by German Zeppelins and later heavy Gotha bombers showed how vulnerable Britain was, especially in the south-east, closest to the Continent. A total of 1,316 people had been killed in 643 German raids. As aircraft development continued this threat would increase exponentially. An inquiry into Britain's aerial defence in 1924 identified deficiencies and, in August 1924, trials began to determine accurate movements of aircraft above Britain. These trials proved successful and led to the formation of the Observer Corps – initially focused on Maidstone and Horsham, although this area was extended following successful observation exercises in June 1925. Volunteer observers were recruited and paid through the police force with observers classed as special constables. In 1929 control of the rapidly expanding Observer Corps was passed to the Air Ministry under Air Commodore E.A.D. Masterman, although observers still retained their special constable status.

As the threat of war increased in the 1930s it soon became apparent that the whole of Britain was vulnerable from the air – not just London and the South-East. The industrial Midlands were now a probable target, as were the transport systems linking these factories with the rest of the country. A conference held in December 1934 confirmed the need for a greater geographic coverage by the Observer Corps and the need for effective communications between observers and the relevant RAF centres. Part of this process would require the Observer Corps to be more closely linked to the RAF Air Raid Warning system.

THE ARMED FORCES - THE ROYAL AIR FORCE & THE ROYAL NAVY

The Observer Corps was officially mobilised in 24 August 1939 and from that date until the end of the war all observer posts and centres were manned twenty-four hours a day, every day. The early days of the war saw little action in the skies over Britain but provided useful training opportunities which would pay off when the Battle of Britain began. The Battle of Britain would give way to the Blitz on British cities which continued until the summer of 1941, although more sporadic raids continued until March 1945.

In recognition of the sterling achievements of the Observer Corps during these times, King George VI allowed the use of the prefix 'Royal' on 9 April 1941. One of the best-known achievements of the

Men of the Observer Corps calculate the height and direction of incoming enemy bombers.
— With permission John Purkiss

Observer Corps was the plotting of the aircraft belonging to senior Nazi Rudolph Hess as it crossed Britain east to west before crashing near Glasgow; the true purpose of Hess's flight remains obscure to this day. 1941 also saw the introduction of women in to the ROC; although they were not paid the same rate as men, they undertook the same duties. While some observer posts were mixed gender many were not, and women were generally not permitted to do night shifts, and certainly never alongside men. Observers were now classed as either, Class A: full-time and working at least forty-eight hours a week, and Class B: part-time working up to twenty-four hours per week. From December 1941 ROC observers were permitted to wear the RAF blue serge battledress uniform instead of their own clothes.

By 1944 members of the ROC had honed their skills to remarkable levels being able to recognise different types of Allied and enemy planes by just a silhouette or even, in cases of limited visibility, by the sound of the engine. These skills would be important during the D-Day landings to ensure that no Allied aircraft were fired on in the confusion of battle. The Air Ministry appealed for volunteers to serve on board merchant ships. Over 1,000 observers volunteered and 796 were chosen, ranging from 17 to 70 years old. These 'seaborne' observers would wear the normal ROC uniform with the addition of 'Seaborne' shoulder flashes and a Royal Navy brassard with the letters 'RN'. They were given the rank of petty officer (aircraft identifier). The seaborne observers were allocated to every US Navy warship and armed merchant ships and controlled the ship's anti-aircraft batteries (although the ship's captain retained overall command and could overrule them). The performance of the seaborne observers was seen as an overwhelming success with only two observers lost to enemy action. Air Chief Marshal Trafford Leigh-Mallory later wrote to ROC personnel stating:

> "I have read reports from both pilots and naval officers regarding the Seaborne volunteers on board merchant vessels during recent operations. All reports agree that the Seaborne volunteers have more than fulfilled their duties and have undoubtedly saved many of our aircraft from being engaged by our ships' guns. I should be grateful if you would please convey to all ranks of the Royal Observer Corps, and in particular to the Seaborne observers themselves, how grateful I, and all pilots in the Allied Expeditionary Air Force, are for their assistance, which has contributed in no small measure to the safety of our own aircraft, and also to the efficient protection of the ships at sea."

At the end of the war the ROC was finally stood down only to be reformed in 1947 as the Cold War escalated.

UNIFORM

HEADWEAR

Initially the Observer Corps members wore the blue Mk.II steel helmet with 'POLICE' stencilled on the front. This was later superseded by a helmet (blue, green or black) with either 'OC' or 'OBSERVER CORPS' stencilled on it or bearing the OC colours. When the RAF battledress uniform was adopted a lack of berets led to black Royal Tank Regiment berets being issued bearing an Observer Corps badge until sufficient stocks of the RAF midnight blue berets became available. This then became the correct beret for the uniform.

CLOTHING

When the Observer Corps began there was no formal uniform and members were identified by a lapel badge with an enamelled border bearing the words 'Observer Corps' and 'Forewarned is Forearmed'. When on duty OC members wore a blue and white striped police duty band bearing the letters 'OC' or 'Observer Corps'. From 1941 the RAF were able to supply battledress uniform to the ROC. Shortages of NCO rank chevrons led to alternatives being used – in this case rank badges intended for the Royal Canadian (Volunteer) Storekeeper Corps. These patches showed rank as a series of horizontal bars within a wreath. ROC personnel who served aboard ships on D-Day were permitted to wear the 'Seaborne' patch throughout their service. RAF shirts, tie and shoes completed the uniform.

CHOOSING AN ROC IMPRESSION

The skill of ROC observers was incredible and their ability to correctly identify aircraft – even by engine sound alone – played a vital part in the defence of Britain against German raids. This is a story which needs to be told and an effective and engaging display of an observation post at work can be achieved with some sandbags and binoculars. Original wartime aircraft recognition books simply add depth and detail to the display.

THE ARMED FORCES - THE ROYAL AIR FORCE & THE ROYAL NAVY

OBTAINING UNIFORM & ACCESSORIES:

Since the ROC uniform was basically the RAF uniform with different insignia added, see under 'RAF' above for suppliers of the basic RAF war service (battledress) uniform. Cloth insignia can be obtained from **'Kelly's Badges'** (www.kellybadges.co.uk).

LIVING HISTORY GROUPS & LINKS

There are few groups specifically for ROC re-enactment but there are a number of groups dedicated to the preservation of specific ROC observation posts although most of these are from the Cold-War era.

'The Royal Observer Corps at War' is a group for those interested in recreating the role of the Royal Observer Corps in the build up to, and during, WW2. www.facebook.com/groups/181480852619547

FURTHER RESEARCH

Royal Observer Corps: The Eyes and Ears and the RAF in WWII (Official History); An Official History; Frontline Books; 2018; ISBN: 1-5267-2488-X. This official history, compiled shortly after the war ended, chronicles all aspects of the work of the ROC. There is a section on the seaborne operations and also on the tracking of Rudolf Hess's aircraft. Detailed and thorough.

ROYAL NAVY

At the beginning of the Second World War, the Royal Navy boasted the largest navy in the world. Such a large navy was needed to ensure the safe movement of trade goods around the British Empire. Such was the traditional dependence on the navy that it was referred to as the 'Senior Service' – a title it proudly retains to this day. Being an island Britain has needed the protection of ships since Saxon times. In 1217 the English were able to put together a fleet to defend against a French fleet threatening the coast; the incident proved that although armies could be raised as needed, it was necessary to maintain a fleet. Indeed, there was no standing army at all until Cromwell's New Model Army during the Civil War. It is for this reason that the navy is the Royal Navy, having been established by the Crown, whereas the army derives from Parliament's forces.

Between 1939 and 1943 the Royal Navy was under the command of the First Sea Lord Admiral Sir Dudley Pound. Early actions added even greater lustre to the navy's reputation with vital roles in the successful evacuations of British troops from Norway, Dunkirk and Crete. However, the reputation of the navy suffered a major blow with the loss of HMS Hood to the German battleship Bismarck. Even the sinking of the Bismarck several days later did not restore public confidence. The navy played a key role in resupplying Malta and allowing it to continue to hold out, also interrupting Axis supplies in the Mediterranean and protecting convoys from U-Boat attacks.

Naval supremacy was essential to operations like the landings in Sicily and Normandy; not just to facilitate the initial landings, but to ensure a steady supply of reinforcements and materiel. The nature of

THE ARMED FORCES - THE ROYAL AIR FORCE & THE ROYAL NAVY

warfare was changing however, and the aircraft carrier became the new symbol of power at sea. The Royal Navy had been a pioneer in the development of these vessels but the United States was now gaining naval superiority and, as the war progressed deeper into Europe, the Royal Navy's role was reduced to convoy escort. Experience had led to developments in combating the threat from U-Boats enabling the Allies to defeat the 'wolf packs' making convoy escort much less dangerous than it had been. In the Pacific, the British Pacific Fleet continued to operate against Japanese targets.

In August 1945 the Royal Navy had some 900 warships and approximately one million people serving in its ranks. A great deal was learned during the war and the navy of 1945 was rather different to the one which started the war.

Royal Navy Petty Officers and Ratings relax outside a pub while on shore leave.

– With permission Andrew Harrison

UNIFORM

HEADWEAR

Ratings wore a blue-top peakless cap with a 'HMS' tally tied around (unofficially but commonly worn with the bow over the right eye). Chief petty officers and above wore a peaked cap. The grey Mk.II steel helmet was worn when at action stations.

CLOTHING

There were few changes made to the naval uniform throughout the war but this apparent advantage has to be set against the number of uniforms that existed.

This section will not address ratings acting as stewards or cooks, but will concentrate on Class I (chief petty officers), Class II (ratings) and Class III (petty officers). Ratings wore the traditional 'square rig' uniform. Bell-bottomed trousers were worn with five or seven near-horizontal creases and a vertical crease at the sides. These creases were pressed from the inside so that they folded inwards when worn. A blue or white square-necked T-shirt was worn under the jumper. Rank and trade insignia were worn on the jumper that also had a large collar which was pulled out to form a neck flap. A black silk square, folded seven times and sewn at one end to form a loop, was worn around the neck, over the jumper but beneath the neck flap and tied at the front. A white lanyard worn around the neck looped around the silk and then inside the jumper.

Class I and III ratings wore very similar uniforms – the main difference being the placement of the trade patches – on the collar for Class

THE ARMED FORCES - THE ROYAL AIR FORCE & THE ROYAL NAVY

A sailor in 'square-rig' uniform.

– With permission
Andrew Harrison

I and on the sleeve for Class III. Both classes wore the standard double-breasted jacket with two rows of three brass navy buttons, trousers and a shirt and tie. Jackets also had three small brass buttons on the cuffs indicating rank. Officers wore a double-breasted jacket with two rows of four gilt buttons, trousers, and a white shirt and collar with black tie. Naval officers also wore an unofficial uniform of blue-black serge battledress blouse and trousers. The blouse had exposed gilt buttons and a button fastening for the waistbelt. Some of these blouses were privately commissioned from tailors while others were dyed army blouses.

CHOOSING A ROYAL NAVY IMPRESSION

Without proximity to a period ship a naval impression can be challenging unless part of a group. Most naval re-enactors tend to portray personnel on leave unless they are with a display of naval uniform and equipment.

OBTAINING UNIFORM & ACCESSORIES

'**The History Bunker**' offers a nice reproduction flat-top ratings cap and HMS tally (thehistorybunker.co.uk) while '**Epic Militaria**' offer a reproduction officer's cap (www.epicmilitaria.com). '**Soldier of Fortune**' (www.sofmilitary.co.uk) offer a range of reproduction insignia and rank shoulder boards as well as the officer's cap (either blue or white top). There are a number of dealers who offer wartime naval uniforms either as reproductions or identical pattern post-war items. Original items can also come up on eBay but the usual caution needs to be used regarding price and, if reproduction, quality.

LIVING HISTORY GROUPS & LINKS

Most people portraying the officers or ratings of the Royal Navy tend to be standalone re-enactors appearing at events either as promenaders 'on leave', or as part of a display of related uniforms and equipment.

FURTHER RESEARCH

Royal Navy Uniforms 1939–1945; Martin Brayley; Crowood Press Ltd'; 2014; ISBN: 1-8479-7844-4. Richly illustrated using period photos and modern colour photos of original uniforms, this book shows the uniform and effects of ratings and officers in great detail. Accompanied by detailed text this is a must-have book for anyone interested in the appearance of the Royal Navy in wartime.

The Royal Navy 1939-45: No.79 (Elite); Ian Sumner and Alix Baker; Osprey Publishing; 2001; ISBN: 1-8417-6195-8. An informative account of the role of the Royal Navy during the Second World War including a very useful and well-illustrated section on the uniforms worn.

Citizen Sailors: The Royal Navy in the Second World War; Glyn Prysor; Penquin; 2012; ISBN: 0-1410-4632-5. The sailors of the Royal Navy saw action across the globe from the Arctic convoys to submarines. Prysor writes a fascinating narrative of the work of the Royal Navy brought to life through contemporary letters and diaries.

WOMEN'S ROYAL NAVAL SERVICE (WRNS)

Originally founded in 1917 and disbanded after the end of hostilities in 1919, the Women's Royal Naval Service (WRNS) was reformed in 1939 under the leadership of Director Vera Laughton Matthews (who had served with the WRNS in the First World War). As with the other women's services, the initial intention was simply to release men from desk duties for active service as shown in early recruitment posters which encourage women to 'Join the Wrens and free a man for the Fleet'. However, as the war progressed women were able to show just how resilient they really were and consequently were given greater opportunities and responsibilities. In addition to clerical and driving duties, 'Wrens' also operated essential radar and communications equipment as well as preparing weather forecasts. Wrens fluent in other languages were sent to coastal stations as part of Special Duties Y Section, where they intercepted and translated enemy communications, and some even served at the Government Code and Cypher School at Bletchley Park, Buckinghamshire. Wrens were also involved in planning the D-Day landings of Operation Overlord – the invasion of Europe.

Following initial recruitment campaigns there were 3,000 Wrens serving by the end of December 1939 and the WRNS reached its peak in 1944 with almost 74,000 women serving, although women were not allowed to serve on Royal Navy ships. Wrens were permitted to operate tugs and harbour launches close to shore and a small number of Wrens served as pilots on D-Day taking over smaller ships and towing back ships with mechanical problems which were often then repaired by WRNS personnel. In addition to working across all branches of the Royal Navy, including the

A member of the Women's Royal Naval Service.

– With permission
Andrew Harrison

Fleet Air Arm, Wrens also served in the Indian Navy as part of the Women's Royal Indian Naval Service (WRINS).

One Wren, Ginger Thomas, became the shorthand typist seconded to work with Lieutenant General Frederick E. Morgan. Morgan was Chief of Staff to the Supreme Allied Commander and, as such, responsible for much of the original planning for D-Day and Operation Overlord. Many Wrens thoroughly enjoyed their period of service and did not relish the return to civilian life. Rozelle Raynes later recalled:

> "when I had to go for my final interview with the Commander of the base when I was being demobbed, I remember him being very kind, and, you know, telling me about a job he would recommend me for, and saying how wonderful I would find civvy street, and I remember bursting into floods of tears and rushing from his office in a terrible state."

UNIFORM

HEADWEAR

Pre–1942 Wrens wore a soft-crowned, broad-brimmed gabardine hat, but post–1942 junior ratings wore hats similar to those of their male counterparts (although it has a soft, unstiffened crown) with the traditional Royal Navy cap tally. Officers and senior ratings wore a tricorn hat. The cap badge bears a light-blue wreath surrounding the fouled anchor motif in place of the gold wreath worn on men's hats.

CLOTHING

From 1939, the WRNS uniform consisted of a course, blue serge double-breasted jacket and skirt based on the the First World War uniform, but updated to be more fashionable. The skirt was worn just below the knee. The uniform was worn over a white shirt (with detachable collar) and a black tie, for all ranks. Black stockings and plain black leather shoes completed the uniform. Senior ratings (petty officers and above) wore a similar uniform but with the addition of gilt buttons, small gilt buttons on the cuff and a rank badge. All insignia, including cap badges and non-substantive (trade) badges, were blue. Wrens were initially issued only a single uniform but by 1943 most had a second, 'best' uniform. Wrens were also issued with a greatcoat of double-breasted, 'lancer' style fastening with a double row of four black buttons. Shoes were of plain black leather with four lace eyelets each side. Wrens also had a variety of workwear and overalls for performing specific tasks such as officers' stewards.

The WRNS officer's uniform was based on that worn by male counterparts. The jacket was a double-breasted tunic made of fine barathea secured by a double row of gilt buttons. Light blue rank lacing was worn at each cuff with the upper length surmounted by a diamond as opposed to the circle used on male uniforms. The skirt was made of the same material but was embellished by the addition of a double box-pleat. Unlike counterparts in the ATS and WAAF, the WRNS tunic buttoned on the ladies' side (i.e. right over left). The officer's great coat was both stylish and functional. It was secured by a double row of six gilt buttons and rank was indicated on shoulder boards.

THE ARMED FORCES - THE ROYAL AIR FORCE & THE ROYAL NAVY

CHOOSING A WRNS IMPRESSION

Unless you are lucky enough to live in a port town and have access to ships you will probably want to portray a Wren on leave, which works well and displays what is widely regarded as the most attractive of the women's service uniforms.

OBTAINING UNIFORM & EQUIPMENT

As ever, eBay is a useful source of material but it is important to be aware of what items generally sell for, since prices can range from very good to extravagant depending on what the seller thinks an item is worth and how many people want it. A good place to look for reproduction items is the relatively new site '**Dressed for Impression (Second World War British Empire uniform reproductions for women)**', which offers a discussion forum to answer questions and offer advice about the best places to obtain items – www.facebook.com/groups/852417575358122.

LIVING HISTORY GROUPS & LINKS

At the time of writing there appear to be no living history groups dedicated to the WRNS, but a number of groups offer multi-service portrayals and these might be worth looking at.

FURTHER RESEARCH

> '**Dressed for Service (WW2 Women's Military Uniforms of the British Empire**' is a site dedicated to the study of Second World War British women's uniforms and a valuable reference source for re-enactors – www.facebook.com/groups/636201423100487.

WWII British Women's Uniforms in Colour Photographs; Martin Brayley and Richard Ingram; Crowood Press Ltd; 1998; ISBN: 1-8591-5032-2. With almost 200 colour photos this is a must-have book for anyone researching any aspect of British women's wartime uniforms. With detailed explanatory text this book documents many rare examples of uniforms from private collections.

Britannia's Daughters: The Story of the WRNS; Ursula Stuart Mason; Pen & Sword Maritime; 2012; ISBN: 1-8488-4678-9. A study of the WRNS throughout its history up to the present day enriched with many personal accounts. The book also includes details of the secret duties some Wrens undertook as well as service oversea.

The WRNS in Wartime: The Women's Royal Naval Service 1917–1945; Hannah Roberts; Bloomsbury Publishing; 2019; ISBN: 0-7556-0198-X. Within the framework of the development of the WRNS from its initial foundation in 1917, this book looks at the impact that key individuals had on its development, and how the changing military and political situation allowed for women to become increasingly involved in the war.

The WRNS in Camera: The Work of the Women's Royal Naval Service in the Second World War; Chris Howard Bailey and Lesley Thomas: Sutton Publishing: 2000; ISBN: 0-7509-1370-3. A very useful source for the re-enactor because, although there is a history of the WRNS provided, the bulk of the book is, as the title suggests, based on period photographs – an invaluable source of information in uniform and insignia.

ROYAL MARINES, COMMANDOS & ROYAL MARINE COMMANDOS

The Royal Marines have a long and distinguished history, tracing their roots back to the Duke of York and Albany's Maritime Regiment of Foot, formed in October 1664. After meritorious service in the First World War (where five Royal Marines earned the Victoria Cross), there was an attempt to completely disband the Marines after 1922. However, instead, the Royal Marine Light Infantry (RMLI) and the Royal Marine Artillery (RMA) were amalgamated with the former ranks of 'private' and 'gunner' respectively, being abolished and a new rank of 'marine' was instituted. Marines were engaged early in the Second World War capturing the approaches to Namsos in Norway in April 1940. As the Royal Marine division, they participated in the capture of Madagascar. Throughout the war the Royal Marines manned many of the guns on naval vessels and also provided detachments on ships as they have traditionally done since the seventeenth century. Men of the Royal Marines Armoured Support Group provided two regiments of Centaur tanks as part of the D-Day landing force and Marines also crewed some Landing Craft.

In June 1940, Prime Minister Winston Churchill ordered the formation of an Army Commando unit, writing in a document dated 18 June 1940:

> "What are the ideas of C.-in-C., H.F., about Storm Troops? We have always set our faces against this idea, but the Germans certainly gained in the last war by adopting it, and this time it has been a leading cause of

RE-LIVING BRITAIN IN THE 1940S

Royal Marine Commandos at a re-enactment.

– With permission Alan Hutchins / Paul Gregory

> *their victory. There ought to be at least twenty thousand Storm Troops or 'Leopards' drawn from existing units, ready to spring at the throat of any small landings or descents. These officers and men should be armed with the latest equipment, tommy guns, grenades etc., and should be given great facilities in motor-cycles and armoured cars."*

Churchill favoured the name Commandos, but the military hierarchy favoured the term Special Service. In the end the two terms would be used synonymously.

Within weeks, the first Army Commando units were raised. The first Commando units comprised ten troops of fifty men each, changed in 1941 to six troops of sixty-five men each. The Army Commandos served in Norway, the Middle East and North Africa, including a raid on Rommel's Headquarters in November 1941. Probably their most famous raid was on the great dry dock at St Nazaire – the only dock large enough to accommodate the German battleship Tirpitz. The Commandos were able to damage the dock sufficiently for it to be out of commission for the remainder of the war, confining the Tirpitz to Norwegian waters where it was later sunk by the RAF. In August 1942 Commandos also participated in the raid on Dieppe.

In 1943 the infantry battalions of the Royal Marine Division were re-designated as Commandos, joining their army counterparts and leading to the division becoming a Special Service command. In all, four Special Service Brigades were created with Royal Marine Commandos represented in all of them. A total of nine Royal Marine Commando battalions were raised (numbered from 40 to 48) seeing action in Sicily, Normandy, the Rhineland, Anzio, Salerno, Sicily, and Burma.

RE-LIVING BRITAIN IN THE 1940S

The service of the Commandos during the Second World War has become the stuff of legend, typified by Corporal Thomas Peck Hunter of 43RM Commando who won the Victoria Cross (VC) in Italy.

Leading a Bren gun group, Hunter noticed that the Troop following him would be an easy target for German machine guns and mortars hidden in buildings ahead. Hunter grabbed his Bren gun and charged, clearing the houses and allowing the Troop to advance. He continued to make himself a target until the greater part of the Troop had reached safety, when he was hit in the head and killed. Part of his citation read:

> "There can be no doubt that Corporal Hunter offered himself as a target in order to save his Troop, and only

Members of the RN Beach Beachhead Commandos at Portsmouth Harbour.

– With permission John Ruffhead

THE ARMED FORCES - THE ROYAL AIR FORCE & THE ROYAL NAVY

the speed of his movement prevented him being hit earlier. The skill and accuracy with which he used his Bren gun is proved by the way he demoralised the enemy, and later did definitely silence many of the Spandaus firing on his Troop as they crossed open ground, so much so that under his covering fire elements of the Troop made their final objective before he was killed. Throughout the operation his magnificent courage, leadership and cheerfulness had been an inspiration to his comrades."

UNIFORM

HEADWEAR

Commandos wore the standard Mk.II steel helmet. A cap comforter was available – a cylinder of knitted wool fitted over the head and fashioned into a hat. This can be either worn as it is or under the steel helmet. Commandos also wore the green beret, which was introduced in 1942.

CLOTHING AND EQUIPMENT

Commandos wore the same basic uniform as other units and carried the same '37 pattern webbing. There were a few small differences however, the trousers were modified by the addition of an attachment on the lower left leg to accommodate the Fairburn-Sykes knife. Commandos might also carry a toggle rope and sometimes used the 'Commando' Bergen in preference to the '37 Pattern large pack.

Commandos retained their traditional dark blue undress uniforms, worn with a peaked cap with a red band for ceremonial occasions and when off-duty.

CHOOSING A ROYAL MARINE OR RM COMMANDO IMPRESSION

The Commandos were – indeed remain – elite units of highly trained soldiers who fully deserve the green beret they proudly wear. Portrayals of commandos are best done as part of a group where the equipment and role of the Commandos can be best demonstrated.

OBTAINING UNIFORM & EQUIPMENT

'**Soldier of Fortune**' offer a number of options from individual garments and webbing sections to complete sets of uniform and webbing. Details can be found at www.sofmilitary.co.uk. The '**History Bunker**' also offers both jackets and trousers at thehistorybunker.co.uk. '**Epic Militaria**' offer individual items or a 'bundle' and they also offer reproduction footwear as well – further details from www.epicmilitaria.com. A good source of original uniform and equipment is '**Militaria Zone**' (www.militariazone.com).

LIVING HISTORY GROUPS & LINKS

'**RNBCR – Royal Navy Beachhead Commando Reenactors**' is a group dedicated to preserving the legacy of the men who served with this elite unit. Details can be found at www.rnbcr.co.uk or www.facebook.com/RNBCR.

THE ARMED FORCES - THE ROYAL AIR FORCE & THE ROYAL NAVY

FURTHER RESEARCH

Commandos: The Definitive History of Commando Operations in the Second World War; Charles Messenger; William Collins; 2016; ISBN: 0-0081-6897-0. Through extensive research supported by interviews with former Commandos the author follows the Commandos through operations from Asia to Normandy.

Commando: Winning World War II Behind Enemy Lines; James Owen; Abacus; 2013; ISBN: 0-3491-2362-4. Using guerrilla tactics these highly trained men spear-headed the Allied assault against the Axis forces. By considering both their failures and successes this book charts the develop of this elite fighting force.

CHAPTER FIVE

CIVIL DEFENCE & EMERGENCY SERVICES ROLES

CIVIL DEFENCE PERSONNEL

On 26 April 1937, during the Spanish Civil War, the city of Guernica was destroyed in a devastating attack by the German 'Condor Legion'. Over a period of three hours the raid, at the request of General Franco to support his overthrow of the Republican Government of Spain, left the city in ruins and 1,654 civilians dead. Newsreels depicting aftermath of the raid were seen throughout Britain and confirmed the view, first voiced after the Zeppelin and Gotha bomber raids during the First World War, that any new war would involve the large-scale bombing of British cities with extensive damage to buildings and infrastructure and potentially huge numbers of casualties. There was also every reason to believe that such raids would make use of poison gas, therefore appropriate precautions had to be taken.

RE-LIVING BRITAIN IN THE 1940S

As early as 1924 the Air Raid Precautions Committee was set up as a sub-committee of the Committee of Imperial Defence, under the leadership of Sir John Anderson. The committee focused on 'passive' air defence – the provision of gas masks (almost 40 million of which would be required), blackouts and the provision of air raid shelters. In March 1935, as the threat of war became ever more real, the committee's work was taken over by a new Air Raid Precautions (ARP) Department of the Home Office. In April 1937 the Air Raid Warden's Service was created with the aim of recruiting 800,000 volunteers. Although early recruitment was slow, the Munich Crisis in September 1938 – created by Hitler's demands for the autonomy of German-speaking people in the Czech Sudetenland – saw numbers quickly swell to 700,000. On 1 January 1938 the Air Raid Precaution Act passed into law and compelled local authorities to create their own ARP services.

A Civil Defence warden on duty. Note the service chevrons on his lower right sleeve.

– With permission WSR

CIVIL DEFENCE & EMERGENCY SERVICES ROLES

With local authorities responsible for the provision of ARP services in their area there was inevitably a lot of latitude in the interpretation of the requirements. Officially an Air Raid Warden would be at least 30 years old but in reality, men and women of all ages (some still teenagers) served in the various specialist branches of the service, although only men were allowed to serve in gas contamination teams, and heavy and light rescue services. From 1941 the ARP officially changed its title to Civil Defence.

Many veterans of the First World War served in the ARP/Civil Defence Services. A small number of ARP wardens were employed full-time from 1 September 1939, but most were volunteers who had full-time jobs of their own and served as wardens in their free time. The expectation was that volunteer wardens would be on duty roughly three nights a week, but this would increase dramatically at times of heavy bombing. There were approximately 1.4 million people involved in ARP/Civil Defence services during the war with a peak of 131,000 full-time staff in December 1940 (of whom some 20,000 were women). This number had dropped to roughly 67,000 full-time staff (of whom 10,000 were women) by 1944 as the threat of German bombing diminished. There were also some 800,000 volunteers serving in 1944.

There were a number of different branches to the ARP services:

WARDENS

Wardens were responsible for policing the blackout to ensure that no lights were showing from a property. If a light was visible then the warden would warn the people responsible – often by simply shouting 'Put that light out' – but persistent offenders could be passed to the local police and prosecuted.

RE-LIVING BRITAIN IN THE 1940S

This role gave rise to the image of the warden as a nosy and interfering individual as personified by the character of Warden William Hodges (played by Bill Pertwee) in the iconic comedy series *Dad's Army*, but in reality the role was important and potentially dangerous. Wardens would also issue gas masks to people in their area and supervise the issue of Anderson and Morrison shelters. The ARP services were particularly valuable during the Blitz, when ARP Control Centres would be responsible for sounding the air raid sirens, directing people into the nearest shelter and watching for bombs falling within their sector. After sounding the all-clear wardens would help to police bomb-damaged areas until rescue services could take over and offer assistance to bombed-out families.

An Air Raid Warden uses a dog to detect signs of life in the ruins of a bombed building. He is wearing the bluette overalls and Mk.II helmet.

– With permission Linda Dodd

MESSENGERS

During air raids the telephone lines were often cut making communications between wardens and their Control Centres difficult. Messengers – often members of the Boy Scouts or Boy's Brigade and aged between 16 and 18 – carried verbal or written messages from wardens back to the Sector Post or Control Centre enabling vital resources to be sent to where they were most needed. This was a vital but dangerous role. The first warden on the scene of a bomb blast would complete a form identified as an 'Express Report', which would be passed as quickly as possible to the nearest Sector Post where the details would then be passed on to the Control Centre. The city of Bristol had recruited some 690 messengers, predominantly Boy Scouts, by September 1940, and this number later increased to almost 1,000. The courage and bravery of the messengers should never be underestimated. Derrick Belfall was only 14 years old but had given his age as 16 to join the messenger service in Bristol. He was on his way to the Central Police Station with a message when he passed a house from which flames were beginning to spread. Forcing open the front door, he stumbled over a stirrup pump which he picked up and turned on the fire, soon bringing it under control. Relieved by the householder, he went on his way, but soon afterwards, hearing cries, rushed into another burning building and rescued an injured and badly frightened baby. He again continued on his way, but as he neared his destination he was hit by a bomb fragment and was found gravely wounded in Nelson Street.

Before he died in the Bristol Royal Infirmary he murmured, 'Messenger Belfall reporting. I have delivered my message.'

REPORT & CONTROL STAFF

These were the staff working at control centres who were responsible for prioritising the allocation of resources for each incident after having received messages from the Wardens in the field outlining the picture in each area.

AMBULANCE DRIVERS & STRETCHER PARTIES

As the name suggests ambulance drivers were responsible for driving the ambulances taking casualties to the nearest hospital – no easy job when many roads were blocked by rubble. Stretcher Parties would help to extricate casualties from damaged buildings and take less seriously injured casualties to the nearest First Aid Post. The most seriously injured would be loaded onto ambulances.

FIRST AID PARTIES

By September 1939 some 15,000 people in Bristol had received basic first-aid training from either the British Red Cross Society or the St John Ambulance. Between March and September

A member of a First Aid Party helps an injured man from a bombed building.
– With permission Red Zebra Photography

1939, suitably trained personnel were organised into First Aid Parties. First Aid Parties comprised four men, including a driver. Their role was to render first aid to casualties of bombing and clear the area of wounded as quickly as possible. To do this they had to work closely with the rescue services and ambulance drivers.

RESCUE SERVICES

Bombing led to many collapsed or seriously weakened buildings and the rescue services were responsible for extracting casualties from these dangerous situations.

In Bristol, the organisation of rescue services was the responsibility of the City Engineer and Surveyor. Volunteers were organised into Heavy Rescue Parties of nine men and Light Rescue Parties of seven men each. At the height of the Nazi air raids of 1940–41 there were, on average, twenty-two Rescue Parties on duty during the day and thirty at night-time in Bristol alone.

GAS CONTAMINATION

After the horrific use of poison gas in the trenches of the First World War, there was every reason to believe that it would also be used in the Second World War, and bombs would be an excellent way to disperse the gases. To combat this threat, gas contamination teams were assembled who specialised in cleaning up after gas or chemical weapons had

CIVIL DEFENCE & EMERGENCY SERVICES ROLES

been deployed. Once the presence of a gas like Mustard Gas had been confirmed by the local Gas Identification Officer, teams would be deployed to deal with the casualties and work to decontaminate the area.

FIRE GUARDS

See Chapter 7: Non-uniformed Voluntary Service roles.

Although not officially used at first, dogs assisted some Rescue Parties by acting in a 'search and rescue' role. The first – and perhaps best known – was a small cross-breed terrier named Rip, discovered alone and hungry in the rubble following a heavy air-raid on Poplar, East London, by a local ARP Warden in 1940. The warden, Mr E. King, took the dog home and the pair soon became inseparable. Rip soon was adopted as the mascot of Post 132, Southill Street ARP Post, and accompanied his owner and the team in their duties. Rip proved adept at locating casualties trapped in bombed-out buildings and soon became their unofficial search and rescue dog – a position later made official. Although never having received any formal training, Rip's instincts led to the recovery of more than 100 people in a twelve-month period and he is generally credited with being the inspiration behind today's highly trained 'search and rescue' dogs. Rip was awarded the Peoples' Dispensary for Sick Animals' (PDSA) award of the Dickin Medal in 1945. His citation read 'for locating many air-raid victims during the Blitz of 1940'.

UNIFORM

HEADWEAR

At the start of the war in 1939, ARP personnel were issued with standard Mk.II British helmets. In general, ARP helmets were black with a white letter on the front (and sometimes also the back). The letters used were '**W**' for Warden, '**M**' for Messenger, '**A**' for Ambulance Driver, '**SP**' for Stretcher Parties; '**FAP**' for First Aid Parties. '**R**' for Rescue Services (later '**LR**' for Light Rescue or '**HR**' for Heavy Rescue) and '**DC**' for Decontamination Parties. Rank was denoted (outside London) by a white helmet with black lettering and a black diamond for head warden, two diamonds for divisional or district warden and three diamonds for chief warden. In July 1942 the system of black stripes running front to back over the helmet, already in use in London, was adopted nationally. A white helmet with a black letter indicated a Post Warden or Rescue/Stretcher Party Leader. One black stripe for district or Divisional Wardens and two stripes for Controllers or Chief Wardens. Although these were the most common markings there were hundreds of variations, including those produced for local authorities and private companies.

After Dunkirk steel was in short supply and so ARP/Civil Defence helmets were made of Grade 2 steel. These can be identified by holes (from one to four) drilled into the rim near the chinstrap attachment to indicate the quality of steel used. The more holes drilled the weaker the steel.

CIVIL DEFENCE & EMERGENCY SERVICES ROLES

CLOTHING

At first there was no official uniform for ARP personnel who were identified only by a silver ARP lapel badge, a helmet (see above) and possibly also an armband – sometimes with the letters ARP. The armbands were unregulated so there are many different designs, some incorporating the local authority's name. ARP personnel would also carry a gas mask made to be rather more robust than the ubiquitous civilian model.

At the start of the war male ARP personnel were issued with a set of dark blue overalls made of heavy cotton drill fabric called bluette. These overalls sported a black, oval, embroidered badge with a red border and the letters 'ARP' also in red, worn above the left chest pocket. The buttons were chrome and were also marked 'ARP'. Rank markings were shown by a combination of red bars and diamonds worn on the lower arm of both sleeves of the overalls starting four inches above the cuff. Female personnel were issued with a dark blue wrap-over overall made of dark blue cotton and fastened with a strap which closed at the rear. The embroidered ARP badge was worn on the left front. Female personnel were also issued with a double-breasted bluette coat with two rows of silver coloured 'ARP' buttons. Again, the embroidered ARP badge was worn on the left front.

In February 1941 the bluette overalls, worn by men in First Aid and Rescue Parties, were replaced with a dark blue battledress blouse and trousers identical in cut to the army pattern battledress. In July 1941 other Civil Defence services adopted the same uniform (though in a slightly lighter-weight cloth). Junior ranks were required to wear the battledress with the neck closed (using a metal hook and eye), but senior ranks could wear it with the neck open, with a light-coloured shirt and dark blue or black tie worn underneath. A wool beret was also added to the uniform to which most personnel attached their silver ARP badge. As the war progressed, and material became scarcer, an austerity version of the battledress was issued. This can easily be identified because the front button closure and breast pocket buttons were exposed to save material and is the most common version seen for sale today.

Women were issued with a single-breasted jacket in the same material as the men's battledress. It was fastened with white metal buttons with either 'ARP' or 'CD' lettering. These buttons were later replaced with black plastic versions from 1943 on. The jacket was worn with a belt of the same material with a slide-through buckle. Slacks and a skirt in the same fabric completed the uniform. Greatcoats were available for men and women and generally carried shoulder titles and rank insignia.

CHOOSING AN ARP IMPRESSION

There is huge scope for developing an interesting ARP impression. Given the regional variation an individual impression can be assembled with patience and research. Even a rather more generic impression can be enhanced by adding appropriate accessories depending on which branch of the ARP/Civil Defence Services you are interested in.

Uniforms come up quite frequently on eBay and, although sometimes expensive, bargains can still be had. The WW2 pattern battledress and trousers continued in use for some years after the war and therefore post-war items can be acquired. It is also worth keeping an eye on sites like Gumtree and Facebook Marketplace.

CIVIL DEFENCE & EMERGENCY SERVICES ROLES

Militaria and Antique fairs can often produce nice items from time to time. Insignia are widely available – both original and reproduction – but be careful over reproduction items passed off as originals. Also beware of post-war insignia (some of which did not appear during the

Stuart from the Frontline Co modelling the ARP.41 Combination Suit.

– With permission The Frontline Co

wars years) passed off as wartime. The lettering of ARP shoulder titles was a golden-yellow on wartime items but brighter yellow post-war.

All ARP personnel would be required to carry a gas mask which was rather more robust than the civilian version. Some carried the ARP General Service Respirator. The gas mask case was worn high on the chest and a hose connected the mask to the filter, which remained in the case. Personnel not issued with the 'General Service Respirator' carried the 'Civilian Duty Respirator' made of moulded rubber thicker than that of the civilian mask and with separate eye-pieces. This mask was carried in a simple light canvas bag, issued with the mask. These come up on sites like eBay from time to time but – as with all gas masks – remember that the filters can contain some unpleasant and dangerous materials (including asbestos) and so they should always be handled with care and never worn or handled by members of the public unless the filter has been removed and professionally emptied or permanently sealed.

Civil Defence personnel would also often carry a whistle stamped 'ARP', commonly on a either metal chain or a lanyard. Some would also carry a penknife which could also be attached to a lanyard or to a belt. Knives – with an integral marline spike – were made by two companies and stamped 'ARP'.

Water bottles were also commonly worn by First Aid Parties and Rescue Parties. Although similar to the military version, the Civil Defence water bottle was provided without a cloth cover and generally embossed with the letters 'ARP' at the top. They were carried in either leather or canvas cradles. There is photographic evidence to show that some Civil Defence personnel were issued with water bottles with a black or dark blue felt cover as used by the St John Ambulance Brigade.

CIVIL DEFENCE & EMERGENCY SERVICES ROLES

OBTAINING UNIFORMS & ACCESSORIES

Royal Navy deck boots are a good substitute for wartime Civil defence boots and sometimes come up on eBay. Modern 'Dunlop' brand wellington boots are also very close to the wartime pattern. The 'Dunlop' branding can be removed from the boots with a small amount of solvent, methylated spirits, white spirit or cellulose thinners.

Original ARP whistles are easily obtainable on eBay for under £20. Original uniforms are becoming harder to source and increasingly expensive but they do still appear on eBay. Post-war garments of similar pattern are cheaper but it is important to ensure that the insignia are changed to wartime design. '**Replica Warehouse**' (www.replicawarehouse.co.uk) offer a range of Civil Defence uniforms. '**Monty's Locker**' (www.montyslocker.co.uk) offer a range of excellent quality reproduction cloth patches. '**The Frontline Co**' (www.thefrontlineco.com) offers an excellent quality reproduction set of ARP overalls or ARP.41 Combination Suit.

LIVING HISTORY GROUPS & LINKS

'**WW2 Civil Defence (ARP) Re-enactors**' – a Facebook page dedicated to Civil Defence re-enacting which puts you in contact with many well-informed, and like-minded, people who are always willing to offer advice and guidance from what to wear to whether items are authentic or modern reproductions. It can be found at: www.facebook.com/groups/793725373978971

FURTHER RESEARCH

'WW2 ARP and Civil Defence Uniforms, Insignia and Equipment'; almost certainly the best source online is Craig Smith's splendid website devoted to all aspects of Civil Defence. This site is kept advert free so please make a donation if you use it: www.ww2civildefence.co.uk

Put That Light Out!: Britain's Civil Defence Services at War 1939– 1945; Mike Brown; Sutton Publishing; 1999, ISBN 0-7509-2210-9 – a very useful account of the Civil Defence Service (including the Fire Service) on the front line interspersed with some very moving, and well chosen, personal accounts.

ARP and Civil Defence in the Second World War; Peter Doyle; Shire Library; 2010, ISBN 0-7478-0765-5 – a small but very useful, accessible and informative overview of the Civil Defence showing how the various elements operated.

A People's Army – Civil Defence Insignia and Uniforms 1939–1945; Jon Mills; Privately published – a detailed overview of the organisation, uniforms and insignia of the Civil Defence Service during the war years. This is currently out of print but copies do come up on eBay sometimes.

CIVIL DEFENCE & EMERGENCY SERVICES ROLES

FIRE SERVICES

In the mid–1930s there were only 4,272 professional firemen in the whole of the United Kingdom, and almost half of those were working with the London Fire Brigade. As the threat of war increased, the Auxiliary Fire Service (AFS) was introduced in January 1938 to increase capacity in order to meet the expected level of threat by working alongside the existing fire brigades. By the time war was declared in September 1939 the AFS numbered some 200,000 members, including a substantial minority of women to address the shortfall created by men volunteering for the Armed

Two NFS firemen use a hose to tackle a fire which has broken out in some wooden sheds.
— With permission Adam Bull

Services. An immediate problem was that the different existing fire brigades had no standardised equipment and there was not even a standardised hydrant valve. Members of the AFS were unpaid, part-time volunteers but they could be called up for full-time service if conditions warranted. Some AFS members were equipped with pumps pulled by cars, or London taxis, painted AFS grey – a reflection of how difficult it was to obtain material. This was made possible by an innovative taxi driver who developed a quick hook-up device which allowed almost any vehicle to be used.

From its inception, an Auxiliary Fire service was set up in every borough and urban district across the country with one in the London County Council area. Each AFS was commanded by a commandant with deputies and assistants in larger areas.

Each service operated its own fire stations commanded by a Section Officer. The area covered by each fire station was divided into 'fire beats', each the responsibility of a Patrol Officer. Services with five or more fire stations divided them into divisions, each commanded by a Divisional Officer. Because this rank structure was not dictated by government there were some regional variations.

During the Blitz on London, the weaknesses of the AFS structure became apparent when different fire brigades called for support from others causing chaos in the command structures and communication. As a result, in August 1941 the AFS was amalgamated with the local authority fire brigades (an estimated 1,600 of them), placed under government control and renamed the National Fire Service (NFS). Many senior leaders of the AFS transitioned across into the new structure. The NFS allowed for standardisation of organisation and equipment across the country.

CIVIL DEFENCE & EMERGENCY SERVICES ROLES

The recruitment of women was a contentious issue and deeply unpopular with many male senior officers, one of whom announced: 'I would rather resign than be made to drill young girls and women to be firemen!' Despite such opposition numbers of women in the AFS continued to rise from 5,000 in 1940 to 20,000 just six months later.

By 1943 there were more than 86,000 women serving in the NFS (32,200 full-time and 54,600 part-time). By the end of the war twenty-five women and more than 900 men had lost their lives in service. Most women in the AFS/NFS were employed as drivers, despatchers and canteen staff and were not expected to actually fight fires. That said, even driving support vehicles and motor bikes in the blackout, during an enemy air raid, was a highly dangerous and risky task. Gillian

A female NFS member maintains the Incident Log at the local Control Room.

– With permission David Purkiss

RE-LIVING BRITAIN IN THE 1940S

Tanner, aged 21, was awarded the George Medal for her courage in delivering petrol to fire pumps near Bermondsey while the docks were being heavily bombed. 'Fetch the Engine', the official history of the Fire Brigade Union (1951) records instances where women did unofficially accompany fire engines and serve alongside men fighting fires. Terry Segars, in Forged in Fire goes further:

> "the reality ... was that firewomen were more widely involved in active work than is generally acknowledged, and they could often be found in the midst of things during the blitz, whether helping out on the pumps, in control rooms close to the centre of the severest raids or delivering supplies to firefighters."

NFS fire appliances arrive to deal with a fire at a rail yard.

– With permission David Moore

CIVIL DEFENCE & EMERGENCY SERVICES ROLES

In reality fire men and women spent long hours waiting for a call. Many performed vital wartime manufacturing roles either in workshops at the stations or close by. This was entirely voluntary but since many of the NFS personnel had come from factories, such work was something they were skilled at and familiar with.

During the 'phoney war' many civilians regarded firemen as contemptible for apparently trying to avoid military service, however the Blitz changed opinions and firefighters were referred to by Winston Churchill as the 'heroes with grimy faces'. Churchill further noted that the fire service 'were a grand lot and their work must never be forgotten'.

UNIFORM

HEADWEAR

Firefighters were issued with a cap with a black peak and a single line of red piping just below the crown. The AFS or NFS badge fixed to the front. When on active duty they wore a green Mk.II steel helmet with the AFS/NFS badge as a transfer on the front and the area number in an oval frame on the rim of the helmet centre-front, or sometimes as a name in a rectangular box stencil e.g. 'SOUTH EASTERN'. Rank was shown by red bands around the helmet. A private purchase Field Service Cap with the 'AFS' or 'NFS' badge was also available.

The first AFS hat for women was a peaked, flat-top pill box hat in very dark blue material with red piping. A cloth neck guard of the same material was folded at the back of the cap and the two ties brought forward and knotted in a bow between the 'AFS' metal badge and the peak. This continued in use but was commonly replaced by the men's peaked cap or the private purchase field service cap.

CLOTHING

The fire services used the traditional dark blue, double-breasted tunic made of heavy serge material. It had two rows of six metal buttons marked 'NFS' with a raised outside edge. Towards the end of the war black plastic buttons of similar design replaced the metal versions. The tunic had two pleats at the back with a button at the top of each pleat. A circular woven, or printed, badge with a red circle surrounding the letters 'NFS' and the area number was worn on the left breast. The trousers were of the same material and were of the same pattern as the Civil Defence uniform trousers. A canvas or leather waistbelt was worn over the tunic. A canvas holder was attached to the belt by two rivetted belt-loops for the fireman's axe. Other equipment might also be added. Black leather shoes were worn with the uniform but these were replaced with heavy rubber boots when fire-fighting. Rubberised, waterproof leggings were available and worn over the trousers. Rank markings were displayed on the tunic epaulettes. A greatcoat was also available for use in adverse conditions.

The first uniform adopted for women members of the AFS involved a single-breasted jacket in very dark blue (almost black) material with a stand-up collar and fastened with four, metal 'AFS' buttons. The embroidered AFS logo was worn on the left breast. There were two large concertina pockets on the front of the tunic skirt. A belt of the same fabric went round the waist, fastening between the third and bottom button of the jacket. It was worn with a plain, two-panel skirt of the same fabric. This design was superseded by adopting the Women's Civil Defence tunic – a more tailored tunic worn open at the neck with a white shirt and tie. The tunic had two flap-fronted breast pockets secured with small metal 'NFS' buttons and two internal flap-fronted pockets on the tunic skirt. The tunic fastened with four, metal or black plastic 'NFS' buttons. A belt of the same fabric was worn fastening between the third and bottom button of the tunic.

CIVIL DEFENCE & EMERGENCY SERVICES ROLES

CHOOSING AN AFS/NFS IMPRESSION

The work of the fire services during the Blitz was a story of remarkable courage and resilience. It is a story that needs to be told but is best told in context – fire fighters do not work in isolation but are part of a team and their work is best commemorated in that way. Somehow, a lone fireman in full kit just seems incongruous.

OBTAINING UNIFORMS & ACCESSORIES

Sadly, both AFS and NFS uniforms and equipment are becoming scarce. Because the numbers of fire service personnel were always relatively small compared to the armed forces few people reproduce material other than the cloth breast patches. Original uniforms do come up on eBay and auction sites and the metal badges are quite common. '**Sentimental Journey**' (www.sentimentaljourney.co.uk) sometimes carry some equipment like the canvas axe holders. Austin Ruddy wrote an excellent article in 2017 on collecting AFS and NFS items and the advice still stands today – www.keymilitary.com/article/collecting-afs-and-nfs-items Austin Ruddy is a regular contributor to the *Britain At War* magazine.

LIVING HISTORY GROUPS & LINKS

> '**The NFS and AFS Vehicles Group**'; a living history group which uses period vehicles and uniforms to recreate the atmosphere and drama of life in the wartime fire service as authentically as possible – within reason! The group is based around Nottingham and takes part in events within a 30–40 mile radius – nfs-afs.org.uk

FURTHER RESEARCH

NFS in Woking and pump-relay competition in Guildford; a colour film from 1942 clearly showing uniforms, equipment and the use of equipment albeit in competition rather than action – player.bfi.org.uk/free/film/watch-the-national-fire-service-in-woking-and-a-pump-relay-competition-in-guildford–1942

The Birth of a Service; a brief film by the NFS Benevolent Fund outlining the origins and development of the wartime fire service with great shots of uniform and equipment. It also shows how water supplies were provided in cities after water mains had been fractured. Good shots of the mobile workshops and voluntary tasks undertaken while not on active duty – www.youtube.com/watch?v=muVNqyiQjcI

A Debt to be Repaid; a short clip by the NFS Benevolent Fund showing the work of the NFS during enemy bombing raids (intermittent sound) – www.youtube.com/watch?v=DXFF7BofLdU

Battle of the Flames; Henry W. Stedman; Jarrolds, 1942 – a moving and dramatic account of almost every major raid of the London Blitz through the eyes of an auxiliary fireman. Great detail on the work and pressures of the job.

CIVIL DEFENCE & EMERGENCY SERVICES ROLES

POLICE

In August of 1939 there were some 60,000 police officers in England and Wales, divided between 182 separate police forces. The largest force was the Metropolitan Police in London with just under 20,000 men. The City of London was served by a separate force of 1,100 men. There were fifty-eight county forces and 122 forces patrolling cities and boroughs. Policing was seen as a man's job and there were fewer than 300 women serving out of a total of 60,000 constables. Women police officers were largely confined to dealing with family problems and particularly with women and children.

The police forces throughout the UK found that an already challenging job became vastly more complex during wartime. New regulations were brought in to meet the exigencies of war which all ranks needed to be aware of, while the blackout provided new opportunities for criminals. Shortages brought about by rationing also led to an active black market, while bombing offered opportunities for looting, resulting in an increase in crime during the war years. The work of the police was also hampered by the early release of convicted criminals with less than three months left to serve and younger offenders who had already served six months in Borstal.

The blackout also provided cover for more hardened criminals. Gordon Cummins joined the RAF in 1935, aged 21. While stationed at Colerne, Cummins frequently spent his leave in London and is suspected of having murdered two women. By 1942 he had built up over 1,000 hours of flight experience and earned a transfer to the Air Crew Receiving Centre in Regent's Park, London, beginning on 2 February 1942. He went on to murder another four women and attempt to

CIVIL DEFENCE & EMERGENCY SERVICES ROLES

Fingered by the Police – an arresting portrait of a wartime 'copper'.
– With permission Andrew Harrison

murder two more over a six-day period in February 1942. Cummins was arrested after leaving his gas mask and haversack (with his service number inscribed inside) at the scene of an attempted murder. Dubbed the 'Blackout Killer' by the media, Cummins was tried and convicted of murder, and hanged at Wandsworth Prison on 25 June 1942.

As well as dealing with 'routine' peace-time crimes, additional, war-specific duties for police constables included reporting for duty at the sound of the air-raid siren and cooperating closely with Civil Defence personnel during and after air raids; supporting the enforcement of the blackout, preventing looting from bomb damaged properties; preventing black-market dealings; cooperating with the military in the recapture of escaped prisoners of war and capture of deserters; protecting key installations essential for national security; monitoring foreigners in case they were foreign agents; monitoring the public's compliance in the use of gas masks and working with local schools to warn children of the dangers posed by bombs and shrapnel.

One trick used by criminals during air-raids was to acquire an ARP warden's helmet and armband and force entry to a shop or warehouse while no one was looking. Seeing the Warden's helmet people would often unwittingly help by assisting in loading stolen goods into a vehicle believing that they were being taken to a place of safety.

Looting from bombed out buildings was another common crime. In the first two months of the London Blitz, 390 cases of looting were reported to the police. The first trials of looters were held at the Old Bailey on 9 November 1940. It is sad to note that of twenty cases tried that day, ten involved members of the Auxiliary Fire Service. The

Daily Mirror, incensed by rising crime figures, noted in November 1940 that, 'Fines and imprisonment have done nothing to stop the ghouls who rob even bodies lying in the ruins of little homes. Looting is in fact on the increase. The country demands that this crime be stamped out ... hang a looter and stop this filthy crime.'

Prostitution increased and so did crime by juveniles who were sent into bombed houses to raid the gas meters. As people were displaced by bombing, fraud increased – one Walter Handy was sent to prison for three years for falsely claiming to have been bombed out nineteen times in five months. Each time he was paid £500 in compensation!

As the threat of war loomed, and many serving officers were likely to be lost to the armed forces, the police forces delayed the retirement of serving officers and called on a number of different organisations to boost its numbers:

POLICE RESERVE

Police pensioners who had been retained on a nominal retainer and were re-employed on normal salary.

WAR POLICE RESERVE

Introduced in 1939, men under the age of 30 in the Police Reserve who were called up for temporary war service (although many were later called up for active service). By 1944 there were 17,000 War Reserve Constables. The serial killer John Reginald Christie enrolled as a War Police Reserve Constable in September 1939 when the authorities failed to check his criminal record; he served until the end of 1943.

CIVIL DEFENCE & EMERGENCY SERVICES ROLES

WOMEN'S AUXILIARY POLICE CORPS

Set up in 1939 and similar to the War Police Reserve except its members were employed chiefly in clerical and driving duties although there were some 500 members who served as WAPC police constables.

SPECIAL CONSTABLES

Unpaid, part-time volunteers who were ineligible for active service by reasons of age or being in a reserved occupation. At the outbreak of war there were around 130,000 Special Constables in service who received additional training in first-aid and how to deal with incendiary bombs.

POLICE AUXILIARY MESSENGERS

Boys between the ages of 14 and 18 who worked as volunteers assisting the police communications by delivering messages on foot or by bicycle.

The work of the police during the bombing was essential in keeping up morale and maintaining order. As one commentator, talking of air raids, put it, 'the calm and authoritative way of the good-natured Bobby did more to dispel panic than any amount of official propaganda'.

RE-LIVING BRITAIN IN THE 1940S

Two Police Constables flank a detective in plain clothes.
— With permission Welsh Bobbies – Bobbies on the Beat / Barry Ward

CIVIL DEFENCE & EMERGENCY SERVICES ROLES

UNIFORM

HEADWEAR

The distinctive police helmet – known as a Custodian helmet – was of cork construction and heavily influenced by the German 'pickelhaube', or spiked helmet. During the 1930s the Home Office attempted to standardise these helmets and their badges. The official pattern was a helmet plate (or Brunswick Star) featuring the monarch's cypher with the name of the force imprinted on the plate (e.g. Metropolitan Police) at the centre front of the helmet. At the top of the helmet is a raised metal 'rose top'. Both the badge and the rose-top were blackened during wartime. The helmet was fastened by a strap under the chin. In reality, attempts at standardisation largely failed and considerable variation remains to the present day. During air-raids police constables would wear the Mk.II steel helmet painted blue with the word 'POLICE' stencilled on the front. A plain peaked cap was also worn by police constables when appropriate.

CLOTHING

The standard police tunic is of dark blue wool, single breasted and buttoned at the neck, with seven buttons up the front. Two pleated breast pockets and a stand-up collar bearing the constable's number on either side. Special constables might have their number prefixed by the letters 'SC' or have a separate metal badge, with the letters 'SC' surmounted by a king's crown. A cloth brassard or arm band, with black and white vertical stripes, known as a 'duty band', was worn on the left forearm while on duty and removed at the end of the shift. The police whistle was worn on the tunic, with the whistle chain hooked over the top button and the whistle itself tucked in between the buttons in a special hidden pocket. Trousers were of similar material with a pocket for the truncheon. The blue colour of the police uniform was a deliberate choice to distinguish the early police from the deeply distrusted local militias who wore the military red uniforms.

In cold weather a double-breasted greatcoat could be worn over the uniform or a three-quarter length cape of Melton cloth fastened at the neck by a hook and chain fixing decorated with a pair of lion's heads.

CHOOSING A POLICE IMPRESSION

There is always something reassuring about the presence of a traditional police officer in the mould of *Dixon of Dock Green* (which ran on TV from 1955 to 1976) and the presence of police either in groups or as individuals at events is always popular. Not only is there a role in protecting visiting dignitaries but also the opportunity to engage with the public and talk about the role of the police in wartime.

OBTAINING UNIFORMS & ACCESSORIES

There are no suppliers of reproduction police uniforms and so it is necessary to either source original items or modify others. Original police Mk.II steel helmets come up on eBay quite regularly or a relic helmet can be refurbished and a 'POLICE' stencil made to copy the original lettering. The traditional domed helmet can sometimes be found on the British Bobby website (www.britishbobby.co.uk). Jackets and trousers can be altered from existing post-war military uniforms. Contact with others already in the hobby is usually the best way to source police items.

LIVING HISTORY GROUPS & LINKS

'Welsh Bobbies – Bobbies on the Beat' – a Facebook page dedicated to this excellent living history group which aims to represent the police force between 1901 and 1955. A very knowledgeable and friendly group – www.facebook.com/profile.php?id=100057630670605

FURTHER RESEARCH

Policing WW2 with Special Constables (1940s) – a short film showing the uniform, roles and training of police constables – www.youtube.com/watch?v=BNL2vMm98wY

CHAPTER SIX
WLA & UNIFORMED VOLUNTARY SERVICE ROLES

WOMEN'S LAND ARMY (WLA)

The Women's Land Army was originally established in January 1917 to increase food production by recruiting 23,000 women to replace the men who had joined the armed forces. The reference to 'army' in the WLA's title is misleading because it was a civilian organisation. Disbanded on 30 November 1919, the WLA was reactivated under the directorship of Lady Gertrude Denman on 1 June 1939 to meet the imminent threat of war.

Between June 1939 and November 1950, the 'Land Girls' of the WLA played an essential role in increasing Britain's food production. The import of food stuffs was seriously diminished by the demands of war and so the amount of land under cultivation had to be substantially increased and existing land made more productive. By autumn 1941 more than 20,000 women had volunteered for service in the WLA –

many from urban areas eager to take up the offer of a healthy outdoor existence which the WLA advertised. At its peak in 1944 there were more than 80,000 Land Girls in the WLA. Although many stayed on the farms where they worked, conditions were often very basic and so a series of hostels were established. By 1944 there were 22,000 Land Girls living in 700 hostels.

Land Girls were paid directly by the farmers for whom they worked. The minimum wage was 28 shillings a week, but half of this was deducted for food and lodgings. By comparison, the average wage for a male farm labourer was 38 shillings a week. The normal working week for the Land Girls was forty-eight hours in winter and fifty in summer, with no holidays. This changed after 1943 when the 'Land Girls' Charter' was introduced which promised one week's holiday annually and raised the minimum wage. Jean Birtles (née Bannister) recalled her typical day as being:

> *5am Milking the cows*
>
> *8am Breakfast (about 30 mins)*
>
> *8.30am Clean out the cow sheds and wash then sterilize the milking equipment*
>
> *12.30 Lunch (about 45 mins)*
>
> *1.30pm Get the cows in from the fields, scrub them down and wash the stone floor*
>
> *5.30pm home for tea (about 30mins)*

Much of the Land Girls' time was spent on animal management. Pigs were valuable sources of meat and their management included mixing

WLA & UNIFORMED VOLUNTARY SERVICE ROLES

the feed, helping with the birth of piglets, keeping records of each sow and her litters right through to preparing the animals for slaughter – never an easy task for Land Girls who had grown attached to the animals they cared for. Land Girls could find themselves responsible for a herd of cows – for some who had never seen a cow before, the distinction between a cow and a bull was soon learned! For them the day usually began and ended with milking and related tasks, included recording the milk yields and delivering milk to the local community.

For those Land Girls involved in arable farming, the work was often hard and involved the use – and maintenance – of heavy machinery. Ploughing was a skilled responsibility and was often learned by watching more experienced farm hands at work. On arrival, many of the Land Girls could not even drive and so handling the tractors and ploughs was a steep learning curve – but many soon mastered the skill and became accomplished at ploughing. In late August and

Little could prepare the Land Girls for the idiosyncrasies of livestock like pigs – but they soon learned!

– With permission Barry James Wilson

September the crops had to be harvested – a task requiring a great deal of labour from the Land Girls, supplemented by members of the local community.

After reaping, the crop had to be threshed to remove the edible grain from the chaff – a very dirty job with small particles of chaff covering them and painfully irritating the eyes. The Land Girls were advised to tie string around their trouser legs to avoid rats and mice from running up inside their trousers. Mobile gangs of Land Girls were employed to kill rats by laying sugared bait and then removing the dead rats afterwards.

As new land was prepared for either cultivation or grazing it was important to ensure that the field boundaries were secure. This involved erecting and mending fences and cutting and laying hedges. Laying hedges was particularly skilled work since any holes would allow sheep or cattle to break through. The land might also need to be irrigated so ditches would need to be dug to irrigate – or drain – the land. One of the largest land reclamation projects was in East Anglia where thousands of acres of fenland were drained using excavators and tractors operated by the Land Girls.

The Women's Land Army also had a number of songs written for it. One was called *Back to the Land* –

> "*Back to the land, we must all lend a hand*
> *To the farms and the fields we must go.*
> *There's a job to be done*
> *Though we can't fire a gun*
> *We can still do our bit with a hoe.*
> *When your muscles are strong*
> *You will soon get along*

WLA & UNIFORMED VOLUNTARY SERVICE ROLES

*And you'll think that the country life's grand;
We're all needed now,
We must all speed the plough,
So come with us – back to the land."*

These songs never truly caught on however, because the women preferred to sing popular songs or parody older favourites. These lyrics were sung to the tune of *She'll be Coming Round the Mountain When She Comes* –

"*If you want to go to heaven when you die, You must wear a green pullover and a tie, You must wear a khaki bonnet, With WLA on it, If you want to go to heaven when you die.*"

A member of the WLA guides a horse in readiness for ploughing the land.

– With permission Barry James Wilson

Britain's war effort required a vast amount of timber for pit-props in mines, telegraph poles and construction work (including the production of aircraft) but after the German invasion of Norway supplies of imported timber were drastically reduced. To make matters worse, ships from Canada were commandeered to carry food and armaments so room for timber was very limited. To address this shortage, a new branch of the WLA was formed in 1942 – the Women's Timber Corps (WTC). Known colloquially as 'Lumber Jills', members of the Timber Corps measured and selected trees for felling, sawed and lifted timber and burned brushwood. In total some 6,000 women worked on the Timber Corps. Although subject to a stricter medical examination than the Land Girls, the Lumber Jills did work a slightly shorter day than their counterparts in the fields which, on occasion, did lead to some resentment. The Timber Corps was disbanded in 1946.

UNIFORM

HEADWEAR

Land Girls were issued with a wide-brimmed, brown felt hat which was to be worn squarely on the head (though rarely was). Often the hat would be rejected in favour of a knotted scarf which was lighter and more versatile. Women in the Timber Corps wore the same uniform as the Land Girls but were issued with a green beret instead of the wide brimmed felt hat.

CLOTHES

Land girls were issued with two pairs of sturdy cotton corduroy breeches which buttoned up on each side of the waist and were tied off just below the knee. These were hard-wearing with plenty of room in the seat to allow full movement. Because the corduroy made a whistling sound as the women walked, the material became known as 'whistling cord'. Three pairs of long socks were issued to cover the lower leg and keep the feet warm and dry. For ordinary wear, Land Girls were issued with plain brown shoes but these would be replaced by wellington boots according to the demands of the tasks undertaken. Three shirts were issued, but these were renowned for being rather itchy and so civilian blouses were often worn instead. Issue shirts were available with long sleeves, or an aertex version with short sleeves for summer wear. The shirt was to be worn with a green tie with yellow stripes emblazoned with 'WLA'. An extra layer of warmth was provided by a V-neck, bottle-green woollen jumper – two were normally issued. Because of

A 'Land Girl' arrives ready for work. – With permission WSR

clothes rationing underwear was often homemade. For some tasks cotton dungarees were worn with adjustable straps and a leather belt. Mackintoshes and overcoats were also issued.

Because they were a civilian organisation, and had many different tasks to perform, a group of Land Girls was rarely uniform in appearance. This fact was lamented in the April 1942 edition of The Land Girl Magazine which noted:

> *"uniform must be uniform or it loses all its point … don't try to express your personality in your uniform… There is no obligation on members of the W.L.A. to wear uniform, but if and when they do, they should let it do its own work, and make its own effect, without any embellishment."*

CHOOSING A WLA IMPRESSION

There are a number of WLA groups around the country and they provide an unusual and popular display at events because they focus on an area of the war that is less well-known than others. It also allows the opportunity for domestic animals and even bees to become involved in the right context. Membership of a group is strongly recommended because the WLA uniform is always best seen in context and loses impact worn in isolation.

OBTAINING UNIFORMS & ACCESSORIES

Soldier of Fortune supply a large amount of good quality, and reasonably priced, uniforms and equipment to living

WLA & UNIFORMED VOLUNTARY SERVICE ROLES

history groups. They offer a 'WLA Women's Land Army Uniform Set' comprising jumper, short-sleeved shirt, WLA tie, WLA armband, tan haversack with shoulder strap, brown leather belt, cord breeches, brown shoes and long socks – www.sofmilitary.co.uk/wla-womens-land-army-uniform-set-25338.html

The 1940s Shop also offers long socks, jumpers, leather belts, WLA ties and several variations of the WLA shirt including the short- and long-sleeved variations. These can be viewed and ordered from – www.the1940shop.co.uk/womens-land-army-uniform They also offer copies of the Timber Corps cap and fabric badges and other accessories – www.the1940shop.co.uk/timber-corps-uniform

Replica Warehouse also advertise a range of WLA uniforms. Contact them directly for a current price list and availability – www.replicawarehouse.co.uk/ww2_costumes_artefacts.htm

LIVING HISTORY GROUPS & LINKS

Daughters of Britain LHS – is a very authentic living history group portraying the many roles undertaken by women during the Second World War with an active group in the Netherlands as well. Further details: www.facebook.com/doblhs

Land Girls at Large – a living history group with an excellent display. A very helpful group for anyone interested in the WLA – www.facebook.com/groups/119520694885040

Women's Land Army – a living history group based in Trowbridge, Wiltshire. The group undertakes research and allows the buying and selling of WLA related material on its page – www.facebook.com/groups/318839220409

FURTHER RESEARCH

Land Girl – A Manual for Volunteers in the Women's Land Army; W.E. Sewell-Cooper; Ministry of Labour; 1941 – reprinted by Amberley Publishing 2011; ISBN: 1-4456-0279-2. A facsimile edition of the original manual given to WLA recruits outlining duties and responsibilities. A must for anyone interested in the WLA.

Women's Land Army & Timber Corps – an excellent website dedicated to the study of the Women's Land Army from initial inception in the First World War to its disbanding in 1950, including an archive and active research programme – www.womenslandarmy.co.uk

Getting Dressed in WW2 – Women's Land Army – a short documentary by Crows Eye Production on the uniform of the Land Girls and their work – www.youtube.com/watch?v=TfFAmckpk18

Land Girls: Cinderellas of the Soil; Amy de la Haye; Royal Pavilion Libraries & Museums; 2009; ISBN: 0-9487-2372-6. A useful introduction with an emphasis on the uniform of the WLA.

They Fought in the Fields: The Women's Land Army; Nicola Tyrer; History Press; 2007; ISBN: 0-7524-4313-5 – a detailed study of the work of the WLA showing the strength, ingenuity and resilience of the Land Girls. Punctuated by photographs and first-hand accounts this is a very valuable tool to understanding the WLA.

WOMEN'S VOLUNTARY SERVICE (WVS)

The concept of the Women's Voluntary Service for Civil Defence was first defined by the government on 16 May 1938. The purpose of enrolling women in the ARP Services was 'to help to bring home to every household what air attack may mean, and to make known to every household what it can do to protect itself and the community'. In effect, the Women's Voluntary Service was intended to serve the ARP Services in the same way that the Women's Auxiliary Services supported the armed forces. The founder of the WVS, Lady Stella Reading (a formidable woman who had served as a nurse in the First World War), was quick to point out the value of volunteers noting that 'too many people think of volunteers as a means to an end, as cheap labour. True voluntary service is nothing of the kind. It is, in fact, the gift of a thoughtful person of their skill, their energy and their time.'

In order to recruit enough women into the WVS publicity was vital and a competition was held to find a poster which would epitomise the service. The competition was won by 19-year-old James Davies of Dagenham in Essex, who claimed the £30 prize. James's winning poster was striking and some 5,000 copies were made, but only two are known to survive. The others were quickly removed (so the story goes) when it was found that the model used was German! Despite this setback, by September 1939 the WVS had attracted 336,000 members.

The WVS was organised using the same twelve geographical regions as used by the Civil Defence. Each region had a regional administrator (paid for by the Home Office). Within the regions, each county had a county organiser with a support staff and each county had a number of centres – during the war years there were almost 2,000 WVS centres. Each centre was placed in a town or village and was responsible for offering support to its local community. Each centre was run by a centre organiser appointed by the WVS HQ in London. In turn the centre organisers were supported by a team of volunteers each leading a specific aspect of the centre's work – for example, evacuation and billeting or food and clothing provision. Each of these 'leaders' was in turn supported by the rank-and-file members. Right from the start it was decided by Lady Stella Reading, the founder of the WVS, that because it was a voluntary organisation there should be no rank structure, although titles would be allowed to define the roles and responsibilities undertaken.

Because of its position at the heart of communities, the WVS was asked to play a key role in the evacuation of children from towns and cities likely to be affected by bombing. WVS members identified 'safe' locations and arranged billeting for the evacuees. This was a very challenging task since evacuee trains did not always arrive at their expected destination, or would turn up unexpectedly. Despite the circumstances the WVS responded to each situation and was chiefly responsible for the relocation of some 1.5 million children and accompanying adults in the first few days of September 1939. Once the bombs began to fall many people were left homeless and without their possessions. The WVS responded by organising clothing for those in need. As early as October 1939, Lady Reading appealed

A WVS Billeting Officer stands next to her car as she awaits the next evacuee train.

– With permission Cheryl Ludgate

to the United States of America to help with the impending clothing crisis. In response to this appeal, the American Red Cross sent large quantities of clothing as part of their 'Bundles for Britain' campaign. This clothing was then distributed from WVS Emergency Clothing Stores to those who had lost their possessions as a result of enemy action and to the thousands of refugees fleeing from Nazi occupied Europe. Clothing Exchanges were also provided by the WVS where outgrown items could be exchanged for larger sizes.

During the Blitz the WVS assumed the responsibility for feeding and refreshing the ARP Wardens and firefighters who were dealing with the immediate effects of the bombing. Mobile canteens were set up close to where the fires raged, placing the WVS members in constant danger from collapsing buildings.

Once the raid had ended, the WVS helped the injured and homeless. WVS records show that their members helped over 10,000 people every night of the London Blitz which lasted fifty-seven nights. Rest Centres were established to accommodate and feed the homeless, who remained there until alternative arrangements could be made – sometimes days and often much longer. One WVS member in Barnes was recorded as having fed 1,200 bomb victims in one day, cooking meals from her own kitchen. WVS members also provided washing facilities for bomb victims. By the end of the Blitz on London, 241 WVS members had been killed and many more wounded.

By 1943 the WVS boasted over one million members and was involved in almost every aspect of wartime life. With so many displaced people the WVS set up Incident Inquiry points where people could find out about their loved ones after a bombing raid, freeing up the ARP services to support the firefighters. Although the bombing raids became less intense as the war progressed there were other pressures. The devastating loss of merchant ships in the Atlantic to German U-boats created shortages which the WVS worked tirelessly to address by collecting everything from aluminium to scrap paper for the war effort. Each WVS centre had its own salvage officer and food leader. The food leader was responsible for assisting in the administration of rationing. The WVS also ran fundraising campaigns such as 'Salute the Soldier', 'Wings for Victory', 'Spitfire Funds' and 'Warship Week'.

After the evacuation of some 340,000 Allied troops from Dunkirk (26 May – 4 June 1940) members of the WVS were on hand to welcome them back with food, drinks and warm clothing. The provision of meals to members of the armed forces coming home on leave, or returning to service, remained an important part of their work. To this day there is a plaque at the railway station in Retford, Nottinghamshire (a major railway hub) commemorating the work of the WVS canteen and restroom at the station. Between 1940 and 1946, almost 2.3 million meals were served – a rate of over 1,000 meals a day! When the American troops started landing in Britain in 1942 the WVS ran 200 'British Welcome Clubs' across the country to help bridge the gap between the American service personnel and British civilians. After the D-Day landings, members of the WVS followed the troops into Europe to continue offering their support.

In 1941, to combat the severity of food rationing, the government set up a series of 'British Restaurants', many of which were run by the WVS, where people could buy cheap nutritious meals off ration. These were set up, where possible, in existing halls and social clubs which already had the tables, chairs and food preparation facilities required. Where this was not possible, prefabricated structures were erected to ensure that there was a British Restaurant in reach of most families. The restaurants were originally named 'Communal Feeding Centres', but Prime Minister Winston Churchill regarded the name as 'an odious expression, redolent of Communism and the workhouse', recommending British Restaurants as an alternative. In 1943 *The Times* reported that there were over 2,000 British Restaurants, increasing at a rate of ten a week.

UNIFORM

WVS personnel had to pay for their uniforms which were designed by the famous Irish couturier, Digby Morton. The fact that the complete uniform cost the equivalent of three weeks' wages for an average worker meant that many members only purchased a few items and the poorer ones wore only their metal WVS badge and/or an armband to identify themselves. Schemes were put in place later to make the purchase of uniform items easier, including making the patterns and material available so that women could make their own.

HEADWEAR

The uniform hat was a trilby style, dark green felt hat with a red band. The metal WVS badge was attached to the centre front of the hatband. The hat was worn in many ways – with the crown flattened or pinched and the brim adjusted to suit the individual wearer. On 28 January 1941 a beret was introduced which, being cheaper to buy than the hat, became popular. Again, made of dark green felt, the beret was worn with either the metal WVS badge, or preferably the grey cloth badge attached over the left eye.

CLOTHING

The first uniform of the WVS consisted of an overcoat and hat but these were expensive, and no member was required to wear the uniform. The coat was grey-green in colour in a herringbone weave, double-breasted with six large buttons. At the back were two pleats and a half-belt. Some overcoats had epaulettes, but these were available separately and could be added if desired.

A tweed jacket and skirt, a red blouse and green overalls were soon added to the inventory. The jacket and skirt were made of the same material as the overcoat but lighter weight in the same herringbone pattern weave. The jacket was single breasted with three large buttons and two expandable pockets, and a half-belt at the back. The skirts were five- panel construction with a buttoned waist band and a zip to the side. The blouse was made of either silk, artificial silk or Viyella. There were six small red buttons arranged in pairs. The blouse was available in either long-sleeve or short-sleeve options. Overalls were made of light green cotton with nine detachable buttons. The pocket placement was the same as for the dress with the breast pocket having the letters 'WVS' embroidered in red. Tailored at the waist, the overall was secured with two waistbelts held by a detachable button. The later wrap-over overall was of similar material. It had the same three pockets but without tailoring. There were no buttons, and the garment was secured by two ties.

In December 1939 the embroidered badges, scarves and white overalls were added. Spring 1940 saw the introduction of a WVS dress in a lighter material, more suited to the warmer weather. The dress is of grey-green wool or wool-blend with six buttons of matching colour, arranged in pairs. There is a small breast pocket on the left side and two larger pockets at the front of the skirt. The dress is tailored into the waist with four darts front and back. The sleeve cup is also buttoned. Most WVS dresses seen today are post-war and can be identified by their bottle-green colour and having eight buttons arranged in four pairs. Otherwise, the dress is identical to the wartime pattern.

By September 1940 knitted sweaters and cardigans were introduced, together with an overcoat. Because the cost of uniform remained prohibitive to many members a second-hand uniform service was created in April 1941, where members no longer able to continue in active service with the WVS could sell on their uniform at a fair price. With the introduction of clothes rationing in June 1941, responsibility for the supply of WVS uniform was passed to the Ministry of Home Security. A restriction of the uniform remained the limited number of sizes available. This was overcome in August 1942 when it became possible to obtain the material required and have the garments tailored (or made up at home) however, strict regulations governed the patterns used and final appearance. In recognition of the need for some WVS members to have use of overalls (for example those working in canteens and British Restaurants) an overall loan scheme was introduced in December 1942. The idea was that there would be a supply of overalls available which members could use while on duty and surrender when they returned home. In the event, these 'loan overalls' were bought jointly by three members who each contributed a coupon and a third of the price. In March 1943 the overalls were finally replaced entirely with a wrap-over overall. For those who still could not afford uniform, arm bands were available of

WLA & UNIFORMED VOLUNTARY SERVICE ROLES

grey felt with the king's crown and letters 'WVS' embroidered in red. Some also bore the letters 'BR' (British Restaurants) or 'RC' (Rest Centres).

CHOOSING A WVS IMPRESSION

A WVS impression is understandably a popular choice given the range of uniforms and roles available. You can represent a 'well-off' volunteer able to afford the full uniform, or simply add a metal WVS badge and armband to ordinary civilian clothing to represent one of the poorer members – and every variation in between! As a 'promenader' you may choose to be uniformed but, with others, you may wish to represent one of the activities undertaken by the WVS – for example providing a washing service, food preparation or running a salvage activity. If you enjoy knitting then making something for service personnel is an easy impression which attracts a lot of interest from the public.

OBTAINING UNIFORMS & ACCESSORIES

'Bygone Days WVS Specialist' – a vintage online clothing store supplying replica clothing and specialising in the uniforms of the wartime WVS manufactured using period sewing machines – www.facebook.com/DanetreesGreenShoppingBygoneDays/

LIVING HISTORY GROUPS & LINKS

'WVS Reenactors Group (Women in Green)' – a Facebook group which prides itself on its friendly and supportive atmosphere, welcoming anyone with an interest in the

WVS during the Second World War. In addition to offering information and support to all members, the group also advertises events as well as sharing patterns, recipes and ideas to enhance an impression. The group can be found at – www.facebook.com/groups/191891204836543

FURTHER RESEARCH

Green Sleeves; The Story of the WVS/WRVS; Katharine Bentley Beauman; Seeley Service and Co; 1977; ISBN: 0-8542-2097-6 – a fascinating and personalised account of the story of the WVS from its inception in 1938, its role during the wartime years and its post-war development.

Women at the Ready: The Remarkable Story of the Women's Voluntary Services on the Home Front; Patricia and Robert Malcolmson; Abacus; 2014; ISBN: 0-3491-3872-9. A delightful account of the work of the WVS in wartime using the diaries of women who served. The diary entries give a very personal feel to the book giving it an intimacy that many histories lack.

Women in Green: The Story of the WVS in Wartime; Charles Graves, W Heinemann Ltd; 1948. An out-of-print book but still available through online book searches. A very useful book because of the many photographs accompanying the text.

A History of the Uniform of Royal Voluntary Service – a very useful video on the history of the WVS uniform from its wartime beginnings with some excellent images of uniform items – www.youtube.com/watch?v=W8POpHATydY

The Introduction and Development of the Uniform of the Women's Voluntary Services for Civil Defence – a fact sheet produced by Matthew McMurray (WRVS Archivist) in 2009 showing the development of the uniform and the regulations governing its usage. Fascinating details regarding the cost of each item and the amount of material (including value in coupons) required to make items like greatcoats. Essential reading for anyone researching the WVS uniform – www.royalvoluntaryservice.org.uk/media/rwzi1so5/wvs_wartime_uniform.pdf

The Women's Voluntary Services (WVS); Jon Mills; Jon Mills Books – available through Jon Mills Books website – jonmillsbooks.weebly.com/jon-mills-the-womens-voluntary-services-book.html. Arguably the definitive reference work for researchers, collectors and re-enactors interested in the uniforms and ephemera of the WVS during the Second World War.

CHAPTER SEVEN

NON-UNIFORMED VOLUNTARY SERVICE & OTHER ROLES

NATIONAL AIR RAID PRECAUTIONS ANIMAL COMMITTEE (NARPAC) & PEOPLES' DISPENSARY FOR SICK ANIMALS (PDSA)

The National Air Raid Precautions Animal Committee (NARPAC) was established in the summer of 1939 as war threatened with the purpose of uniting animal welfare groups, the veterinary profession, and local authorities in the event of war. The organisation was to provide information to the public about protection during air raids for domestic, farm and working animals. As the name suggests, NARPAC was organised through the Home Office Air Raid Precautions Department and was chaired by Howard Edward Dale CB. The organisations under the NARPAC banner were:

Home Office (Air Raid Precautions Department)

Ministry of Agriculture & Fisheries (Animal Health Division)

Commissioner of Police of the Metropolis (Head of London's Metropolitan Police)

National Veterinary Medical Association

National Farmers' Union

Royal Society for the Prevention of Cruelty to Animals (RSPCA)

People's Dispensary for Sick Animals (PDSA)

Our Dumb Friends' League

National Canine Defence League

Scottish Society for the Prevention of Cruelty to Animals

Glasgow & West of Scotland Society for the Prevention of Cruelty to Animals

The Dog's Home, Battersea

The Home of Rest for Horses

For administrative purposes, NARPAC divided the country into districts each with a 'District organiser' overseeing affairs. Beneath the district organiser was a 'Chief Guard' who oversaw the work of local 'Animal Guards'. The Animal Guards were to provide shelters and veterinary care for animals caught up in air raids. Secondly, they would

A mobile NARPAC Ambulance attached to the rear of a 1936 Austin 7 Ruby Deluxe.
— Author's collection

create a central register of pets, giving each one a numbered collar tag, to allow lost animals after a raid to be identified and returned to their owners where possible.

The 'Animal Service' was responsible for farm and working animals through the work of 'Animal Stewards'. NARPAC would also undertake research to evaluate the impact that domestic animals would have on food supplies given the impending rationing of food. It was estimated that there were between six and seven million dogs and cats in Britain which could impose a burden on increasingly stretched food supplies.

In addition to the registration of pets, NARPAC established a series of first aid posts for animals, generally at the clinics or hospitals of animal welfare societies or private veterinary practices. Animal

RE-LIVING BRITAIN IN THE 1940S

Guards were to serve as the liaison between the local residents and first aid posts after an air raid. Animal Guards would ensure that local residents were aware of the address of the nearest first aid post and, after a raid, assist in ensuring that injured animals were given necessary treatment as soon as possible. Animal Guards were also

NARPAC Animal Guards with an improvised mobile animal carrier and home-made catch pole.
— With permission Ethan Reuben

NON-UNIFORMED VOLUNTARY SERVICE & OTHER ROLES

required to assist with the disposal of dead animals but were not expected to be out on the streets during an air raid. To facilitate the work of NARPAC, any vehicle bearing the NARPAC logo was allowed to travel unchallenged.

Almost from its inception, NARPAC courted controversy. As an organisation reliant on donations there was an immediate conflict between all of the component organisations and NARPAC itself, all competing for the same limited pool of donations. This inevitably led to different charities accusing each other of 'poaching' on the charitable fundraising of others, which then led to further conflict and division. Amid accusations of financial irregularities, Battersea Dogs' Home began to distance itself from NARPAC, and the RSPCA withdrew completely in July 1941. The RSPCA's decision was also influenced by conflict between itself and the PDSA who were regarded as extremists because of their opposition to fox hunting. This infighting also had a detrimental effect on recruitment and retention of volunteers. In 1939 NARPAC boasted some 47,000 Animal Guards, but boredom and friction meant that this number had fallen to 16,000 by October 1940. It did not help that many pet owners were more concerned with feeding their pets, given the constraints of food rationing, than finding the NARPAC animal registration fees.

A government announcement was, inadvertently, to lead to the unnecessary deaths of hundreds of thousands of pets. The government concluded that pet owners in larger cities should relocate their pets to the countryside and published their advice in the pamphlet 'Advice to Animal Owners'. The pamphlet contained the advice that 'If at all possible, send or take your household animals into the country in advance of an emergency.' However, it concluded with the statement:

'If you cannot place them in the care of neighbours, it really is kindest to have them destroyed.' This advice was echoed in 'Air Raid Precautions Handbook No. 12', which stated that the evacuation of pets was the personal responsibility of their owners and 'owners should make up their minds whether they can take away their dog or cat themselves. If this is impossible, they should decide whether the animal is best destroyed or evacuated to the care of friends in the country.' The BBC announced this conclusion and almost every newspaper printed it. Although, several weeks later, a supplementary pamphlet was issued making clear that 'those who are staying at home should not have their animals destroyed' the public had already taken the advice, as they saw it, to heart – especially in the absence of any official provision for pets, unlike farm animals.

With the declaration of war on 3 September 1939, pet owners thronged to RSPCA and PDSA hospitals to have their pets euthanised. They genuinely believed that they were doing their patriotic 'bit' for the war effort and helping to preserve precious food supplies. The RSPCA's magazine *Animal World* had reported in October 1939 that 'the work of destroying animals was continued, day and night, during the first week of the war'. One animal shelter had a half-mile long queue of people waiting to have their pets euthanised. Crematoria were overrun with the corpses of dogs and cats. The problem was further compounded by the fact that the crematoria could not run at night due to blackout conditions. Animal welfare societies soon ran out of chloroform, and shelters ran out of places to bury the corpses. One local sanatorium offered the use of a meadow, where half a million pets were buried. Within the first week of the war, it is estimated that some 400,000 pets were destroyed. Not only pets were sacrificed to save food – many animals in London Zoo were also killed. In November 1939 *The Times* newspaper noted that 'there is daily evidence that large numbers of pet dogs are still being destroyed for no better reason than that it is inconvenient to keep them alive — which, of course, is no reason at all, but merely shows an owner's inability to appreciate his obligations towards his animal.'

The start of the Blitz in 1940 led to another round of killing and another 350,000 animals had been destroyed by VE Day. There were protests against the killings by the RSPCA and the PDSA, and Battersea Dog's Home cared for 145,000 dogs during the war. Other individuals made their own safe havens for animals. Nina, Duchess of Hamilton, created her own sanctuary for pets at a heated aerodrome in Ferne, Dorset. The Duchess apparently sent her staff to the East End of London to rescue strays and unwanted pets – and the Ferne Animal Sanctuary continues to this day in Somerset.

NARPAC continued to operate throughout the war and wound itself up in 1945 with all assets being passed to the PDSA. Despite lofty and noble ambitions, NARPAC will always be associated with the pet massacre. This is rather unfair since they never did actually advocate mass euthanasia. Arguably, as historian Hilda Kean notes, the responsibility lies with the government whose:

> *"failure to acknowledge in timely fashion the presence of dogs, cats, budgerigars, and other companion animals would have severe repercussions for such animals… Although the state was not directly responsible for the decision of people to kill their pets, its lack of action made it easier for a positive animal-human relationship to be so drastically broken in September 1939."*

NON-UNIFORMED VOLUNTARY SERVICE & OTHER ROLES

Two NARPAC Animal Guards treat an injured dog.
— With permission Ethan Reuben

Although the PDSA, founded by Maria Dickin, was involved in NARPAC as a member organisation it continued to function as an independent body as well.

During the First World War, Maria Dickin toured the poverty-stricken slums of London and was appalled by the levels of deprivation she saw. She was also shocked by the suffering on animals in the slums whose owners were too poor to seek veterinary aid for them. Her response was to set up the PDSA with the first clinic opening in Whitechapel in 1917. Outside the door she placed a sign which read 'Bring your sick animals. Do not let them suffer. All animals treated. All treatment free.' Such was the demand for her services that she soon had to move to larger premises, despite the opposition of veterinary practices. By 1922 there were seven clinics across London and by 1927, fifty-seven new clinics had been established and three mobile clinics.

During the Second World War the PDSA saved more than 250,000 pets injured and/or lost during enemy bombing raids. PDSA Animal Rescue Squads scoured bomb sites in an attempt to locate animals in the debris. Perhaps the best known of these was Superintendent Bill Barnet who led one of the Animal Rescue Squads. Bill was often accompanied by Beauty – his wire-haired terrier. One night Beauty started to dig near to Bill and minutes later the team helped Beauty uncover a cat buried beneath the rubble. By the end of the war Beauty had saved sixty-three animals from being buried alive. In January 1945 Beauty was awarded the 'Dickin Medal' (introduced by Maria Dickin in 1943 to recognise the importance of military service animals and the sacrifice they make).

CHOOSING A NARPAC OR PDSA IMPRESSION

A NARPAC or PDSA impression is always one to attract the attention of the public, and a good impression to choose if you have a pet that you want to involve in your hobby. NARPAC was a voluntary organisation with no uniform – members were identified by a metal badge and an armband. NARPAC members engaged in house-to-house collections wore a card 'Authorised Collector's Badge' on a length of string and worn around the neck. Some NARPAC personnel appear to have been issued with the civilian 'Zuckerman' helmet, introduced in December 1940 and produced throughout 1941, with a transfer of the NARPAC logo on the front.

PDSA Animal Rescue Squad members wore dark blue cotton overalls with heavy work boots or wellington boots. They also were issued with the Mk.II steel helmets bearing the 'Animal PDSA Rescue' text on three lines. NARPAC personnel used the civilian high-domed Zuckerman helmets with the NARPAC logo on the front.

There really is no limit to how far this impression can be taken. NARPAC Animal Guards used a wide variety of cages and enclosures to contain animals. An old bird cage would be appropriate, as would a hand-cart with old pram wheels bearing the NARPAC logo. If an appropriate vintage vehicle is available, then an 'animal ambulance' can be built and added. Alternatively, a collection of reproduction paperwork lends itself to a NARPAC pet registration point display. The Facebook page 'NARPAC Animals and the Blitz' detailed below gives a lot of ideas as to what is possible, and members are always willing to share their experience. Since most people today are completely unaware of the wartime 'pet massacre', it is a topic which solicits a great deal of interest – especially if a pet is involved!

NON-UNIFORMED VOLUNTARY SERVICE & OTHER ROLES

OBTAINING RELEVANT ACCESSORIES:

There is very little original wartime material surviving from these organisations, but original Animal Guard badges come on the market from time to time (although they tend to be rather expensive). They are sometimes listed on eBay, but bidding can elevate the price. Sally Bosley's Badge Shop (www.sallybosleysbadgeshop.com/home.php) is always worth checking.

Copies of NARPAC paperwork – envelopes, ARP Handbook No.12 and other documents – come up on eBay from time to time. A reproduction card 'Authorised Collector's Badge' is available from Somme Poppies Repros - www.facebook.com/sommepoppiesrepros.

Original Zuckerman helmets are readily available, and relatively cheap for an example in poor condition. Stripped down and repainted these can be finished off with a decal available from eBay (www.ebay.co.uk/itm/WW2-AFS-NFS-Fire-Service-St-Johns-Abulance-Ministry-of-Food-NARPAC-Helmet-Decal/222614493051). Reproduction NARPAC armbands are also generally available on eBay.

LIVING HISTORY GROUPS & LINKS

'NARPAC Animals and the Blitz': a Facebook page for people interested in animal welfare during the Second World War. A good source for research but also for meeting like-minded living historians. The page can be found at – www.facebook.com/groups/NARPAC

FURTHER RESEARCH

Bonzo's War: Animals Under Fire 1939–1945; Clare Campbell; Constable; 2013; ISBN: 1-4721-0679-2 – a deeply moving account of the experiences of animals in war; from animals under fire to homeless pets trying to survive a ruthless government campaign against them. Includes the role of NARPAC and other agencies.

The Great Cat and Dog Massacre: The Real Story of World War Two's Unknown Tragedy; Hilda Kean; University of Chicago Press: 2017; ISBN: 0-2263-1832-X – a detailed and thoughtful consideration of the background to these tragic events right back to attitudes forged in the First World War, written in a lively and engaging style. The only major criticism would be the focus on London without contrasting that experience with that of other cities and areas.

150 years on: the story of Maria Dickin and PDSA – part of the PDSA website devoted to the history of the charity and the role of its iconic founder, Maria Dickin. It includes a short film showing footage of the slums of 1917 and a commentary by Maria Dickin herself.

NON-UNIFORMED VOLUNTARY SERVICE & OTHER ROLES

STREET FIRE PARTY/FIRE GUARDS

With the start of the Blitz in September 1940 the 'Fire Watchers Order' was introduced, and it was made compulsory for the owners/occupiers of commercial and business premises to have fire watchers on duty at all times. As the bombing continued, the compulsory recruitment of civilian men and women was introduced. These people were required to join part-time fire-watching and fire party duties. Supplementary Fire Parties, organised by local fire brigades, comprised trained volunteers, in groups of three or five, who were equipped with stirrup pumps and trained to tackle small fires, including those caused by 1kg magnesium incendiary bombs. It was compulsory for all males, aged 16 to 60 years old, to register for forty-eight hours of service per month. Fire watchers would monitor business and industrial

A Fire Guard rests after a busy night shift.

– With permission
Andrew Harrison

premises in the same way that Supplementary Fire Parties (organised by the fire brigades) and Street Fire Parties (organised and recruited by the ARP) monitored residential buildings.

In August 1941, with the formation of the National Fire Service, the 'Fire Guard' was formed under the supervision of the ARP Wardens' Service. Fire Guards were full-time paid positions under the command of the local Chief Warden. Fire Guards organised local volunteer Street Fire Parties. 'Fire Guard' armbands then replaced the 'SFP' armbands worn by the previous Supplementary Fire Parties. Fire Guards were often responsible for a specific area or building and were required to monitor the fall of incendiary bombs, dealing with them if possible, and passing on details of any fires which had broken out to the National Fire Service.

The Fire Guards were reorganised again as a separate service under control of a local authority Fire Guard area officer from April 1943 – a reflection of the success of the Fire Guards during the 1942 'Baedeker Raids'. The Baedeker Raids concentrated on particular English cities, with the name deriving from the series of German tourist guidebooks used to determine targets. The cities were not industrial centres, but rather of great historic and cultural value. The idea was that the loss of such cities would weaken British morale and bring about an early end to the war.

By December 1943 some 6 million people were enrolled in the Fire Guard organisation and compulsory service was extended to 63 years old, with voluntary enrolment for men between 16 and 70, and women 18 to 60. The Fire Guards also worked closely with the Fire Services. A note in the author's collections from the 'Bristol Fire Guard service: Redland Division, Sector 314', informs Fire Guards that

NON-UNIFORMED VOLUNTARY SERVICE & OTHER ROLES

'a demonstration of practical help by Fire Guards to the N.F.S. (Third Stage Training) will be given at the Static Water Tank on Sunday 27 February at 10.30 a.m.'.

As the Allies began to push into Europe after D-Day, enemy air raids became less frequent and the requirement for daytime fire-watching duties was relaxed. However, we should never underestimate the role that Fire Guards played. Each night four Fire Guards assumed their posts on the roof of Canterbury Cathedral. During the course of enemy bombing raids many incendiary bombs landed on the cathedral roof, which could have caused devastating damage were it not for the courage of these Fire Guards, who located them and threw them off so they could be extinguished on the ground.

CLOTHING

While volunteer Fire Guards had no uniform, senior ranking personnel were entitled to wear the standard civil defence uniform of battledress and trousers with shoulder titles identifying them as Fire Guards and badges indicating their rank.

While there was no uniform for volunteer Supplementary/Street Fire Party personnel, they were issued with an armband of dark blue cotton with the letters 'SFP'. Similarly, Fire Guard personnel were identified by a similar dark blue cotton armband with the yellow/gold words 'Fire Guard'. From September 1944 members of the Fire Guards were allowed to add war service chevrons to their armbands. The chevrons were to be placed to the left of the writing (as seen by another person).

Fire Watchers could choose from a bewildering array of enamelled metal lapel badges (many of which were produced by private companies for those staff involved in fire watching) to identify themselves.

Supplementary/Street Fire Party and Fire Guard members were issued with the civilian Zuckerman helmet. These were high domed and relatively cheap to manufacture. The helmets were painted grey and adorned with the letters 'SFP' or 'FG' in black. Higher ranking Fire Guard personnel were identified by black bands around the helmet, which was painted white.

CHOOSING A STREET FIRE PARTY / FIRE GUARD IMPRESSION

The advantage of a Street Fire Party or Fire Guard impression is that it can be used to enhance a civilian impression because there was no uniform per se – merely an armband and a helmet. Together with a few props (like a stirrup pump and a galvanised bucket with sand) an impression can be created which will attract the interest of the public and encourage questions.

OBTAINING ACCESSORIES

Because the SFP/FG had no formal uniform it is perfectly possible to add this to a standard civilian impression by acquiring a worn Zuckerman helmet (readily available from eBay) and adding a stencil of the required letters (or you might be fortunate enough to find an original already lettered). Reproduction armbands can be found on eBay at www.ebay.co.uk/itm/222307064919. Accessories like a galvanised bucket and stirrup pump can often be found at junk shops, vintage fairs or antique fairs reasonably priced. When buying a stirrup pump try to ensure that the hose still retains its original hose and brass nozzle rather than a later piece of hosepipe added as a replacement.

NON-UNIFORMED VOLUNTARY SERVICE & OTHER ROLES

LIVING HISTORY GROUPS & LINKS

'**WW2 Civil Defence (ARP) Re-enactors**' is a group dedicated to supporting those who re-enact ARP and later Civil Defence at events. As Street Fire Parties and Fire Guards were under the banner of Civil Defence they would be a most helpful group to contact at www.facebook.com/groups/793725373978971

FURTHER RESEARCH

'**WW2 Fire Guards & Fire Watchers Insignia, Armbands, Lapel Badges & Helmets**' – a well-illustrated overview of the various helmet markings and armbands of these organisations. www.ww2civildefence.co.uk/fire-guards-watchers.html

MINERS – 'BEVIN BOYS'

At the beginning of the war Britain was heavily dependent on coal as a source of power for transport and also to generate electricity. However, ignoring the fact that the demand for coal was likely to increase dramatically with the demands of war, by mid-1943, 36,000 miners had been lost to the armed forces and largely not replaced. The government had already tried releasing former miners from the armed forces, recalling retired miners, and appealing to unemployed men, and boys of school-leaving age, but without success, and a further 50,000 miners were required over the next eighteen months. On 12 November 1943 Bevin, the wartime Minister of Labour and National Service, made a radio broadcast aimed at school sixth-formers saying:

> *"We need 720,000 men continuously employed in this industry.... This is where you boys come in. Each one of you, I am sure, is full of enthusiasm to win this war. You are looking forward to the day when you can play your part with your friends and brothers who are in the Navy, the Army, the Air Force.... But believe me, our fighting men will not be able to achieve their purpose unless we get an adequate supply of coal.... So when you go to register and the question is put to you 'Will you go into the mines?' let your answer be, 'Yes, I will go anywhere to help win this war'."*

The term 'Bevin Boys' is thought to derive from this broadcast.

From 26 September 1942, men under the age of 25 called up for active service could choose to do their service underground and were referred to as 'optants', but on 2 December 1943, Bevin announced the introduction of a new scheme which would allow young men to complete their National Service in Britain's coal mines instead of joining the armed forces. Under the new scheme the option of choice would be taken from them. There would now be a ballot and miners chosen by this method were referred to as 'ballotees'.

On registering for National Service, young men between 18 and 25 years old would be selected according to the last digit of their registration number. Numbers were drawn on a fortnightly basis and there were no grounds for appeal. Refusal to go down the mines would lead to a heavy fine and possible imprisonment under the Emergency Powers Act. By 31 May 1944, 285 conscripts had refused to serve in the mines; 135 of those had been prosecuted and thirty-two given a custodial sentence.

NON-UNIFORMED VOLUNTARY SERVICE & OTHER ROLES

Many people at the time treated the Bevin Boys as dodging military service, and they were often treated as Conscientious Objectors. This was to some extent understandable since some Conscientious Objectors were sent down the mines as an alternative to military service under a totally different scheme. The new recruits were similarly regarded with suspicion by regular miners who were suddenly confronted with an influx of inexperienced young men who had no real interest in the work they were forced to undertake. The fact that they were young men of military age without a uniform also led to many being stopped and questioned by police under suspicion of avoiding military service.

A miner at the end of his shift relaxes next to a collection of miners' lamps.
– With permission Paul Gregory

Training was undertaken at one of thirteen training centres nationally. Upon arrival the new recruit would be allocated either to a Miners' Hostel, or billeted in the local community (for which over a third of their weekly wage was deducted to cover costs). The pay was a constant source of complaint and some 140 trainees went on strike in Doncaster for two days.

To add insult to injury, although some conscripts were issued with overalls, many were expected to wear ordinary clothes paid for out of their ration coupons. They even had to pay for their tools, which led many to complain that since the army did not pay for their rifles why should they pay for their picks and shovels?

Bevin Boys would then receive six weeks training. The first four weeks were based in a classroom and the following two at the colliery attached to their training centre. Once they had completed training, the new miners were sent off to begin work at one of the nation's collieries; for the first four weeks they would be supervised by an experienced miner. Except in South Wales, the newly trained miners were required to serve four months underground before being allowed to work at the coal-face. In most cases, the Bevin Boys were not directly involved in cutting coal from the coal-face, but instead were responsible for filling wagons with the newly mined coal and taking them to the shaft for transportation to the surface, either using cables or pit ponies. Pit ponies were especially useful for the new miners if their lamps went out because if they could grab the pony's tail it would lead them to safety. The ponies had no fear of the darkness since many were stabled underground for life and never saw daylight. The work was hard in very tough conditions anything up to a mile underground. There were no toilets, and the constant noise of machinery, risk of injury or even explosion challenged even the toughest nerves. Although the war ended in 1945, the Bevin Boys were not released from their service until March 1948.

CLOTHING

There was no formal uniform for miners – some wore overalls while others were expected to wear their own clothes down the mines. Overalls would have been of heavy cotton denim, button fronted without an elasticated waist. Ordinary clothing will be older outworn garments – corded or corduroy fabric – high waisted and button-fronted. Trousers might be secured with a belt or braces. A collarless shirt and old waistcoat might complete the appearance.

An exhausted miner at the end of his shift.

– With permission Sue and Tony Horton

CHOOSING A MINING/'BEVIN BOY' IMPRESSION

In many ways this is a very good choice for an impression because relatively little is known about the Bevin Boys today. All official records of their service were destroyed in 1950. The miners received no medals and little recognition for their work. The 'Bevin Boys Association' was not formed until 1989, and they did not receive official recognition until 1995 when Queen Elizabeth II acknowledged their service in a speech. Only in 1998 were the Bevin Boys permitted to march in the Remembrance Day parade at the Cenotaph in London. This means that there is a lot to engage the public with, however, to some extent such an impression is limited to places where mining took place or is at least represented. Suitable locations include the former colliery at Blaenavon – now Big Pit National Coal Museum in Gwent.

OBTAINING EQUIPMENT & ACCESSORIES

Suitable clothing can often be sourced from charity shops or vintage fairs. Some garments might need a little alteration (for example replacing a zip with buttons) but finding appropriate clothing should not present a challenge. Sadly, there are no dealers specialising in vintage mining equipment. There is no substitute here for research – identify exactly what equipment you need and then try to source it. Flea markets in former mining areas remain a good source of material, as does eBay, but patience is a virtue when it comes to getting the right piece at the right price. No matter how hard you try, there will always be the one piece that eludes you. According to one living historian with an extensive knowledge of mining equipment, the 'Holy Grail' of mining memorabilia of the period is the canary resuscitator.

Canaries were used in mines to detect poisonous gases like carbon monoxide. The resuscitator had a circular door which would allow air in. If the canary reacted to any gas present then the door would be closed and a valve opened on the small oxygen cylinder above allowing the canary to revive while the miners evacuated the area.

LIVING HISTORY GROUPS & LINKS

There are a number of individuals around the country who portray miners but no formal group. A good place to visit and make contacts is the Blaenavon Ironworks Wartime Weekend (usually held in July) – location of the BBC TV series *Coal House*. Blaenavon is a World Heritage Site and includes the Big Pit National Coal Museum.

FURTHER RESEARCH

> **'The Forgotten Conscript'**; website dedicated to the Bevin Boys with film clips, copies of original documents and a wealth of information on every aspect of their work, including the Bevin Boys Association and a Remembrance record. This can be found at www.theforgottenconscript.co.uk.

> **'Mining People'**; Frederick Sykes; HM Stationery Office; 1945 – a contemporary booklet detailing the work of the miners but also their education and welfare opportunities. Emphasis on the support given to miners rather than on their work but a useful insight into aspects of wartime mining often neglected.

CHAPTER EIGHT
CIVILIANS

CIVILIAN ROLES

The civilian experience of war was clearly very different depending on where a person lived. Someone living in any of the major cities would be subject to air raids and the fear, destruction and the constant threat of danger, whereas those living in rural areas would find that the war had substantially less of an impact on their lifestyles. For those in areas targeted by the Luftwaffe, the threat of death or injury was very real. Many civilians in such areas chose to wear identification bracelets to facilitate identification in the event of injury or death. Many such bracelets had St. Christopher charms attached to offer the wearer some spiritual reassurance if not protection.

Year	1940	1941	1942	1943	1944	1945
Dead	23,767	20,885	3,236	2,372	8,475	1,860
Seriously injured	30,529	21,841	4,150	3,450	21,989	4,223

Bombing casualties in Britain 1940-45.
From figures provided by the Ministry of Home Security and the 'Bombing of Britain 1940–1945 Exhibition', University of Exeter.

In order to establish an accurate population check (since the last census had been in 1931 and next not due for a further two years), Parliament passed the National Registration Act 1939. This Act set up a National Register and was the basis for issuing identity cards. Householders were issued forms in advance and required to complete the details of every resident as of 29 September 1939. Every household was visited, the information provided was checked and some 45 million identity cards issued. The identity card was to be carried at all times. On 8 January 1940 food rationing began and although things like fruit and vegetables were not rationed there were shortages, and imported items such as lemons and bananas basically disappeared. The 'Dig for Victory' campaign encouraged people to grow their own, but clearly those people living in the rural areas generally had a better diet than those in cities – although even their rations could be supplemented by the black market.

After the experience of WWI there was a real fear of poison gas being used in bombs dropped from aircraft. This led to the government manufacturing and issuing gas masks to every person in the country and it was expected that the mask should be carried with them at all times. Masks were issued in a cardboard box with a string threaded through for suspension round the neck or over the shoulder. These boxes would not take a lot of use (especially when wet) and certainly did not look fashionable! Manufacturers soon started to produce a range of gas mask cases that resembled ladies' bags in faux leather, or actually were bags with a container for a gas mask built in to the bottom. Similarly, the blackout each night created a market for fashionable accessories that would make a person more visible to drivers and other pedestrians. Manufacturers produced a range of items, such as flowers which could be pinned onto clothing and which would glow in the dark, and luminous coat buttons. Stores like Selfridges offered a wide range of items to choose from. Even white coats were produced to increase visibility.

As the air raids began in earnest, people became accustomed to leaving their beds to head for the nearest shelter whenever the 'raiders overhead' siren sounded. If a family had their own Anderson or Morrison shelter then it didn't really matter what they wore, but if they lived in a tenement block with access to a communal shelter then some degree of modesty was required. A simple one-piece suit referred to as the 'Siren Suit' was produced which could be quickly pulled on over night clothes when the siren sounded. The suit had a drop-down panel at the back to facilitate using the toilet and some were even embellished with padded shoulders. An example in the Imperial War Museum collections has padded shoulders, flared trouser legs and a fitted hood. With piping in a contrasting colour and a separate belt, the overall garment was both practical and fashionable. One of the greatest supporters of the 'Siren Suit' was Winston Churchill, who was often photographed wearing his own tailor-made version of the suit.

One of the things that draws many people into an interest in the '40s is the glamour and fashion of the time. This is perhaps surprising at a time of rationing and shortages, but is an outstanding feature of the period. Many people anticipated that the demands of war would mean an end to fashion as the materials needed for civilian clothing became scarcer or, in the case of silk, simply unobtainable. Prices rose and attention turned to the imminent threat of air raids and German invasion, but fashion was not forgotten and the government recognised the importance of fashion in keeping up morale.

Arguably men's fashions changed far less than women's. Men had something of a uniform in that a suit and a hat was the everyday clothing for most, other than manual and factory workers who often wore coveralls or old trousers and a shirt. The introduction of clothes rationing in 1942 meant that single-breasted jackets replaced double-breasted (to save on material) and the size of lapels was limited. Furthermore, fashionable turn-ups on trousers were forbidden, but this could easily be overcome by buying a pair of trousers that were too long and having them altered. The length of shirt tails was limited and double cuffs were abolished. An article produced by the Imperial War Museum calculates that some 4 million square yards of cotton

This gentleman has gone for a golfing impression complete with set of clubs. The lady's stylish dress shows just a hint of petticoat which might encourage someone to quietly tell her that 'Charlie's dead'. This was a warning that some petticoat was showing and appears to originate from the time of Charles II when, out or respect, women were said to have flashed their petticoats when news of his death was announced!

– With permission Andrew Harrison

were saved each year through these measures alone! Many suits were also now made with a wool-rayon blend rather than the pre-war pure wool. The new materials were also commonly patterned (especially with stripes). Knitted sweaters with a V-neck (often adopting a Fair Isle pattern) were worn for a more casual look. At home a sweater might be worn over a collar-less shirt for relaxation.

A hat was still considered an important accessory during the '40s (although their popularity declined in the years after the war ended). The fedora, made of felt, was one of the most popular hat styles and often worn at a jaunty angle, whereas a homburg hat might be worn for more formal occasions. In the summer heat, wide-brimmed straw hats were popular. Workmen, and men at leisure, would favour the flat cap. As at any time, the older generation could be a little more conservative in their clothing and it was not uncommon to see 1930s suits still in use, and also bowler hats retained some popularity. Even top hats were still worn on more formal occasions. Both Neville Chamberlain and Winston Churchill wore top and bowler hats respectively. The comic duo Laurel and Hardy also both wore bowler hats throughout their stage and movie careers.

At the end of the 1930s British women's fashion was designed around knee-length dresses and skirt and blouse combinations. These were made from colourful fabrics and involved a lot of flounces and surface embellishment. For more formal wear these might be finished with a jacket or bolero, or by a cardigan or jumper for a more casual look. These items were worn over foundation garments such as girdles to create a flat stomach, and bras designed to produce the rather pointed, uplifted bust fashionable at the time. The effect was to create a triangular silhouette from the shoulders to the narrow waist. The outbreak of war in 1939, and the resultant shortages, would have a profound effect over the next decade.

Women felt the restrictions of clothes rationing and austerity rather more than men did. Clothes rationing was introduced to Britain on 1 June 1941. An adult ration book contained a series of coupons with sixty-six coupons for clothing per year (although this figure was reduced to forty-eight in 1942, thirty-six in 1943 and twenty-four in 1945). Blocks of coupons within a book were coloured differently and the government announced when each colour could be used to prevent people using all their coupons in one go. Each item of clothing was allocated a value in coupons depending on the amount of material and effort used to make it. For example, a dress was worth eleven coupons while a pair of stockings was worth two. There was some flexibility in the system to reflect need – for example a new mother would receive an extra fifty coupons to meet the needs of a rapidly growing baby. Parents were also encouraged to buy larger sizes so that children could 'grow into the garment', thereby making them last longer. To support this system clothing exchanges were set up at which people could exchange outgrown items of clothing for some that fitted the growing child.

Item of Clothing	Women	Girls
Lined Mackintosh or Coat over 28'	14	11
Under 28' Short Coat or Jacket	11	8
Frock, Gown or Dress made of Wool	11	8
Frock, Gown or Dress made of Other Fabric	7	5
Bodice with girl's skirt or Gym Tunic	8	6

CIVILIANS

Item of Clothing	Women	Girls
Pyjamas	8	6
Divided Skirt or Skirt [Full]	7	5
Nightdress	6	5
Dungarees or Overalls	6	4
Blouse, Shirt, Sports top, Cardigan	5	3
Pair of Slippers, Boots, Shoes	5	3
Other Garments including Corsets	5	2
Petticoat, Slip, Knickers/combo	4	3
Apron or Pinafore	3	2
Scarf, gloves, mittens or muff	2	2
Stockings per pair	2	1
Ankle Socks per pair	1	1
1 yard wool cloth 36' wide	3	3
2 ounces of wool knitting yarn	1	1

List of rationed clothing items for women and girls and the number of coupons required.
From an article by Pauline Weston Thomas at www.fashionera.com

Given the demands of the war, people understood rationing, and were prepared to accept it, even though it was not popular. New clothing was very expensive – clothing prices more than doubled between 1939 and 1941. What was needed was clothing which was designed to be fashionable yet met the austerity provisions imposed to save material. The introduction of purchase tax in October 1941 added to the pressure to reform clothing since items were now taxed according to the amount and type of material used. To address the need for quality, cheap clothing a new CC41 Utility mark was introduced. Today no one is entirely sure what the 'CC' stands for. Some people argue that it has no meaning at all and is simply a design feature, but the similarity of the design to the letters 'CC' have led others to suggest that it stood for 'Civilian Clothing' because it was introduced by the Directorate of Civilian Clothing. Given that the mark also appears on shoes, crockery and furniture, others have suggested that the 'CC' stand for 'Controlled Commodity'. We shall probably never know for certain! If it was possible, through connections in the Royal Air Force or through the Black Market, to obtain a piece of parachute silk then more luxurious garments could be made from underwear to blouses or even a complete wedding dress, despite the fact that the acquisition of such material for civilian use was a crime. Weldon's Patterns however did include guidance for using parachute panels to ensure minimum wastage when their use became legal in 1945.

In January 1942 the Board of Trade and a number of leading fashion designers met together to form the Society of London's Fashion Designers. The inspiration behind this move came from the editor of British Vogue magazine, Alison Settle. The new organisation was tasked by the Board of Trade with designing a suit, a dress and an outdoor

1942-43 CLOTHING BOOK

This book may not be used until the holder's name, full postal address and National Registration (Identity Card) Number have been plainly written below IN INK.

NAME ANNIE. E. THOMPSON
(BLOCK LETTERS)

ADDRESS AVENUE HOTEL
(BLOCK LETTERS)

(TOWN) MINEHEAD (COUNTY) Somerset

NATIONAL REGISTRATION (IDENTITY CARD) NUMBER

WOJD. / 85 / 2

Read the instructions within carefully, and take great care not to lose this book
Page 1

1942–43 Clothing Ration Book.
— Author's collection

coat which met the new Utility specifications but would appeal to fashion-conscious buyers. In all, thirty-two designs were submitted by the eight designers (Captain Molyneux, Norman Hartnell, Digby Morton, Victor Stiebel, Ang le Delange, Peter Russell, Madame Bianca Mosca and Hardy Amies) and regarded as a great success. The wartime shortages had led to a new streamlined style which was an immediate hit with the public. *The Daily Mail* lauded the fact that 'suburban wives and factory girls will soon be able to wear clothes designed and styled by the Queen's dressmaker'. Some early Utility products were not always especially well-made, and some retailers resented the reduced profits which added to the negative image soon acquired by Utility garments. Even the name 'Utility' clothing was resented but, as more and more garments appeared on the market in a variety of styles and colours, Utility clothing soon became known for being hard-wearing and of good quality. Part of the popularity of Utility clothing was the March edition of *Picture Post* magazine, which featured the actress Deborah Kerr modelling Utility clothing. Not only did this allow the working classes access to better quality clothing at prices they could afford, it also served to conceal the social divide since all women could now own something that was both fashionable and glamourous. All Utility clothing bore the CC41 mark but did not carry the name of the designer. There was another reason for getting the designers to create new styles – the Paris designers were now all under Nazi control and therefore unable to dominate the world fashion scene and so Britain was keen to show the United States that British fashions were a worthy replacement. This was so successful that even after the war ended, exports of fashions to the United States remained five times what they had been prior to the war.

As the war continued and shortages became more severe a number of changes took place. Far greater use was made of new synthetic materials such as rayon, nylon and viscose, and style increasingly gave way to practicality with practical, functional clothing replacing the more flamboyant attire. Women getting married increasingly chose to wear suits which could be worn for work, or wore their service uniforms if they had one. As the number of coupons provided continued to decline it became fashionable to 'Make Do And Mend'.

The government backed 'Make Do And Mend' campaign was introduced to extend the life of clothing items by encouraging people to learn the skills of darning socks and repairing or reusing worn-out garments. Even Boy Scouts were taught to sew and patch tears in clothing. In Autumn 1942 the 'Make Do And Mend' campaign was boosted by support from the Department of Trade, with the introduction of the character 'Mrs Sew And Sew', who appeared on a

CIVILIANS

series of posters and advisory leaflets and was even brought to life in animated films designed to show how various items were used and to illustrate different techniques of repair. A wartime leaflet encouraging people to darn moth holes and small tears actually stated that 'a neat darn is a real badge of honour'. People were encouraged to recycle clothes and so old suits (no longer used by men away serving in the armed forces) became skirts and jackets.

The war years also saw a resurgence in knitting and many garments – including underwear – could be made this way, saving valuable coupons. Some people chose to buy material and make their own clothes. Paper patterns were widely available, if relatively expensive, and were sold by dress size with guidance on how to alter the pattern

Separation was a major feature of life during the war and is poignantly illustrated in this photograph. – With permission Black Cloth Photography

to accommodate individual shapes. Patterns with different markings for different sizes did not appear until some years later.

Women in poorer areas of the country like the East End of London often had large families to support and needed all of their coupons simply to keep the family clothed. Younger children would have clothes which their older siblings had outgrown. Women often wore garments that had been fashionable in the previous decade but now served as a house dress – generally covered by a wraparound pinafore.

Some items remained in very short supply – especially stockings. Silk was unavailable and, although the American company DuPont had begun manufacturing nylon stockings in 1939, these would remain unavailable to British women until America entered the war. To maintain the impression of stockings being worn, women would use gravy browning smoothed onto the legs to replicate the colour and a carefully drawn pencil line to

Original lingerie is often difficult to source and rarely a good fit. This lady models reproduction 40s lingerie from 'What Katie Did' - www.whatkatiedid.com.

– With permission 'What Katie Did'

CIVILIANS

represent the seam. Another method was to soak a cotton bag with old tea leaves to achieve the same effect. Hair care products and cosmetics were also in short supply since many of these used rationed ingredients. Lipstick was used and red was the most popular colour. However, this effect could also be achieved using cherry juice and beetroot. Beetroot could also be used as rouge to enhance the cheeks. Eyebrows were very hard to maintain and so were often shaved off completely and full-brows drawn in using a charcoal pencil. The drawn in eyebrows could then be enhanced by the use of petroleum jelly which would make them shine. Petroleum jelly was also used on the eye-lids as a form of eye shadow. Mascara was not generally used during the war years. If it was required, it could be made from a combination of coal dust stiffened with petroleum jelly and applied with a fine brush. Some toiletries, however, remained available through the 'black market' which

A smartly dressed young lady pushes her bike along the platform while waiting for the next train.

– With permission
Tim and Asia Wetherell

flourished throughout the war years.

Managing hair was a challenge during the 1940s because shampoos and other hair products were very hard to obtain. For women in service hair had to be styled to be off the collar while on duty and so shorter styles, which could be contained under a hat, were popular. Women working in factories also needed to style their hair in such a way as to ensure that it could not get caught up in machinery. The overall result was far more variety than seen in previous decades, reflecting the woman's taste and wartime role. No matter what hair style was chosen, hair was always set in order to achieve the lift and movement demanded by the different styles.

The wealthier could afford to have their hair permed at a hairdressers but most women used pin- or barrel-curls to set it. Probably the most recognisable element of '40s hair styles was the roll, because it was so versatile. A roll could be placed at the top, side or back of the head or more than one roll could be worn on each side of the face. The best known roll was the 'Victory' roll. Rhoda Woodward noted in the BBC 'People's War' online archive that:

> *"our hair had to be kept above our collars on duty. We used to make a head band out of the top of an old stocking and roll our hair round the band. This style was known as the 'Victory Roll'. Afterwards, when brushed out, our hair turned under into a pageboy style quite easily."*

Keeping long hair clean and contained remained a challenge. Hair could be washed with a tablespoon of baking powder in a small cup of warm water. Dry hair could be made shiny by rinsing in beer, and dirt could be removed from hair using lemon juice (if you could obtain it). Keeping

CIVILIANS

up appearances was not only good for morale but a patriotic duty, and magazines continually implored women to 'Keep Up Appearances' and 'Put Your Best Face Forward'. Snoods (often home-made crocheted bags) were used to keep the hair neat and away from machinery, but a hair net achieved the same goal and was regarded as more sophisticated, being less visible. Scarves were also worn for the same reasons, either worn around the head and knotted under the chin or fashioned into a turban. Hats were very popular fashion accessories and could lift even the plainest dress. Hats came in many styles including the pillbox, beret and fedora – all usually worn at a jaunty angle and often embellished with flowers, ribbons, feathers or beads.

A couple relax in the countryside while the baby sleeps. Note that the gentleman carries the ARP gas mask as opposed to the civilian one shown in the basket on the pram. The lady wears a Women's Institute badge and also has a WVS Housewives Section armband.

– With permission Harriett Norris

CHOOSING A CIVILIAN IMPRESSION

A civilian impression is ideal for individuals and couples who want to embrace the atmosphere of '40s events but without being tied either to a larger group or to a fixed display. Such an impression allows considerable scope for individuality, ranging from the fashionable to the poor in appearance. While it is tempting – and very satisfying – to wear the most fashionable items (including fur stoles) it is also important that ordinary, working-class people are represented as well. Movies have perpetuated the view that wartime people were all slim but a study of contemporary photos shows that this is not the case. While a higher percentage of people compared to today would have had a healthier diet imposed through rationing, and supplemented by frequent exercise, many others did not have access to such a diet because of shortages in the cities, and also had less reason to move around, so the full range of body shapes and sizes were present then, as now.

As with all impressions, it is the details which makes the impression convincing – and also offers opportunities to engage with, and educate the public. All citizens were required to carry an Identity Card and to produce it, when instructed, by any official. The card was often placed in a protective case inside a handbag or jacket pocket. Similarly, a woman would often carry her food ration books with her in case the opportunity arose to take advantage of a new delivery at the greengrocers or butchers. Clothing ration books might also be carried. It was expected that all people would carry their gas mask so this is something a wartime impression should have as standard. Little details also add depth to an impression. A man might wear an ARP badge on his jacket lapel to reflect his service as a local warden, while a woman might sport a WVS badge. Little details like these all help to 'flesh out' an impression and stimulate questions from members of the public.

Some civilians might carry a book or a newspaper to read while sitting on a park bench or on the train. In choosing a newspaper think carefully about the date of it. Most events have American troops present so a newspaper report of the success of the Dunkirk evacuation would not fit. Better to choose a paper dated 1944 which would explain the American presence. Wrist watches were commonly worn in the '40s but were not digital – a modern watch and bracelet can easily spoil an otherwise detailed and accurate impression.

If in doubt, older men might still wear a pocket watch on a chain. Other useful accessories might include period coinage and bank notes,

Paul Collings has built his impression of a shopkeeper around an impressive collection of original and reproduction shop merchandise which appears as the 'Victory Store' at many heritage events. – With permission Liz Elmont

which are always a good talking point and also allow a discussion of what things cost in those days. Smokers might carry a pack of cigarettes or a cigarette case and either a period matchbox or lighter. All of these little touches make an impression more real and rounded. A young couple might find a period pram and use that to involve their baby in the event. There have been a number of impressive mother and baby impressions at recent events and these always attract the attention of the general public.

OBTAINING RELEVANT ACCESSORIES

Vintage markets and antique fairs/shops are an excellent source of 1940s clothing – often at very reasonable prices, but it is important to remember that the full skirts of the Christian Dior 'New Look' style, with it's voluminous skirts and rounded shoulders, was not introduced until 1947 and so would not be appropriate for a wartime impression. Ebay is another good source of clothing but it is important to remember that original garments were not sized as modern clothing is and so it is very important to check measurements before committing to buy. There really is no substitute here for research to ensure that what you are buying is actually of the period. The 'CC41' mark continued in use until 1952 so there is no guarantee that an item bearing that mark is wartime or even 1940s! A good understanding of the wartime styles will help to narrow choices and produce an accurate impression. There are companies who market 'retro style' garments online. While some of these are very acceptable, others use the period as a starting point but also incorporate more modern design features – such as zips in men's trousers. Treat garments sold as 'retro' with caution. It is perfectly possible to make your own clothing if you are a confident 'sewer', since many wartime patterns are now available reconfigured for modern sizes and shapes. If you are going to produce your own clothing then pay particular attention to the fabrics used since a modern synthetic fabric will not handle, or look the same, as a period one. 'Apple Tree Vintage' provide original vintage garments and accessories alongside a range of reproduction items at www.facebook.com/Apple-Tree-Vintage-156253907746547. 'Distressed Damsels' specialise in the design and production of 1940s clothing and accessories with a range of prestigious clients. They can be contacted at www.facebook.com/distresseddamsels1. Quality reproduction men's clothing can be found at 'Froggy Went Courting' (froggywentcourting.co.uk). 'WW2 Civilian Buy and Sell' is a great site for finding everything from hat pins to clothing – www.facebook.com/groups/285899881542680. Authentic reproduction knitwear is available from Vintage Stitches Historical Knitwear – www.facebook.com/vintagestitches1940s. If you are a competent knitter then a good source of 1940s knitting patterns available as PDFs can be found at '1940s Knitting Patterns – For Sale' – www.facebook.com/1940sKnittingPatternsForSale.

Men's hats of the period have never really gone out of fashion and there are still many companies which manufacture felt trilby, fedora, homburg or even bowler hats which are very acceptable copies of period examples. Sometimes the external ribbon is of a modern polyester fabric but that can easily be replaced. Good sources of well-made '40s style hats include Hicks & Brown (www.hicksandbrown.com) or Vintage Hats (www.hatsandcaps.co.uk) both of which carry a wide range of quality hats for men and women. It is still important to check the material used, however, since many hats today are made of a polyester blend which would not have been the case in the 1940s. Antique and vintage fairs are a good source for women's hats – if in doubt, never be afraid to ask for assistance on dating. A question asked before purchase is always much better than embarrassment later on.

Gas masks are frequently offered on eBay or found at antique or vintage fairs. It is vitally important to remember that these masks should never be worn by yourself or a member of the public because many of them used compressed asbestos as part of the filter system. Over time the asbestos may have broken down and fibres might be inhaled. Either seal the filter of the mask – the Imperial War Museum suggests using white glue (Polyvinyl Acetate or PVA) mixed with water and poured slowly into the bottom of the filter. Epoxy resin is also used to seal the filter and arguably provides a longer lasting and stronger seal. It is well worth reading the article on 'Decontaminating our gas masks' on the 'NFS and AFS Vehicles Group' (nfs-afs.org.uk/2014/09/14/decontaminating-our-gas-masks). There are people who produce 3D-printed facsimile filters which can be added to replace the original filter, while others manufacture complete replica gas-masks which are completely safe for adults and children to wear. Gas mask boxes and cases are also commonly offered for sale on eBay and help to really round off a period impression.

Original identity cards and ration books are still easy to acquire but are quite fragile these days and there really is no need to use them when so many good quality facsimiles are available which allow you to add your own details. It is, however, important to check prospective purchases carefully because some, apparently good, reproductions are badly spoiled by having a very large

CIVILIANS

and prominent barcode on the reverse side! An adult ID card and ration books (food and clothing) can be purchased either individually or as a set from Pete Bainbridge's 'Love of the '40s' shop (/loveofthe40s.co.uk/shop).

LIVING HISTORY GROUPS & LINKS

Most civilian living historians tend to be couples or individuals and there are few groups which cater to them as a body. However, there are a number of sites which provide links to events and are a forum for like-minded people to communicate and make new friends.

> '**1940s Events and Social Space**' does exactly as it suggests in that it provides an up-to-date list of heritage events around the country and also a forum for those interested in the period to exchange news and views with others – www.facebook.com/groups/387972647928436. The same admins also run a very useful and informative website www.loveofthe40s.co.uk which is invaluable for keeping up with events and friends.

> '**Home Front History**' is a great resource for researching any and all aspects of life in Britain during the '40s with some very well-known and respected contributors. The site can be found at www.facebook.com/groups/homefronthistory.

FURTHER RESEARCH

CC41 Utility Clothing: The Label that Transformed British Fashion; Mike Brown; Sabrestorm Publishing; 2014; ISBN: 1-7812-2005-0. This is the essential guide to the background and evolution of the utility clothing scheme. He carefully charts the expansion of the scheme to include a wider range of garments and also how the Utility reputation gradually changed to become synonymous with quality and good value. Well-illustrated throughout.

'**Women's 1940s Hairstyles: An Overview**'; an extremely useful overview of the different styles of the time and the limitations imposed on women in the services. Also includes a useful consideration of accessories used to enhance hairstyles. Can be found at: hair-and-makeup-artist.com/womens–1940s-hairstyles

Fashion in the 1940s; Jayne Shrimpton, Shire Library, 2014; ISBN: 0-7478-1353-1. This book documents the changing focus of fashion from Paris to London during the war and then back to Paris again with Dior's 'New Look'. It also looks at the new, less formal styles adopted by women involved in war-work. A very useful overview.

Women's Lives and Clothes in WW2: Ready for Action' Lucy Adlington; Pen & Sword History; 2020; ISBN: 1-5267-6646-9. Focusing initially on the lives and clothing of the British women in the Second World War, the book expands to look at other countries as well as a comparison and contrast. Well-illustrated and an engaging read.

1940s Fashion: The Definitive Sourcebook; Charlotte Fiell; Welbeck; 2021; ISBN: 1-7873-9891-9. Contrasting the thrifty utility designs of the war years with the explosion of elegance in the latter half of the decade this book charts the season-by-season changes in fashion. It also provides useful biographies of the principal designers of the period. The book is well-illustrated with photographs (many previously unpublished) and drawn illustrations.

SPIV

No one is really sure where the term 'spiv' actually comes from. It appeared in a crime novel in 1934 (*School for Scoundrels*). The Oxford English Dictionary suggests that its origins lie in the words 'spiffy' (well-dressed) or 'spiff' (a bonus for salespersons for managing to sell excess or out of fashion stock – often this was achieved by the seller splitting his commission with the customer to offer a discount).

In Britain the 'spiv' was a petty criminal who sold rationed items on the black market out of a suitcase. Despite their illegal activities the spiv maintained a degree of support and sympathy because they made available items otherwise out of reach of the general public. The popular image of the spiv is of someone well-dressed, with a moustache (modelled on that of the actor Clark Gable), trilby hat worn at a jaunty angle and a garish tie. The intention was to fly in the face of wartime austerity as an advertisement for their activities. Perhaps the best-known fictional spiv was the character of Private Joe Walker (played by James Beck) in the TV series *Dad's Army*.

Although seen today as a harmless and almost comedic character, the reality was often different. Crime rates soared by 57 per cent during the Second World War, from 303,771 offences in 1939 to 478,000 offences in 1945. This was not helped by the early release of

Iain Dawson brings to life 'Viv the Spiv' as he attempts to sell some top quality ('knocked-off') watches.
— With permission Derek Hayward/Iain Dawson

many prisoners who had already served the bulk of their sentences.

One example was the London gangster Billy Hill. In his biography, *Boss of Britain's Underworld,* published in 1955, Hill noted 'that big, wide, handsome and, oh, so profitable black market walked into our ever-open arms.... It was the most fantastic side of civilian life in wartime. Make no mistake. It cost Britain millions of pounds. I didn't merely make use of the black market. I fed it.' Hill realised that the enlistment of many experienced police officers would weaken the force, which it did. Hill sold everything he could from whisky to sausage skins and, despite several spells in prison, emerged from the war a wealthy man with considerable influence in criminal circles.

It was not just career criminals who took advantage of the wartime opportunities. Rationing led to widespread abuse by people who would, under normal circumstances, never consider themselves as criminals. By 1945 there had been more than 114,000 prosecutions for black market activities. One of those convicted was the composer Ivor Novello, who served four weeks in jail for misuse of petrol coupons which had been offered to him by a female fan. Professor Dick Hobbs of the London School of Economics noted that the war:

> *"introduced people to crime and the possibilities of crime that they hadn't necessarily been aware of before, whether it was actually doing the crime itself – going out and stealing or poaching rabbits and selling them to the butcher or the neighbours – or whether it was just buying and selling stolen goods."*

The traditional image of the spiv is of a loveable rogue, but there is little evidence to support this image. In reality, so much money was at stake through crime that there was a much darker side to the way in which the black-market merchandise was obtained and distributed. Many criminals who started out selling a few black-market items 'off the back of a lorry' went on to clearing entire warehouses of their stock at gunpoint, becoming the foundation of the crime gangs which emerged in the 1950s and 1960s, despite the threat of £500 fines, and even imprisonment. That said, the small pleasures gained from 'under the counter' luxuries created the popular, and enduring, image of the spiv robbing from the establishment to sell to the needy.

No '40s event is complete without a spiv to supply the needs of the public in these times of austerity. The best-known spiv is Viv the Spiv (brought to life by Iain Dawson). With his unique brand of comedy and charm Viv also supplies a wide range of quality merchandise off ration including nylon stockings with a free fitting service. As he is keen to point out, the goods he sells are 'not stolen, simply not paid for yet!'

CHOOSING A SPIV IMPRESSION

The spiv is always a popular character at events. Based on a regular diet of similar characters (such as George Cole as Flash Harry in the *St Trinian's* films, and James Beck as Private Walker in *Dad's Army*) the public have an expectation of what the spiv should be. Understanding and challenging that expectation is both entertaining and an opportunity to educate the public about the impact spivs actually had and the reality of crime in wartime. The secret of a successful spiv impression is in the patter — encouraging normally law-abiding citizens to tweak the law in order to get luxuries otherwise forbidden or in desperately short supply.

OBTAINING ACCESSORIES

The spiv would have made every effort to dress inconspicuously and thus be able to merge quickly into the crowds when threatened with arrest. A suitcase or briefcase would be used to carry items for sale. A spiv is traditionally portrayed as being very smart – if anything rather flamboyant, but spivs came in many shapes and sizes as do criminals today.

LIVING HISTORY GROUPS & LINKS

Given that the spiv was an isolated character, on the fringes of the criminal fraternity and operating out of sight of the law, there are no groups dedicated to them, but inspiration can be gained from following the progress of 'Viv the Spiv' – www.facebook.com/vivthespiv

FURTHER RESEARCH

> *Crime in the Second World War: Spivs, Scoundrels, Rogues and Worse*; Penny Legg; Sabrestorm Publishing; 2017; ISBN: 1-7812-2009-3. This book scratches beneath the traditional view of the wartime spirit and exposes an underworld of organised crime and even murder. Well-illustrated throughout the book is a must read for anyone wanting to understand the spiv and their place in the wartime criminal fraternity.

CHAPTER NINE
ROLES FOR CHILDREN

EVACUEES

The attack by aircraft of the German Condor Legion on the Spanish town of Guernica in 1937 during the Spanish Civil War showed in graphic detail what would happen to British towns and cities once war started. To protect the children and vulnerable people living in these locations, the government divided the country into three types of area – Evacuation, Neutral and Reception.

Evacuation areas were those deemed high risk targets from which children should be removed; Reception areas were those identified as suitable for the reception of evacuees, while Neutral areas were those that would see neither evacuation nor reception. Those deemed eligible for evacuation were: school-aged children; the infirm; pregnant women and mothers with babies and/or pre-school children. The Camps Act of 1939 created the National Camps Corporation to build residential camps which would provide opportunities for outdoor education and serve as evacuation centres once the war

ROLES FOR CHILDREN

In the early days of the war parents wait for their children outside a school.

— With permission John Purkiss

started. These centres could accommodate more than 200 children and their teachers and were built in more than 30 locations around the country.

The process of evacuation had been determined by report, generated by a committee chaired by Sir John Anderson during the summer of 1938. By November 1938 the report's findings, together with those of other bodies (including the London County Council), had evolved into the official Evacuation Scheme. The London County Council commissioned buses and trains, and a registration of evacuees and potential billets in readiness for the inevitable outbreak of war. The Evacuation Scheme was to be known as 'Operation Pied Piper'. However, evacuation was not compulsory although many parents, aware of the devastating impact of bombs, did choose to send their children to safety. The government however had overestimated the numbers – they had planned on 80 per cent of children being evacuated, but in fact the number was closer to 47 per cent, although this figure varied from place to place. More than 60 per cent of children were evacuated from cities like Birmingham and Manchester but elsewhere the figure was as low as 15 per cent.

As the threat of war increased, the evacuation order was given for 1 September 1939. Children began assembling at their schools early that morning as Operation Pied Piper commenced. London alone had 1,589 assembly points so the whole process was incredibly challenging. Many children boarded trains at their nearest railway station but there were still trains leaving London's main stations every nine minutes for nine hours. Some children even left London by ship for Great Yarmouth, Felixstow and Lowestoft. In addition to railway staff, local authority personnel and teachers, there were also 17,000 Women's Voluntary Service members providing support and refreshments. In the first three days 1.5 million people were relocated. In England this included 673,000 school age children, 406,000 mothers with young children and 3,000 pregnant women.

Evacuated children were expected to carry their basic essentials which were detailed in a Ministry of Health leaflet. These included:

> *"a handbag or case containing the child's gas mask, a change of under-clothing, night clothes, house shoes or plimsolls, spare stockings or socks, a toothbrush, a comb, towel, soap and face cloth, handkerchiefs; and, if possible, a warm coat or mackintosh. Each child should bring a packet of food for the day."*

Upon arrival at the assembly point, each child had a luggage label pinned to their coat with their name, school and evacuation authority in case they got lost. The actual point of departure must have been very traumatic for parents and children alike. Not knowing where they were going, or when they would return, the children bade a tearful farewell to their parents who then endured a wait of several days before receiving a postcard notifying them of the child's arrival and location.

The plan was for evacuated children to be billeted in homes in the communities to which they had been evacuated as well as in residential camps. It was compulsory for people with space in their homes to accommodate one or more evacuees. Places were decided by available

ROLES FOR CHILDREN

space rather than suitability, which led to some children being hosted by very reluctant homeowners. This caused some youngsters to try and make their own way home. Many children described the experience of arrival at a reception centre as a 'cattle market', with children chosen by looks and some siblings forcibly separated. Some children, coming from homes with indoor toilets, found conditions rather more rustic in the countryside with newspaper, and even leaves, substituted for toilet paper.

During the so-called 'Phoney War' (the period after the declaration of war in September 1939 until the start of the German bombing campaign in May 1940, in preparation for the invasion of Britain, code-named Operation Sea Lion) many children returned home, but once

A young evacuee, waits patiently for the train to take her away from danger.
— With permission Jeff Wharton

France fell bombs soon started to land on Britain and the evacuation began again. The threat of German invasion also led to the south coast of Britain being redesignated as an evacuation area and a further 200,000 children relocated. The final evacuation in 1944 was code-named 'Operation Rivulet' and was a response to the new threat posed by the V-1 and V-2 missiles.

The end of the war in Europe allowed the evacuees to return home, but for many it was a difficult transition. Some returned to find their homes had been destroyed, sometimes with the loss of family members. Some returned to find that their families no longer wanted them. All who returned were very different from the young children who had left. They were now five years older and no longer had much in common with those family members who had remained. Some even spoke differently, having picked up the accent of the place where they had been living. Some had suffered abuse, but many had enjoyed their experience and no small number later returned to settle in the areas to which they had been evacuated.

CLOTHING

Where appropriate, children would wear their school uniform, but most schools did not have one. The children simply wore their everyday clothes – often handed down from older siblings. The iconic view of the evacuee is of a young child carrying their gas mask and a bag, or small suitcase, with their clothes, possibly an apple and a few favourite toys, and wearing a luggage label pinned to their coat. Remember that school aged boys (up to the age of 14) wore short trousers. Girls did not wear trousers.

CHOOSING AN EVACUEE IMPRESSION

This is an excellent way to engage younger children with the hobby. Many will have learned something about this period in school and will already have some understanding of the evacuee experience. Reading books like Goodnight Mister Tom (see 'Further Research' below for details) will help give a greater understanding and enable the child to feel some empathy with the evacuees. Evacuee children are always a welcome sight at heritage railway events where a steam train ride adds to the experience.

OBTAINING CLOTHING & ACCESSORIES

As ever, eBay is a good source of period clothing but be careful; there are very cheap 'fancy dress' sets which are made of the wrong materials and look wrong. It is always worth taking the time to get the right 'look' and using the correct materials is an important part of that. There are also many period patterns available online either as originals or reprinted. With a little skill, making your own clothes is an easy solution and if they don't look perfect then all the better. An online search for '1940s children's clothing' will access many original photos and other sources of information and patterns.

Period pressed cardboard suitcases are also readily available via eBay. Reproduction luggage labels, ration books and identity cards are available from Memorabilia Pack Company through their website (www.mempackcompany.com/shop) or via Amazon. Other companies also sell reproduction paperwork on eBay – just try to avoid reproductions with a large bar code on the back! Reproduction gas mask boxes are also available. A comprehensive set of documents comprising an identity card, ration book, luggage label, gas mask box and a postcard to send home is available through eBay. If you have an original gas mask it is strongly recommended that you do not use it because of the potentially dangerous asbestos in the filters.

LIVING HISTORY GROUPS & LINKS

There are no formal groups for evacuees but many heritage railways offer opportunities for evacuees to recreate a train ride to a new destination. These are always popular both with participants and the general public.

FURTHER RESEARCH

Evacuees: Evacuation in Wartime Britain 1939 – 1945: Mike Brown; History Press; 2005; ISBN: 0-7509-2537-2. Liberally illustrated with contemporary photographs and related ephemera this book proved a well written factual account of the experiences of evacuees – good and bad – drawing on contemporary accounts. A fascinating insight into the experience of evacuation and the Home-Front generally.

Goodnight Children Everywhere: Monica B. Morris; History Press; 2011; ISBN: 0-7524-5282-7. Rich in personal experiences this book is a testament to the strength and courage of the children who left their parents for an unknown world. Although few died, some suffered the most unendurable heartbreak separated from all they knew and loved.

Child from Home: John Wright: History Press; 2009; ISBN: 0-7524-5229-6. The author was 4 years old in 1939 and evacuated to a large house in North Yorkshire, requisitioned as a nursery school. This book is his story of happiness and heartache, cruelty and joy against the background of his exploration and understanding of his new environment. An insight into one boy's experience but typical of so many.

The Evacuees: Children of War DVD; Pegasus Entertainment; 2010. A documentary film which intersperses contemporary stock film footage with interviews with surviving evacuees giving an interesting range of perspectives on the evacuee experience.

The Daily Life of A... World War II Evacuee; Alan Childs; Wayland; 2008; ISBN: 0-7502-5564-1. This book is ideal for young children to help them understand the role better. A combination of skilful artwork and well-chosen photos allows the young reader to spend the day in the company of this fictional evacuee.

Goodnight Mister Tom; Michelle Magorian; Puffin; 2014; ISBN: 0-1413-5480-1. The story of fictional character Willie Beech. Willie is a sad and deprived child evacuated from London to stay with reluctant host, old Tom Oakley. As their relationship builds, the reader is offered an insight into the living conditions of many poor, working-class children and the experience of evacuation. A touching story for children aged 9-12 which engages, but also encourages them to ask questions and dig deeper into the topic. Also available as a DVD starring John Thaw.

BOY SCOUTS

The Boy Scout movement was started by Lieutenant-General Robert Baden-Powell in 1908 with the publication of the first instalment of his book 'Scouting for Boys'. This was eagerly received by boys who had grown up listening to stories of Baden-Powell's heroic defence of Mafeking (during the Boer War). Baden-Powell wrote a military guide, *Aids to Scouting*, in 1899, which captured the imagination of youngsters, encouraging Baden-Powell to write a version for boys – *Scouting for Boys*. Such was the success of this book that Baden-Powell established a Boy Scouts Office to register new scouts between 11 and 14/15 years of age, and design a uniform. Some 60,000 Boy Scouts were registered by the end of 1908 with the first national meeting at the Crystal Palace, London in September 1909, attended by 10,000 Scouts, including a large contingent of 'Girl Scouts'. The movement soon began to appear in other countries around the world.

Baden-Powell's concept was of groups of six or seven boys under a Scout Leader (patrol and patrol leader) who would be trained in mapping, signalling, knotting, first aid, camping and other outdoor activities. This training would be underpinned by the Scout Law of loyalty to country and honesty and respect to all people. As the popularity of the movement spread, Baden-Powell introduced the Wolf Cubs in 1916 to attract younger members. This was inspired by Rudyard Kipling's *Jungle Book*. The first World Scout Jamboree was held in 1920 at Olympia, London, attracting 8,000 Scouts and confirming the international status of the scout movement.

During the Second World War Scouts were trained to undertake more than 170 tasks to help the war effort. These were commemorated

ROLES FOR CHILDREN

in a Scout booklet called *They Were Prepared* (a title inspired by the Scout motto 'Be Prepared') published in 1941. Many Scouts were evacuated under Operation Pied Piper in 1939. Where possible, Cub Packs and Scout Troops were evacuated together so that the children would have something familiar in their new environments. Older Scouts helped to organise the evacuation by supervising groups of children, carrying luggage and helping to comfort those in distress. In urban areas Scouts assisted in preparing for the blackout by painting the kerb stones white to make them easier to see in the dark, thus reducing accidents. As preparations for war continued, Scouts assisted householders in the potentially difficult task of erecting air raid shelters – either the Morrison Shelter inside buildings or the Anderson Shelter dug into gardens. By January 1942 over

A wartime scout Patrol Leader with gas mask.

– With permission
Edward Parrish

half a million Morrison Shelters had been issued across Britain and Northern Ireland.

Once the bombing started, Scouts supported the Air Raid Warden's Service and other emergency services. Scouts acted as fire-watchers, messengers and stretcher-bearers and also carried out basic first aid on casualties. Many Scouts showed exceptional bravery in carrying out these duties and this was rewarded through the Scouts gallantry awards. One recipient of the Gilt Cross (the fourth highest gallantry award) was Patrol Leader John Flinn of Sheffield. Flinn was awarded his Gilt Cross on 30 April 1941 and his citation read 'For his gallantry and resource in rendering valuable assistance at fire-fighting and rescue work during a heavy air raid on the Sheffield area on the night of the 12/13 December 1940.'

Sadly, some Scouts made the ultimate sacrifice in performing their duties. Frank Davis (aged 17) was serving as a messenger when he rescued a fellow messenger who had been injured by an incendiary bomb. Having carried the injured boy to safety Davis returned to put out the incendiary bomb but was killed when another bomb exploded nearby. He was awarded the Bronze Cross (known as the 'Scout's Victoria Cross') for his courage and devotion to duty, epitomising the Scout values.

When the Home Guard was formed in 1940, Scouts assisted in teaching tracking skills, first aid and bushcraft to the new recruits. They also assisted by supporting a number of national initiatives aimed at increasing food production and recycling. The 'Dig for Victory' campaign urged people to grow their own food to reduce dependence on imported foodstuffs. Bomb sites and abandoned plots of land were converted into gardens which the Scouts helped to maintain. Scouts also helped the farmers to gather in their crops; 600 Scouts picked more than one million pounds of plums in Worcestershire alone in 1942. Some Scouts assisted the Women's Timber Corps with tree felling. Scouts also contributed greatly to the campaigns to collect waste paper and scrap metal for the war effort. Between March and April 1944 Scouts collected over 300,000 tons of waste paper.

One of their lesser-known duties was scouring the countryside for plants which could be used in medicine. Sphagnum moss has antiseptic qualities and can be used when dressing wounds. The seed pods of opium poppies were widely collected – when split while green they exude a milky white latex which contains 15 per cent morphine, while foxgloves were a source of Digitalin, used in heart treatments. Deadly Nightshade could be processed to provide Atropine Sulphate which was used to counter nerve agents used in gas attacks. During the First World War the government had requested 50 tons of Deadly Nightshade, but that figure rose to 200 tons during the Second World War. The Ministry of Health published guidelines on the medicinal uses of different plants and Scouts played an important part in their collection.

UNIFORM - BOY SCOUTS

HEADWEAR

Scouts wore the wide-brimmed, khaki felt 'lemon squeezer' hat with four indentations in the crown. The hat has a brown leather band and is secured by a cord worn under the chin.

CLOTHING

The Scout shirt was a short-sleeved garment made from khaki cotton (although dark blue, green or grey can also be found). There were a number of suppliers and a number of variations in pattern can be found. Most shirts were designed to be pulled on over the head and fastened up with a line of generally three buttons on a partial placket extending down in line with the bottom of the sleeves. Other shirts, however, have a full placket with buttons all down the front. There were two pockets each with a buttoned flap. The pockets were frequently pleated but photographs and surviving examples also show plain pockets. Shoulder epaulettes were also present. The shoulder knot (in the Patrol colour) was attached to the left epaulette. A single white strip on the left side of the pocket denoted 'PS' (Patrol Second) while two white strips, one each side of the Scout badge, identified the 'PL' (Patrol Leader). Proficiency badges were worn on the right sleeve.

A scarf in the troop colour was worn tightly rolled around the neck and secured with a woggle (a term used but not formally accepted until 1945), commonly made of leather. Short trousers were worn in a variety of colours and fabrics. The wartime uniform specifications required dark blue, khaki or grey shorts. These appear to have come, like the shirts, from a variety of manufacturers and can be found in plain or corded fabric. Shorts were button-fronted and came to just above the knee. They were held up with a leather belt with the Scout emblem on the buckle. The belt was passed through belt loops on the shorts. Socks should be of any plain colour, worn turned over just below the knee with a green-tabbed garter showing on the outside. Boots or shoes should be brown or black in colour.

UNIFORM - CUB SCOUTS

CAPS

The Cub Scouts wore a bottle green cap with yellow piping.

CLOTHING

Unlike the older Scouts who wore a shirt displaying proficiency and other badges, the Cub Scouts wore a plain, dark-green or blue-coloured jersey with long-sleeves and a round-neck. A small triangular patch of cloth in six colours was sewn at the top of the left sleeve immediately below the shoulder. A shoulder badge indicating the pack was worn on the right shoulder. In all other respects the uniform was as for the older Scouts – a scarf in the pack colour, dark blue shorts, blue, green or grey socks worn turned down just below the knee with a green-tabbed garter showing and brown or black shoes or boots.

CHOOSING A SCOUT IMPRESSION

Given the many roles that Scouts undertook during the war there are many opportunities for individual and group impressions which reflect different aspects of the Scout roles – acting as messengers, collecting wild plants for medicinal purposes (a great way to engage the interest of the public) or collecting scrap paper and aluminium for the war effort.

OBTAINING UNIFORMS & ACCESSORIES

At the time of writing there are no sources for reproduction 1940s Scout uniforms. However, original examples do come up on eBay and other sites from time to time. Alternatively, if a basic cotton shirt can be either made or adapted, period badges can be added. Leather belts and other accessories can also be sourced quite easily from eBay. Original hats can be found but patience may be required since they appear like buses – either none or several at the same time.

LIVING HISTORY GROUPS & LINKS

Sadly, although there are a number of individuals portraying Scouts in the '40s, there are no organised groups at the time of writing.

FURTHER RESEARCH

>'**Explore – The Scout Association Archive**' offers a selection of records from the archive reflecting the different roles undertaken by scouts including individual acts of bravery. Individual articles rather than a more developed history but useful none the less. The archive can be found at www.scoutsrecords.org/explore.php?dil=&icerik=84&bparent=CB6FCCF1AB7A8F1765FC3A9D09C9ACAE&.

>'**Scouting on the Home Front: They Were Prepared**' is an extremely well-illustrated article showing the many roles undertaken by Scouts during the war including fire-fighting and collecting waste. Some rare photos which also offer excellent views on contemporary uniforms and their variations as well as photos of related ephemera. heritage.scouts.org.uk/exhibitions/scouting-during-the-second-world-war/scouting-on-the-home-front-they-were-prepared

'WW2 People's War – a Boy Scout at War' Is a fascinating account of the wartime experience of Boy Scout Alan Sandall of Reading, Berkshire until he joined the Royal Navy in 1944 – www.bbc.co.uk/history/ww2peopleswar/stories/95/a8067495.shtml

GIRL GUIDES

When around a thousand girls attended the first national Scout meeting at the Crystal Palace, London, in September 1909, calling themselves 'Girl Scouts', it became clear that the idea of scouting was not just for boys. The girls were inspired by none other than Robert Baden-Powell, founder of the Scout movement, who had commented in his book *Scouting for Boys* (published in instalments in 1908) that 'Scouting is equally suited to boys and girls.' Baden-Powell had already responded positively to Girl Scouts noting in **The Scout** magazine, January 1909, that 'some of them are really capable Scouts'. Scout rallies were organised across the country to which girls were invited and welcomed.

Although the intention was for Girl Scouts to meet and drill separately from boys, a few groups allowed girls to participate alongside boys and without female chaperones, which was widely condemned. Baden-Powell tried hard to distance the Scout movement from this controversial publicity and even approached the Red Cross Society to see if they might take the fledgling Girl Scouts under their care. When this failed, he asked his sister Agnes to lead a new, separate organisation and, in 1910, 'The Girl Guides Association' was created. The term 'guides' derived from the military guides who had undertaken hazardous raids on the north-west frontier of India. Baden-Powell thought that the name reflected the pioneering organisation he envisaged for girls. As the movement evolved, the Brownies were established in 1914 (originally called Rosebuds) followed by a group for seniors in 1916 which became Rangers in 1920. The Guides movement helped to break down social barriers because different social classes worked side by side within Guide companies and arguably contributed substantially to the campaign for women's emancipation.

Guides soon showed their worth during the First World War where they made an important contribution to the war effort by assisting in hospitals, factories and soup-kitchens, in addition to

A Girl Guide sits at a table surrounded by books to help advance her skills. The Girl Guide standard is propped in the corner behind her.

– With permission John Wickham

growing food and acting as messengers. By the start of the Second World War there were 750,000 Guides in the United Kingdom. Guides were earning badges in a wide range of skills which would benefit the war effort including mechanics, electronics, first aid and telegraphy. The telegraphist badge was awarded to those who could build their own wireless receiver and send messages in Morse code at a rate of thirty letters per minute. Many of the tasks undertaken by Guides mirrored those carried out by their male counterparts in the Boy Scouts – helping with evacuation, whitewashing kerb stones to reduce accidents in the blackout, fundraising and helping with the collection of jam jars for recycling. During one week in 1940, Guides raised over £50,000 to pay for two air ambulances and even a life boat which was used at Dunkirk.

It wasn't just men who were called up – women joined the Women's Auxiliary Air Force (WAAF), Women's Royal Navy (WREN) and the Female Aid Nursing Yeomanry (FANY) leading to a shortage of teachers and nursery nurses. Girl Guides readily stepped in to take on these responsibilities. Girl Guide training was also in demand in the bombed-out cities, where Guides helped to maintain morale. Their experience with cooking over open fires was also utilised when the Ministry of Food requested that Guides demonstrate how to cook under Blitz conditions. This involves using bricks from bombed buildings to build emergency ovens and demonstrating how to create meals from whatever was available. One recipe used showed how to cook 'mock fish cakes', using potatoes and anchovy sauce. Many of the recipes used had been created by the Guides themselves. The skills learned in sewing and knitting were also used to help knit socks and other items for servicemen.

Girl Guides also helped in the collection of wild plants and herbs for use as medicines. The extent and importance of the Guides' work was such that, at the Lord Mayor's Show in 1942, Winston Churchill saluted the Guides by removing his hat as they marched past. The Guide movement proved so popular that the Trefoil Guild was set up in 1943, for members aged over 21, who still wanted to remain part of the movement. Ninety Girl Guides, aged between 14 and 16, worked for MI5 as messengers. Some of the messages relayed were classed as 'top secret', which is a measure of the high regard the establishment had for the Guides.

Brownies also did their bit for the war effort. In 1941 a collection by Brownies yielded 15,000 used cotton reels, reputedly for a secret

A Guide practices using a 'Blitz oven' as part of her training.
— With permission Vanessa and Megan Poxon

RAF job. The recent release of declassified documents has shown that the cotton reels were used by MI9 to assist in the escape of allied prisoners of war. The cotton reels were hollowed out and the space filled with silk maps of Europe, paper German money and even lists of contacts. The reinstated reels were then sent to PoW camps in relief parcels.

UNIFORM - GUIDES

HATS

The official hat had a wide brim and was made of navy-blue soft felt and bore the hat badge (also in navy blue) with the official stamp. However, a blue cotton version of the hat was available for summer use and at camp.

CLOTHING

The principal uniform was either an overall dress (of Headquarters blue cotton) with two patch pockets and shoulder straps or a jumper (of Headquarters blue cotton) and skirt (of navy-blue serge). From 1940 on, the skirt became shorter as a result of shortages of fabric. For summer wear, a light-blue cotton dress with short sleeves was available. Knickers were to be navy- or light-blue. The uniform was to be worn with a tie – triangular in shape and either light-blue or in the appropriate company colour. The tie should be worn folded neatly into a narrow fold worn under the collar, but not under the shoulder strap. The belt should be of brown leather with the official buckle. Shoes could be either black or brown (but the whole company had to wear same colour stockings to match shoes). Only brown shoes were permitted after 1943. Light-blue or white ankle socks could be worn with the summer dress. A shoulder knot in the correct patrol colour should be worn on left shoulder. The emblem (showing the patrol flower or bird) should be worn above the left-hand pocket. The company name and number should be shown on a title tape worn on left arm, covering juncture of the shoulder knot with the shoulder strap. A tenderfoot brooch should be worn on the tie. Long hair should be plaited and held in a ribbon coloured black or navy-blue. The use of navy-blue scarves was introduced in 1943.

UNIFORMS - BROWNIES

The uniform was either a brown overall dress with patch pockets or a jersey and kilted skirt. For summer-wear a brown cotton dress with short sleeves was available. Knickers were to be brown in colour. The belt should be of brown leather. The tie should be either a brown or gold 'triangular' (and the whole pack must wear the same colour). Shoes and stockings should be brown, although white socks may be worn with the summer dress. Hair should be tied back with a brown ribbon. The Sixer Distinguishing Mark should be two horizontal gold stripes on a brown background, worn 2 inches above left elbow. The Second Distinguishing Mark should be one horizontal gold stripe on a brown background, worn 2 inches above the left elbow.

HATS

There was a plain, knitted brown cap or a hat of either brown cotton or Melton cloth. The cloth cap, introduced in 1934, soon became the preferred option.

ROLES FOR CHILDREN

CHOOSING A GIRL GUIDE OR BROWNIE IMPRESSION:

The wartime role of the Girl Guides and Brownies is a story which needs to be told. Their contribution to the war effort was huge and varied and allows for a wide range of impressions to be created. A static display recreating a 'Blitz oven' would attract a lot of public interest and stimulate some interesting conversations, but so would a simple display of knitting for the troops. Many original knitting patterns are available for the army, Navy and Air Force and many are also available as reproductions. Taking orders from fellow living historians might even generate a modest income!

OBTAINING UNIFORMS & ACCESSORIES

As with the Scouts, there are no places that supply reproduction uniforms. While it is possible to obtain original uniforms, these are quite rare now and tend to be very expensive. The design of the uniform is relatively simple to reproduce from photographs and other sources. The uniform belt can be obtained from the likes of eBay, as can other brass badges. The badges on Megan Poxon's uniform (illustrated above) were actually hand embroidered by her mother to match designs in the 1935 Girl Guide badge book.

LIVING HISTORY GROUPS & LINKS

There are no known Guide re-enactment groups but hopefully there are enough enthusiasts to form a group, if only to support each other and encourage others to take on this very worthwhile impression.

FURTHER RESEARCH

'Leslie's Guide Uniform History': a website dedicated to the changing uniforms worn by all personnel involved in the Guide movement from Brownies through to commissioners. Detailed and well-illustrated it is a valuable reference tool for those trying to replicate the look. lesliesguidinguniformhistory.webs.com.

How Girl Guides Won the War: Janie Hampton; HarperCollins; 2011; ISBN: 0-0073-5632-3. The role of Girl Guides in the war is one of the forgotten stories of history and this book redresses the balance. With many well-chosen anecdotes. the wartime years, and the massive contribution that Guides made to the war effort, are brought vividly to life.

CHAPTER TEN

MUSIC AND ENTERTAINMENT

As late as May 1940 there had been a powerful group of MPs and Ministers led by the Foreign Secretary, Lord Halifax opposed to continuing the war. With the British Expeditionary Force falling back in retreat on Dunkirk with the imminent loss of both the entire army and of France itself, Halifax favoured a peace with Hitler brokered by the then neutral dictator of Italy, Benito Mussolini. On 27 May a memorandum proposing an approach to Mussolini threatened to split the War Cabinet. Only by gaining the support of Churchill's twenty-five member 'outer Cabinet', and previous Prime Minister Neville Chamberlain, was Churchill able to overcome this opposition.

This confusion and anxiety were shared by the general public. Former soldiers who had fought Germany in the First World War knew all too well the horrors of war and would now have to face sending their own children into that same hell. There was also a sense that the many failings of the Versailles Treaty needed some rebalance, and that appeasement of Hitler's wishes would right the wrongs of Versailles and prevent a further war. Only when Hitler invaded Poland on 1 September 1939 did people realise that Hitler would never stop and that war was inevitable.

Given the tension and fear that existed, entertainment was vital in keeping up morale and the lifeblood of entertainment was music. Most British homes had a radio or a gramophone or both, and music became the medium through which the spirits of the masses were raised. Cheerful songs rallied a people in times of hardship and sentimental songs reminded people of what they were fighting for. The popular songs 'We'll Meet Again' and 'The White Cliffs of Dover', both sung by Vera Lynn, struck a nerve with the public. Both songs have maintained their popularity to the present day. Other songs, like Jerome Kern and Oscar Hammerstein's 'The Last Time I Saw Paris' (1941) reminded people of life before the war in this beautiful and iconic city, now under Nazi occupation. One song, 'Lily Marlene' – known as 'the song the 8th Army captured' – became a hit with both sides of the conflict. Originally performed by Marlene Dietrich, the song had lyrics in both German and English. The comedy duo Flanagan and Allen produced a series of entertaining songs including 'Run Rabbit Run' and 'We're Going To Hang Out The Washing On The Siegfried Line'. Whether at home, in a camp, factory or hospital music raised the spirits of the nation.

Before the war the trend had been for 'Big Bands', but as more and more musicians joined the armed forces, some bands shrunk while others simply disbanded, creating a new trend towards soloists. British Dance Band music grew out of the dance halls and hotel ballrooms of the 1920s and 1930s and merged elements of jazz with a rhythm and style derived from the dance halls. Jazz had first been introduced to Britain when the original Dixieland Jazz Band first toured the country

MUSIC AND ENTERTAINMENT

in 1919. Louis Armstrong first toured Britain in 1932 but his music was not universally popular. There were British jazz pioneers too, Ken 'Snakehips' Johnson was a 26-year-old jazz bandleader, leading an all-black orchestra. On 8 May 1941 his career sadly ended when a Luftwaffe bomb fell through a ventilation shaft at the Cafè de Paris during his performance, killing Johnson and dozens of others.

The pre-war popularity of dance halls continued into the war years and played a major role in keeping up morale and professional dancers emerged with the evolution of dance contests. Every town, and even villages, had some venue where dancing could take place. Larger venues often had sprung dance floors and their own resident dance bands but even the smallest venues had a piano or gramophone available even if the dancing surface was a wood plank or concrete floor.

Crowds celebrate at a dance at the West Somerset Railway '40s Weekend 2018.
– With permission Julia Amies-Green

Once America joined the war, the British people were exposed to a whole new set of experiences from chewing gum to new musical influences and dances. Jazz, blues and swing music followed the American GIs and gained immediate popularity with the younger generation in Britain. Various types of swing dance emerged such as the 'Jitterbug' – so named because the lack of formal dance steps made it look like someone drunk having the jitters. 'Lindyhop' and 'Jive' were popular dance styles, but ultimately the term 'Jitterbug' came to cover them all.

Today, Jive and Lindyhop dancers help to recreate the '40s atmosphere at most heritage events and almost all live music acts (from soloists to Big Bands) will soon gather anything from a pair of dancers to a dance floor full. Many will encourage this by offering basic tuition to encourage more passive observers to try a few steps. For those who want to learn, there are Jive and Lindyhop classes in many towns and cities across the UK. Lindyhop certainly requires more skill and coordination than Jive, but both are great fun to learn and offer good exercise and good company in the process! Age is no restriction and events soon attract dancers of all ages from teens through to more senior citizens, some into their 70s!

THE BIG BANDS

No commemoration of the 1940s would be complete without either a Big Band or other vintage musical performance. There are vintage performers across the country and each has his or her own following of fans. Styles cover everything from the Big Band sound to vocal harmonies and soloists. Some performers replicate the music and

MUSIC AND ENTERTAINMENT

style of particular entertainers like George Formby while others offer a broader and more generic range of '40s popular music.

Three of the most popular British dance bands of the 1940s were those of Bert Ambrose, Joe Loss and Billy Cotton. Cotton's Swing Band entertained people throughout the war and later toured newly liberated France. Joe Loss's Orchestra was one of the most successful bands of the 1940s and its signature tune was the iconic 'In the Mood'. The Joe Loss Orchestra still tours today although Joe Loss died in 1990. Ambrose and his Orchestra stopped performing live in 1940 but continued to make recordings throughout the war. Bert Ambrose is also credited with having discovered Vera Lynn, who later married one of the clarinettists from the orchestra! However, the most iconic Big

The Kalamazoo Dance Band plays to another packed house.
– With permission Kal Vaikla

Band was that of American Glenn Miller. Such was Miller's popularity that *Time* magazine observed (27 November 1939) that 'of the twelve to 24 discs in each of today's 300,000 U.S. jukeboxes, from two to six are usually Glenn Miller's.' Miller fully understood the power of music to comfort soldiers far from home, but also to inspire patriotism.

In 1944 Miller wrote from London to his friend and former drummer, George T. Simon, explaining that 'we didn't come here to set any fashions in music. We merely came to bring a much-needed touch of home to some lads who have been here a couple of years.' Even Nazi Germany had a jazz band – Charlie and his Orchestra. Under the control of Josef Goebbels, the band's role was to cover popular British and American jazz songs with lyrics altered to give a propaganda message. Far from threatening, Churchill himself found their lyrics hilarious!

Today, one of the best-known Big Band sounds at heritage events is that of the 'Kalamazoo Dance Band', founded in 2015, by Kal Vaikla. Dressed in US Army Air Force uniforms, complete with vocalists, the band conjures up the sound and image of the famous Glenn Miller Band. Swing dance instructors help to ensure that the audience becomes fully immersed in the experience. Kal explains that he was brought up in a musical environment and, having played in swing and big bands for some thirty years, he wanted 'to set my own big band in action and create a real physical spectacular stage presence that would create an immediate wow factor, and so The Kalamazoo Dance Band was born'.

All big bands had their own unique quality and Kal undertook a lot of research to bring the Kalamazoo Dance Band to life and accurately recreate the feel of the period. As Kal states:

MUSIC AND ENTERTAINMENT

> "we are all passionate about the era and want nothing more than to have the audience members leaving at the end of the performance saying 'wow, they were fantastic' and 'that was a brilliant night – can't wait to see them again'. With that principle in mind, (wanting to wow the audience) I set about recreating that very atmosphere. Our uniforms are representative of the Glenn Miller USAAF style, but since none of us are US military by background, I didn't feel it was right for us to wear the exact same uniforms, and therefore we wear uniforms that put us in the spirit of the 40s' era – the badges aren't true to any particular military division and the US sleeve patch is worn on the opposite shoulder so that it is representative, but we don't believe we have the right to wear exactly as those fine young soldiers wore. We have enjoyed a 100 per cent success rate of sell-out events at every performance we have played, which we believe is true testimony to the fact that guests truly enjoy what we do."

In order to bring even greater authenticity to the sound and feel of the band:

> "many of the band's instruments, for example saxes, are indeed from the 40's or earlier and really quite rare. Our bandstands show a spotlight shining on the Chicago city skyline and even the band name 'Kalamazoo Dance Band' obviously originates from the song 'I've Got a Gal in Kalamazoo' performed by Glenn Miller."

MUSIC AND ENTERTAINMENT

Kal Vaikla – founder of the Kalamazoo Dance Band.

– With permission Kal Vaikla

Playing to an audience who really know and understand the music of the '40s – and the historical context behind those tunes – imposes a great responsibility to get it right. Kal's principle is:

> *"I firmly believe that every event we play at should be considered in the very same attitude as if it was our very first or very last event, so much so, that I just will not compromise on any aspect of our delivery from uniforms to stage set up and lighting to music repertoire – this ensures that the consistency is always the same with the intention of exceeding customer expectation every time. It is evident from the audience reaction when they arrive at the venue and see the set-up we have in place, with even smaller details such as US flags all pressed and aligned to the same direction across the entire stage, that they know that they are in for a great night."*

Sometimes, however, the best concerts are those little is expected of:

> *One year, at Pickering '40s Weekend, we had been playing at Whitby Metropole over the weekend and I suggested to the band that we roll into the high street in Pickering and play an impromptu concert. We pulled up near the market place and quietly and deftly set up the band stands and PA system. Of course, the public started to wonder why there were US soldiers setting up all this*

gear. We also had our Andrews Sisters tribute trio in RAF uniforms with us and, of course, this was gathering quite a lot of interest. Now, the area in question is quite spacious but as soon as we started playing 'In The Mood' the whole area suddenly filled with no space left whatsoever. It was probably one of the best concerts we have ever played, and the atmosphere was beyond the scale. Swing dancers appeared dancing on the cobbles and the audience were singing along. It's moments like this that you just wish would go on for ever.

SOLO ARTISTS

Solo artists were popular in Britain during the '40s and often performed with Big Bands. Some artists were known for their comedic songs such as Gracie Fields. Gracie Fields' career began in the 1920s and she remained popular throughout the war years although she was forced to leave Britain in 1940 because of her marriage to film director Monty Banks, an Italian national. Fields did, however, perform extensively for the Entertainments National Service Association (ENSA). Two of the best-known solo artists of the period are Vera Lynn and George Formby. Their music is still well-known to this day.

VERA LYNN

Today, Vera Lynn, more than anyone else in Britain, is regarded as synonymous with the sounds of the war years, yet she came from a background far removed from showbusiness – her father was a

MUSIC AND ENTERTAINMENT

plumber and her mother a dressmaker. Vera was born 20 March 1917 and soon revealed a natural talent for singing. She was so successful that she became the family breadwinner at the age of just 7 by singing in working men's clubs. By the age of 11 Vera had left school and was working as a dancer and singer in a touring music hall show. At this point the young Vera Welch became Vera Lynn by adopting her grandmother's maiden name. Vera had no formal voice training as a child and, when she did seek help to extend her vocal range the teacher, having heard Vera sing, proclaimed: "I cannot train that voice, it's not a natural voice." So I said: "Well thank you very much madam", and left' as Vera later recalled. Aged 15, Vera was spotted by a local talent scout and signed immediately.

Vera fronted a number of bands but found fame performing with the Joe Loss Orchestra. This, in turn, led to regular radio

Lorrie Brown as Vera Lynn poses by a Spitfire.

– With permission
Lorrie Brown

appearances. Her easy charm soon endeared her to audiences and, in 1936 Vera had her first solo record with the song 'Up the Wooden Hill to Bedfordshire'.

Vera feared that announcement of war with Germany in 1939 would prematurely end her career but, when the *Daily Express* asked British service personnel to name their favourite musical performers, she was top of the list and acquired the unofficial title of 'the Forces' Sweetheart'. A key part of her ongoing popularity was her radio programme *Sincerely Yours*, which started in 1941 and soon became a massive success, receiving over 2,000 letters a week. In February 1942 the show was taken off air because it was feared the sentimental nature of the songs would undermine morale. A programme of more traditional music replaced Vera Lynn's show, although it did return to the air eighteen months later. The iconic songs 'We'll Meet Again' and 'The White Cliffs of Dover' have forever connected Vera Lynn to the war years, and her work with ENSA in Egypt, India and Burma confirmed her status as 'the Forces' Sweetheart'.

Today Vera Lynn is represented by Lorrie Brown whose tribute act evolved from performances in residential homes. Producer Harry Brookes heard of her and asked her to join his 1940s themed show, performing Vera Lynn songs. While on tour Lorrie acquired an original ENSA uniform and has continued to present as Vera Lynn ever since, to great acclaim. While performing, Lorrie met veterans who had seen Vera Lynn on tour, including the man who had driven her to the different performance venues. In 2013 Lorrie was winner of the National Tribute Music Awards in recognition of her skills. Hearing of this award Vera Lynn invited Lorrie to her home:

MUSIC AND ENTERTAINMENT

> "I was so nervous. It's hard enough performing in front of her fans, who know her songs back to front, but then to actually meet the person you are performing as? In the end, she was wonderful and welcoming. When I walked into the room, she gave me a hug and congratulated me on my award. I sat and talked for three hours with Dame Vera and her daughter, Virginia. We had tea and cake and she showed me some of the dresses she wore during her shows. I also took my ENSA uniform and asked her to inspect it and check that it was correct, and thankfully, she said it was."

As with all tribute acts, Lorrie fully understands the responsibility that such a role carries.

> "It's a massive responsibility, performing as an entertainer enormously loved by generations of fans. You are being watched by her fans who probably own many of her albums and know her voice inside out. It's a great honour when they come up and say they enjoyed the show. You have to totally respect the artist you are portraying."

Having met Dame Vera, Lorrie offered to help her charity, The Dame Vera Lynn Children's Charity, which helps children with cerebral palsy and their families. The charity was actively promoted during all of the shows on the 'Sincerely Yours: Vera Lynn Story' tour and raised £10,000 for the charity. Lorrie and her husband became ambassadors for the charity in 2018.

GEORGE FORMBY

It is hard to imagine that George Formby – the cheeky, yet unassuming ukulele playing lad from Wigan – was, in 1939, the most popular and highest paid entertainer in the United Kingdom. With his infectious sense of humour and natural warmth, Formby could quickly capture an audience and leave them crying out for more. Born 26 May 1904, George was the eldest of seven children. His father was an entertainer and determined that his children would not enter the same profession. Having left school at the age of 7 unable to read or write, George was sent to be trained as a jockey. On the death of his father in 1921, George decided to use his father's material under the name George Hoy (his mother's maiden name). George met with little success until 1923 when he started playing the ukulele and met his future wife Beryl Ingham – a champion clog dancer and actress. Although Beryl did not enjoy George's act, the two hit it off personally and married on 13 September 1924.

Beryl, a shrewd businesswoman, took over management of George's act and made changes to the songs and even his appearance on stage. She encouraged George to take formal lessons in playing the ukulele which soon paid off and George secured a revue contract giving him guaranteed work for five years. In 1932 George produced a record with the Jack Hylton Band. Once released, the public soon embraced the 'B' side, a song called 'Chinese Blues', which featured a character called Mr Wu whose adventures were recounted, to an increasingly enthusiastic audience, in a series of further records. Beryl then directed George into films; his first film, *Boots! Boots!*, soon led to contracts for a further eleven films despite limited critical acclaim.

MUSIC AND ENTERTAINMENT

Each film included three or four songs which were then released on record and as sheet music, including 'The Window Cleaner', 'Fanlight Fanny' and, probably his most famous song, 'Leaning On A Lamp Post'. A review in the *Manchester Observer* of George Formby in the film *No Limit*, released in 1935, commented: 'our Lancashire George is a grand lad; he can gag and clown, play the banjo and sing with authority.... Still and all, he doesn't do too bad.'

With the outbreak of war in 1939 George applied to join the newly formed ENSA and made his first overseas tour in March 1940 to France, performing for the British Expeditionary Force (BEF). George continued to make films during this period and *Let George Do It* became an international success, even playing to packed houses in Moscow! He continued to tour extensively with ENSA and even joined his local Home Guard, serving

Kyle Evans as George Formby leaning on a lamp-post...

– With permission
Andrew Harrison

as a despatch rider whenever his schedule allowed. In 1942 an organisation called the 'Lord's Day Observance Society' began legal actions to prevent non-religious songs being performed on Sundays. Many performers had already given in to this pressure but George was adamant stating:

> *"I'll hang up my uke on Sundays only when our lads stop fighting and getting killed on Sundays… as far as the Lord's Day Observance Society are concerned, they can mind their own bloody business. And in any case, what have they done for the war effort except get on everyone's nerves?"*

Pressure from the group ended shortly after, such was George's influence. In August 1943 George began a gruelling fifty-three-day tour of North Africa with ENSA, and he followed the troops into Europe in July 1944. After the war ended George continued to tour and make further films and records. Indeed, by the end of 1946 George had cut more than 200 records and his 1936 hit 'When I'm Cleaning Windows' sold over a million copies. His fundraising and efforts to keep up the nation's morale earned him the award of OBE in 1945. In 1949 he undertook a coast to coast tour of Canada, which took its toll on George's health but did not see an end to his career.

Although George Formby died on 6 March 1961, he is still instantly recognisable today and, although few remember his films, his records are still played. It is no surprise therefore that George's songs and comedy are in popular demand at '40s events.

Kyle Evans now takes on the responsibility for representing George Formby having been attracted to 'Formby's amazing banjo-ukulele skills as well as his massively funny comic talents.' Of all aspects of George Formby's performance, Kyle believes that the hardest to replicate was:

> "his playing techniques as his style of playing wasn't like any other style at the time and is very challenging to mimic. The next step was to copy how he used to interact with his audience when he performed on stage, that is play one song, then have a joke before the next number."

Kyle understands well that his audiences already 'know' Formby, and therefore there is a requirement to recreate his performances as closely as possible in order to keep his spirit and character alive. Kyle uses the public reaction as a measure of his success and is proud to note:

> "since I started my George Formby Tribute in February 2019, the public's reaction has been very positive and complimentary. A lot of people were quite surprised at first when I told them what I do, but when they saw me perform, they would come up to me saying how good I was and how much like George I sounded. That's the best praise I can get!"

RE-LIVING BRITAIN IN THE 1940S

FEMALE HARMONY GROUPS

Female harmony groups were not well established in Britain before the war but that changed with the arrival of American troops, who brought with them the music of the Andrews Sisters. Having been signed to Decca Records in 1937, the Andrews Sisters were at the height of their popularity, becoming the first million-selling female group with their song 'Bei mir bist du schon'. Today they are best-known for their 1941 song 'Boogie Woogie Bugle Boy' (ranked number six on the Recording Industry Association of America (RIAA) 'Songs of the Century'). The Andrews Sisters also recorded with stars such as Bing Crosby with the million-selling 'Don't Fence Me In'. The sisters later joined the United Service Organisations (USO – the American

The Liberty Sisters perform for crowds at the annual event at Slapton Sands.
– With permission Raymond Goldsmith

equivalent to ENSA) entertaining and inspiring homesick troops, and reminding them who they were fighting for. As Patty Andrews noted, 'we were such a part of everybody's life in the Second World War. We represented something overseas and at home – a sort of security.' In 1946, the American Billboard magazine observed that 'no matter how pop tastes have switched from boogie to ballads, sagebrush to sambas, waltzes and calypsos to be-bop, The Andrews Sisters have continued to be faves. In discs, they rank second only to Bing Crosby on the Decca lists.'

Heritage events today have a number of vocal trios providing entertainment. One well-established trio is the 'Liberty Sisters' – Ruby, Rose and Dolly – who began performing together in 2015 having met as members of a gospel choir. The Liberty Sisters repertoire is

Ruby, Rose and Dolly in playful mood enjoying a ride in a jeep.

– With permission Raymond Goldsmith

heavily influenced by the legacy of the Andrews Sisters and includes the joyful 'Boogie Woogie Bugle Boy' and 'In The Mood', the romantic 'I'll be With You in Apple Blossom Time', the cheeky 'Oh Johnny, Oh!', together with the poignant 'Shoo Shoo Baby' and the 1945 hit 'Rum and Coca Cola'.

On stage the Liberty Sisters appear in the uniforms of the USO. Performers with the USO wore officer grade uniforms and were allowed the privileges that went with that rank. Being effectively uniformed civilians, USO performers were afforded considerable latitude in how the uniform was worn. The Liberty Sisters wear the USO cloth badge on shirts, tunics and mackintoshes as well as on their side caps. They also wear the US army brass lapel pins. For variety the Liberty Sisters also have a colourful civilian wardrobe, including evening dress.

Claire Fairburn of the Liberty Sisters is keen to point out that getting the sound and image of the period correct is vital but takes hours because, 'as each performance is a blend of civilian and military influence the information needed requires hours of reading and listening – there is no rule-book to follow.' Claire goes on to explain:

> *"we take our performances extremely seriously in order to honour the original performers, and also not wanting to run the risk of critical comments from today's audience. If we can't find backing music which sounds uncompromisingly authentic then we don't do the song. Our vocal style is as correct as it can be, with the same vocal ranges and responsibilities as the originals."*

Performances by the Liberty Sisters are always well-received and the group has a very loyal fan base. They even have a group of swing dancers who add yet another dimension to shows. As Claire observes, 'all age groups respond well to our performances, but those who lived through those turbulent times, and their immediate families, express the greatest appreciation for truly being taken back in time'.

The Entertainments National Service Association (ENSA) was formed in 1939 and performed valuable service throughout the war providing entertainment for troops in locations all across the globe and keeping up their morale. The comedian Tommy Trinder joked that ENSA meant 'Every Night Something Awful' but, although mocked, performers included stars such as Harry Secombe, Tommy Cooper, Eric Sykes, George Formby and Gracie Fields. Top film stars like John Gielgud and Ralph Richardson also contributed their talents. Vivienne Leigh, star of the 1939 hit movie 'Gone With the Wind' also joined in, at one time performing in front of 8,000 men in North Africa. Ballet and performances of Shakespeare were also offered to broaden the appeal of the shows.

RADIO

While ENSA entertained the troops, the general public relied on the wireless and a gramophone for their entertainment. Radio was certainly the cheapest form of entertainment, and consequently the most popular during the war years with its ability both to entertain and also inform the public. In the 1940s ownership and use of a radio required a licence and by 1945 there were almost 10 million radio licences across Britain. Unlike today, the British Broadcasting Corporation (BBC) offered just two programmes – The Home Service and The Forces Programme – which, between them, held a

Late 1930s radio set which has been adapted to play period music through a Bluetooth connection. Such radios add real atmosphere to any event.
— With permission Author's Collection

virtual monopoly. The content varied from educational to comic – most notably the popular show ITMA ('It's That Man Again'). ITMA had been launched in 1939 but received such poor reviews that the show was almost axed; however, by 1945 it is estimated that 40 per cent of the population listened every week. The star of the show was comedian Tommy Handley who played the Minister of Aggravation and Mysteries at the Office of Twerps. The radio series was based in the Ministry of Twerps. One reason for the show's success was that it poked fun at the myriad petty regulations that dictated every aspect of life in wartime.

Radio was also the principal source of news and official announcements, but the authorities were worried about the impact

MUSIC AND ENTERTAINMENT

of accurate reporting on morale when things were not going well. To measure morale the government turned to a social research organisation called 'Mass Observation', which had been set up in 1937 to study the lives of ordinary people and which still continues its work today. Five hundred people had been selected as a cross-section of society and were regularly asked to give feedback on a huge range of issues, including how they felt about bad news. Whereas some people craved any news, others avoided it. One woman, Adelaide Poole from Sussex, even blamed bad news for her sister's death stating:

> *"I have had a last letter from my sister who died suddenly in Rochester, NY. She wrote ... how they had listened to the guns over London as broadcast direct from London ... saying 'I do wonder if you are losing sleep night after night?' Within two days she was dead, but we are still alive and I was sleeping quietly at the time. The vicarious suffering she went through on our account helped to kill her. The radio accounts keyed her nerves to an unbearable pitch."*

The skill was to present bad news in such a way that the national spirit remained intact. The classic example of this is the way in which the evacuation from Dunkirk – a military disaster by any standard – was presented as a triumph of British character when confronted by the Nazi juggernaut.

Workers in factories and on production lines were essential, and maintaining their morale was regarded as a vital function of radio. While such entertainment might not actually help increase productivity it would serve to relieve the monotony and boredom. *Music While You*

Work provided a stream of non-stop music with a beat which would accompany repetitive work. This flew in the face of traditional BBC broadcasting which had played heavily on personality. A BBC memo dated 10 July 1940 outlined what was required:

> *"from the point of view of the general listener we are asking for a bad piece of programme building. There must be as little variation of tempo as possible, the ideal being to maintain the same beat through the whole programme. Artistic value must not be considered. The aim is to produce something which is rhythmically monotonous and repetitive; a 'sustaining' background of brisk, cheerful but unobtrusive music."*

According to BBC records this approach certainly worked and, by mid–1945, more than 45,000 factories and workshops were listening in along with between 10 and 20 per cent of the general population!

It is still possible to get the feel of '40s radio by tuning in to one of the current radio stations recreating the sounds of the '40s. The original internet station playing music exclusively from the 1920s to the 1940s is the '1940s Radio Station' (www.1940sukradio.co.uk) which began broadcasting in 2010. The station is managed by Shaun Moncaster who initially set it up in response to a family member's dementia, as he explains:

> *"often, after a bereavement, a person losing their life-long partner finds themselves living alone. I found this happening to my father who had been diagnosed with dementia and was also losing his sight. This prompted me to load his MP3 player with lots of old-time radio*

MUSIC AND ENTERTAINMENT

shows and also 1940s and 1950s music which he enjoyed listening to. Noticing the beneficial effect in Dad being calmer and more settled led to me thinking about starting the radio station, thinking that it might provide some comfort to others."

Shaun goes on to explain that the station has 'an excellent line-up of presenters from the UK and the USA, many of whom have worked in broadcasting for many years, and some of who have embarked on the career more recently. The common denominator linking the presenters is an unstinting love of the music.' Shaun explains the station's success by noting that 'all the station's presenters provide their expertise and time on a voluntary basis which allows the station to succeed in today's competitive online entertainment radio industry.' The same team also produce 'The British Home Front Radio Service' (www.1940sukradio.co.uk/BHFR) which concentrates mainly on British music and worldwide original news broadcasts which could have been heard in Britain at that time.

The Utility Radio or Wartime Civilian Receiver introduced in July 1944. It only received medium wave broadcasts and the tuner only listed BBC stations.

– With permission
Author's Collection

FILM

The British film industry in the Second World War was influenced by the Ministry of Information whose task was to create films which would inspire the public – no small task at a time when defeat looked a realistic possibility and the people were subjected to nightly, and demoralising bombing raids! The bulk of the viewing audience were women and so it was important that films were created which women could relate to. This required women scriptwriters, and led to a host of strong female characters emerging, from actresses such as Margaret Lockwood, Phyllis Calvert and Anna Neagle. Inspirational war films were also produced such as *Went the Day Well?* (1942) and *Fires Were Started* (1943). There remained a desire for more light-hearted films and George Formby starred in a number of comedies such as *Turned Out Nice Again* (1941) and *Much Too Shy* (1942). Possibly Charlie Chaplin's greatest film, *The Great Dictator* (1940) was one of those films produced in Hollywood but popular in Britain. The films of Laurel and Hardy continued to entertain audiences on both sides of the Atlantic with catchphrases such as 'Well, here's another nice mess you've gotten me into!'

LAUREL & HARDY

Stan Laurel was born Arthur Stanley Jefferson on 19 June 1890 at Ulverston, Lancashire, to theatrical parents named Jefferson. By the age of 19 he was working as an understudy to Charlie Chaplin. In 1912 Laurel left Britain on a tour of the United States, and stayed. By 1920 he was using the stage name Stan Laurel and officially adopted that name in 1931.

MUSIC AND ENTERTAINMENT

Laurel worked in theatre and film, appearing in more than fifty films before he partnered with Oliver Hardy. Hardy was born Novell Hardy on 18 January 1892 in Harlem, Georgia, USA, and was a successful stage singer by his late teens. Branching into films, Hardy was known by one of his nick-names – 'Babe' – and appeared in the credits as Babe Hardy. Having enjoyed watching comedy, Hardy decided to try it himself and began working with Lublin Films in 1913. He soon became known for his versatility starring or co-starring in over 250 silent 'shorts'. Having failed to be accepted for the US Army during the First World War (because of his size), Hardy moved to California in 1917 and went to work for Hal Roach. When Roach also hired Laurel, the two worked together in a film and a partnership was born. Unlike most comedy duos both Laurel and Hardy were comedians and both could play a straight role when required.

Laurel and Hardy's comedy was based on slapstick and visual humour which was compounded by the physical differences between the two. Their first movie together was called *The Lucky Dog*, released in 1921. By 1930 the pairing of Laurel and Hardy was official. Whereas many actors failed to survive the end of the silent movie era, Laurel and Hardy thrived, although the frenetic pace of their comedy slowed to a more natural speed. The pairing and the format were so successful that little changed over the next thirty years. During the Second World War the duo supported the war effort, including producing a short film for the US Department of Agriculture, called *The Tree in a Test Tube* (1942), stressing the need to conserve domestic timber supplies. Also in 1942, they took part in the Hollywood Victory Caravan Show on its nationwide tour before touring with USO.

Gary Slade and Rob Graham bring Laurel and Hardy back to life for a new generation of fans.

– With permission Rob Graham

MUSIC AND ENTERTAINMENT

Although Laurel and Hardy did not visit Britain during the war years, their work was immensely popular and they were well-known stars throughout the '40s. In fact, they had visited Britain in 1932 at the height of their success, and again in 1947 by which time their Hollywood careers were almost at an end. Today's visitors to heritage events may still catch sight of the pair brought back to life by Gary Slade and Rob Graham. They both love Laurel and Hardy and Gary has always been a dedicated fan. As Rob observes, 'Gary has been a fan all his life, and is almost Stan even when out of character. He

Laurel and Hardy take a well-earned break from entertaining the crowds.

– With permission Rob Graham

just looks and sounds the part. He knows all the history and all the characters in most of the 107 movies that Stan and Ollie performed in!'

Getting the behaviour of Stan and Ollie right has taken a huge amount of work, since their humour is effortless. As Rob says, 'we always do our best at every show. Stan and Ollie would not have performed any other way and we follow their mantra of practice, practice, practice.' Because Laurel and Hardy are still so well-known even today it is essential that Rob and Gary are convincing in role. The fact that they remain so popular is useful, as Rob observes, because 'when members of the public see us they automatically take to us. We start by making them laugh with zany antics then perform amazing tricks, where all the emphasis is on laughing and making ourselves look foolish.' Both Rob and Gary regret that they never had the opportunity to see their characters in real life because they were such comedy icons, but they do try to take the comedy forward. On one occasion they were working with a real star but persuaded the audience that the star was actually a tribute act like themselves. At the end of the evening, he said that it had been an amazing event and such a relief not to have to sign autographs all night! 'Laurel and Hardy were such iconic comedians – just a look into the camera would make you smile' says Rob 'I hope we can give a small percentage of the happiness to our audience that they did. It's always good to leave someone with a lasting impression!'

MUSIC AND ENTERTAINMENT

RECORDS & GRAMOPHONES

Shellac records were another common form of entertainment played on a wind-up gramophone player. The term 'gramophone' properly refers to the products of the Gramophone Company, but by 1910 the term had become generic and covers all wind-up record players. Today, shellac records are widely referred to as 78s – a reference to the standard speed of 78.26 revolutions per minute (RPM) – but that term did not come into use until the 1950s when vinyl took over from shellac and a slower speed of 33.34 rpm was introduced. Vinyl had already begun to replace shellac in America during the Second World War, partly because vinyl was stronger but also, and possibly more importantly, because shellac was also used in the production of explosives, leading President Franklin Roosevelt to order a 70 per cent cut in the production of new shellac records. Popular records in Britain were commonly either comedic (for example 'Run Rabbit Run' sung by Flanagan and Allen, or 'Kiss Me Goodnight Sergeant Major') or sentimental (for example 'There'll Always Be An England' or 'We'll Meet Again' both sung by Vera Lynn). American imports took a while to take off. The song 'Coming In On A Wing And A Prayer' was initially condemned for using religious terminology with a foxtrot melody! As the public became more familiar with American Dance Bands, sales of their records increased.

LIVING HISTORY GROUPS & LINKS

Anyone wishing to hire a vintage entertainer or particular tribute act should visit Marie and Pete Bainbridge's excellent website '**Love of the '40s**' at loveofthe40s.co.uk. This essential site has links to everything from solo artists to Big Bands and tributes.

FURTHER RESEARCH

Glenn Miller Declassified; Dennis M. Spragg; Potomac Books Inc; 2020; ISBN: 1-6401-2308-3. The music of Glenn Miller and his orchestra still resonates with audiences today. On 15 December 1944 Miller boarded a plane from Britain to Paris but never arrived. The mystery of his death has simply added to the legend that he became. This book strips back the legend to reveal the man while also examining the circumstances of his death.

Keep Smiling Through: My Wartime Story; Vera Lynn with Virginia Lewis-Jones; 2018; Arrow; ISBN: 1-7874-6011-9. Vera Lynn has become synonymous with the Second World War and fully deserves her reputation as 'the Forces Sweetheart'. This is her story in her words and well worth the read.

George Formby: The Biography; David Bret; CreateSpace Independent Publishing Platform; 2016; ISBN: 1-5397-6345-5. Formby was an unlikely candidate for stardom and owed much of his success to the drive of his wife Beryl. The book examines Beryl's role in Formby's career but also reveals the man himself with his dedication to charity work and support for the troops. A good introduction to a complex icon.

Wartime Broadcasting; Mike Brown; Shire Books, 2018; ISBN: 1-7844-2264-6. This is an excellent introduction to the challenges faced by the BBC as the sole radio broadcast company in Britain. The book looks at the stars and the iconic programmes like ITMA, but also considers the challenges faced in reporting the news accurately while still maintaining morale and not becoming simply a vehicle for propaganda.

'**Workers' Playtime: Archive Wartime Radio Recordings by Workers' Playtime**'; Audio CD. A selection of wartime radio broadcasts which offer a good insight into the sort of programmes presented for workers in factories.

'**Guide to Collecting 78 RPM Records**'; online article. Although from an American source the article contains extremely useful advice about not only collecting 78 RPM, records but also about the best ways to play them. Useful guidance for any collector. The address is: vibrations.ca/fr/record-collecting/item/1-guide-to-collecting-78-rpm-records.

Great Songs of World War Two; Michael Leitch (editor); Music Sales Ltd; 1985; ISBN: 0-8600-1041-4. For anyone wanting to learn the lyrics or music of thirty-one of the best wartime songs this book is a must. Contains historical context and is well-illustrated with 160 photographs of the Home Front.

CHAPTER ELEVEN

TRANSPORT

No commemoration of the '40s is complete without period vehicles, which help to add realism and depth to any event. These vehicles are privately owned and maintained by enthusiasts. Although not a requirement, many vehicle owners choose to dress in uniform or civilian clothing appropriate to the vehicle they own. Many vehicle owners attend rallies organised by the clubs to which they are affiliated, but many also attend heritage '40s events. Each vehicle has been lovingly and carefully restored and has its own story to tell.

MILITARY VEHICLES

The work of entertainers and organisations like ENSA was essential in maintaining morale among the troops serving far away from their homes and families. Moving performers, their equipment and staff between shows was no small undertaking, and vehicles had to be adapted for that purpose. This unique 1939 Ford Mercury Eight series 99A Estate Car was originally owned by Sir Malcolm Campbell (winner of the World Water Speed Record with his boat 'Bluebird').

He acquired the vehicle to carry the equipment needed to maintain the boat and for his mechanics to sleep in. Campbell had a large estate

George Formby's 1939 Ford Mercury Eight series 99A Estate Car.

— With permission H&H Classics

car body fitted and the rear seats constructed so that they folded into the floor to provide a sleeping area. Sadly, war broke out before he had the opportunity to use the vehicle. Later, he was introduced to George Formby and learned of Formby's planned trip to North Africa with ENSA. Offered the Mercury for his use, Formby had the Royal Electrical and Mechanical Engineers (REME) adapt the vehicle for desert work with new paintwork, partially tinted windows to reduce glare, and larger wheels and tyres to grip the sand. Formby and the Mercury then embarked on an exhausting fifty-three-day tour through Italy, Sicily, Malta, Libya, Tunisia, Egypt, Lebanon and Palestine. During the tour Formby entertained 750,000 troops and dined with Field Marshall Montgomery, becoming the mascot of the Eighth Army. Formby sold the Mercury in 1946, but thankfully its rich history has been preserved and maintained.

TRANSPORT

The range of military vehicles used in the Second World War is vast and includes vehicles purpose built to meet specific military needs. This ranged from heavy armour (tanks and self-propelled guns and artillery), armoured cars (smaller wheeled vehicles for reconnaissance use), transports (for moving the vast amounts of materiel needed to meet the needs of an advancing army), amphibious vehicles (for crossing rivers and waterways) and motorbikes (for despatch riders). There were also mobile repair trucks, ambulances and other specialist vehicles.

Originally termed the US Army Truck, ½ ton, 4 x 4 Light Reconnaissance vehicle, the Jeep is the most recognisable, and most loved, military vehicle of the period. It takes its name from the acronym for 'GP' for 'General Purpose'. In June 1940 the US Army sought bids from vehicle manufacturers to make this new 'Light reconnaissance' vehicle. The first model – known as the Willys MA – was largely

1943 Jeep with .30 calibre machine gun and windscreen and canvas frame lowered.
– With permission Louis Brzozka

shipped to England and Russia under Lend-Lease and only about thirty examples remain.

In July 1941 Willys Overland was awarded the contract to produce 16,000 MB models. Wartime reporter Ernie Pyle, speaking of the Jeep, said that 'It did everything. It went everywhere. Was as faithful as a dog, as strong as a mule, and as agile as a goat. It constantly carried twice what it was designed for and still kept going.' Highly versatile, the Jeep remains a popular vehicle for military vehicle enthusiasts. This Jeep, owned and driven by Louis Brzozka, came off the production line of the Ford Motor Plant at Louisville, Kentucky on 28 April 1943 with the hood number 20372272 and serial 111633. Before it came to England it was in Washington State, USA. The owner at the time was hoping to restore it but fell ill and, eventually, the vehicle was imported to Britain for restoration by a company in Leicestershire.

Heavier than the Jeep were the 'Beeps' or 'big jeeps', manufactured by the Dodge motor company in its premises near Detroit, Michigan. Known as the Dodge 'WC' series, they are also often referred to as 'Weapons Carriers' although, in fact, the 'W' represents 1941 and the 'C' a nominal payload of ½ ton. This model code was continued after 1941 to include all ¾ ton and 1½ ton models as well. Other than size, the main difference between the Jeep and the Dodge series was that the Jeep was a standard vehicle which could be modified in the field to meet specific requirements, whereas the Dodge series included a range of purpose-built, mechanically uniform variants. The Dodge series included cargo trucks, ambulances, weapons carriers, field workshops and others – a total of fifty-two model versions. The vehicle illustrated is a Dodge WC51. Together with the WC52 (same model but with a Braden winch fitted to the front) there were 255,195

1942 Dodge WC51. With the canvas covers removed a .50 calibre machine gun can be added for defence.
– Author's photograph

vehicles made. The WC51/52 could transport up to ten fully equipped men on benches along either side, or carry stores and equipment.

This vehicle is thought to have been built in 1942 before shipment to Europe. It must have served during the war as it was in Germany at the end of the war where it received a rebuild by the Waiblingen Ordnance Rebuild Shop, operated by Daimler-Benz. After being shipped back to Britain the vehicle received a further rebuild at the Rootes Ltd Factory, Manchester, in February 1955. The Dodge was then sold to Norway where minor modifications were made before returning to Britain where it was restored by Roy Emberson of Surrey, before being purchased by the author.

RE-LIVING BRITAIN IN THE 1940S

The M3 White Scout Car is an armoured car produced by the American White Motor company of Cleveland, Ohio, between 1937 and 1944, for the American Army. It was also supplied in large numbers to all of the Allied forces under the Lend-Lease scheme; the British Army in particular receiving large numbers of them. The White Motor Company made around 20,000 Scout Cars. Weighing four tons unladen and up to six tons fully loaded and designed to carry an eight-man infantry squad, the Scout Car could reach 55mph, although its off-road ability was limited. When the American Army moved to a ten-man squad the Scout Car was no longer fit for purpose. As a result, the American Army switched to using mainly Halftracks and so many Scout Cars found their way to the Allied forces who put them to use mainly in support or reconnaissance roles rather than in the front line.

M3 Scout Car with paratrooper manning the .50 calibre machine gun.

– With permission Andy Norman

TRANSPORT

The M3 Scout Car was used in many different roles and in many different theatres of war, in its original specification it carried seven troops plus a driver, had a 'skate rail' to carry weapons around the inside of the armour and was armed with one .50 calibre and two .30 calibre machine guns. The intention being that the machine guns would support the infantry crew members who would 'debus' and move forward under their firing cover. As the vehicle's use was changed from a frontline role it was reconfigured into many different forms to suit the use to which it was being put. This particular vehicle represents a British Army vehicle in use by the Support Squadron (C Squadron) of the 6th Airborne Armoured Reconnaissance Regiment RAC (6th AARR), which was an independent unit within the Parachute Regiment.

As a support vehicle, this example has a centre pintle mounting to carry either a British Vickers Medium machine gun or an American .50 calibre machine gun, racking on the rear to hold a ground-mounted 3-inch mortar and a WS19 Radio for communication. Two of its seats have been removed to allow more space inside as it carried a smaller crew of four. This particular vehicle is thought to have been brought back to the UK from Greece during the 1990s where it sat in storage for around twenty years. Between 2010 and 14 it was totally rebuilt to 'as new' standard by its previous owner who had a no-expense-spared professional rebuild completed, including new armour and running gear. When purchased by its current owner in 2015 it was as good as a vehicle fresh from the production line down to the last detail, only needing repainting and some finishing touches. The M3 Scout Car is now owned by Andy Norman.

For upwards of £300,000 you could acquire the ultimate in military vehicles – a tank! Actually, it is not illegal to own a tank (as long as

Fully restored Sherman tank outside the Cobbaton Combat Collection building.
— Author's photograph

the weapons are deactivated in line with current legal requirement or are registered as live weapons). This example is the American made Medium Tank, M4 – better known as the Sherman – named after the American Civil War General William Tecumseh Sherman. Mass-produced, tens of thousands of these tanks were issued to British and Commonwealth forces under the Lend-Lease programme. Equipped with a 75 mm gun, the Sherman's design emphasised reliability and ease of both production and maintenance. The weight was designed to allow shipping and not exceed the limits of bridging equipment currently in use by the Allied forces. The Sherman's heavier armour and superior firepower outclassed German and Italian light tanks in use at the time of its introduction in 1942.

Because the Sherman was relatively easy to repair, many disabled tanks were able to be recovered, repaired and returned to service, giving Allied forces a significant numerical advantage overall. Despite the introduction of heavier tanks on both sides of the conflict, the Sherman remained in widespread use.

The Sherman shown here has a welded steel hull as opposed to the later cast hull. It was acquired and remained as a wreck in the children's play area at Cobbaton Combat Collection until revised health and safety regulations meant that it was no longer deemed safe for children to climb on. Instead it was fully restored and went on to have a role in the Brad Pitt film 'Fury' where it can be seen having its turret blown off after a direct hit from a Tiger tank.

GROUPS & LINKS

The largest military vehicle club in the UK is the **Military Vehicle Trust** (MVT) – also the largest military vehicle club in the world. The MVT is a charity dedicated to the preservation of former military vehicles of any age. There is a network of thirty-three local MVT 'areas' across the country in which members organise meetings, social events and shows. There are also close links to ex-servicemen's associations and the Royal British Legion's annual Poppy Appeal. Many members' vehicles are used in film and TV work. The MVT also offers an authentication service to assist members in correctly registering such vehicles for the first time. Further details can be found on the MVT website at www.mvt.org.uk.

Invicta Military-Vehicle Preservation Society (IMPS) is also UK based but with strong links with many European and smaller UK preservation groups. The club is involved in many large-scale events including the annual Combined Ops Show at Headcorn Aerodrome, in Kent. Their website address is www.imps.org.uk.

COLLECTIONS

The Tank Museum. Based at Bovington, Dorset, this is the largest collection of tanks in the world tracing the history of the tank from the earliest surviving combat tank through to the armour of today. There are almost 300 vehicles on display at Bovington which is also the museum of the Royal Tank Regiment and the Royal Armoured Corps. See the website for further details at tankmuseum.org.

Armourgeddon Military Museum. Based near Husbands Bosworth in Leicestershire, the museum displays a wide range of military vehicles including tanks, artillery, guns and militaria from the First World War to the Cold War. A number of the vehicles have appeared in films and TV series. There is even the opportunity to drive a tank on selected days. Further details from militarymuseum.uk.

Muckleburgh Military Collection. An extensive collection of tanks and other military vehicles maintained in working condition located near Weybourne, Norfolk. Together with a large display of militaria, the collection offers a great introduction to the vehicles of the Second World War. Further details on the website at www.muckleburgh.co.uk.

Cobbaton Combat Collection. Located near Chittlehampton in North Devon this collection is literally a hobby that got out of hand. Housed in a number of former hangars, military vehicles and related uniforms and equipment fill the space to the brim. There is also an extensive home-front exhibition. The website address is www.cobbatoncombat.co.uk.

FURTHER RESEARCH

Allied Armoured Fighting Vehicles of the Second World War; Michael Green; 2017; Pen and Sword Military; ISBN: 1-4738-7237-5. A full inventory of the armoured fighting vehicles used by the Allies – all expertly described in words and captioned images.

Allied Tanks of the Second World War; Michael Green; 2017; Pen and Sword Military; ISBN: 1-4738-6676-8. This book offers a full inventory of the tanks used by the Allies and their development throughout the war years. This is a companion volume to *Allied Armoured Fighting Vehicles of the Second World War* immediately above.

World War Two Military Vehicles Transport and Halftracks; Pat Ware; Ian Allen Publishing; 2007; ISBN: 0-7110-3193-2. A very comprehensive account of the development of military transport during the war years. Superbly illustrated, the book covers both Allied and Axis vehicles in detail.

World War Two Military Vehicles Transport and Halftracks; G.N. Georgano; Osprey Publishing; 1994; ISBN: 1-8553-2406-7. A useful overview of the vehicles produced by the major countries on both sides of the conflict, and the difficulties they faced.

WW2 Allied Vehicles Military Portfolio 1939–1945; R.M. Clarke; Brooklands Books Ltd; 2000; ISBN: 1-8552-0546-7. A well-illustrated book containing lots of new material on the characteristics and use of Humber staff and Scout cars, Morris Mk. I light reconnaissance vehicles, Daimler Scout and armoured cars, Jeeps, amphibians, staff cars, half-tracks and Austin light utilities, together with features on driving techniques and desert warfare.

CIVILIAN VEHICLES

By 1930, car production in Britain was dominated by Austin and Morris which produced some 60 per cent of total British output between them, becoming Europe's largest car manufacturer in 1932. In 1937 Britain produced 379,310 cars and 113,956 commercial vehicles. The outbreak of the Second World War in 1939 brought a halt to the production of civilian vehicles, moving instead to military vehicles, aircraft and aircraft engines. In September 1939 petrol was rationed to roughly 200 miles worth per month, but from July 1942 the ration was withdrawn completely. Only essential users could apply for fuel coupons. A reduced basic ration was reintroduced in June 1945.

The blackout imposed further restrictions on motorists, requiring all lights to be dimmed by the addition of 'blackout light covers', which covered the lights allowing only a narrow, diffused beam of light to be seen. While theoretically making life harder for the German air force it also led to a dramatic increase in road casualties. The king's surgeon, writing in the *British Medical Journal* in 1939, complained that by 'frightening the nation into blackout regulations, the Luftwaffe was able to kill 600 British citizens a month without ever taking to the air'. By the end of September 1939 there had been 1,130 deaths attributed to the blackout and the highest number of deaths on the roads was in 1940, with 9,169 casualties. Pedestrians were urged to carry a newspaper or something white to make them more visible, and luminous white discs were available to buy which could be pinned to clothing. One Birmingham coroner told old people to keep off the streets after dark, suggesting that their evening visits to the pub should be sacrificed for the war effort. This was because so many were killed as they left the pub to walk along a darkened street. White paint was widely used to help people 'see' in the dark. Stripes were painted on kerbs, and around the edges of car bodies to make them more visible. Car crashes were frequent even after the speed limit was reduced to 20mph. Many vehicle owners without access to petrol simply stored their vehicles for the duration of the war.

After the Austin Motor Company went into receivership in 1921 it underwent restructuring enabling it to survive, but the emphasis was placed on producing smaller vehicles than had previously been the case. Sir Herbert Austin wanted a car that young families could afford. Opposed by the company's directors and creditors (the company still being in receivership), Sir Herbert Austin decided to progress the project using his own funds and with the support of 18-year-old draughtsman Stanley Edge (ironically a cousin of the author). While Austin was responsible for the vehicle's design, Edge designed the engine and gearbox. The product was the Austin 7 (nick-named the

'Baby Austin'). Nearly 2,500 Austin 7s were produced in the first year and by 1939, when production ended, 290,000 had been sold, saving the company and seeing it through the depression of the 1930s. Numerous models were produced including tourers, saloons, sports, coupès and vans.

This is the 1936 Austin 7 Ruby Deluxe. The vehicle was originally purchased for £165 and first registered to Mr George Nicklin of The School House, Eckington, near Pershore in Worcestershire on 1 January 1937. George was married to Ella Nicklin, then the Headmistress of Eckington School. As a teacher, George was permitted fuel vouchers and so the car was used throughout the war. In March 2017 the car returned to Eckington School and was displayed to the current Head and pupils. The car is now owned by the author and used as part of a National Air Raid Precautions Animal Control (NARPAC) mobile ambulance display.

1936 Austin 7 Ruby Deluxe. — Author's photograph

TRANSPORT

1930 Austin 7 Box Saloon car.

– With permission Phil Dunford

This beautifully maintained maroon vehicle is a 1930 Austin 7 Box Saloon car owned by Phil Dunford. The car displays the common white painted stripe along the wings and the edge of the running board to make the vehicle easier to see in the blackout. It also has the dimmed headlamps.

The Austin 10, as the numbering suggests, was a small car which fitted between the Austin 7 and the larger Austin 12. Introduced in April 1932 the Austin 10 soon became the best-selling car of the decade. This vehicle has the white visibility strip but also clearly shows the dimmed headlights.

The Austin 10 car in full 'black out' order. — With permission Phil Dunford

TRANSPORT

Immaculate deluxe Ford 8.

– With permission Eric Umpleby

The Ford Motor Company also produced vehicles in Britain. The Ford 7Y was produced between 1937 and 1939 with a total of 69,420 being produced. The car was actually marketed as the Ford 8 and was the last Ford model produced with the 'kink' in the front bumper to accommodate a starting handle. The model shown here is the deluxe version with running boards and a spare wheel at the rear and was first registered in 1937 in Reading. Today it is owned by Mr Eric Umpleby of Cheshire.

A less well-known car manufacturer today was the Standard Motor Company which operated from 1903 until 1963. Standard bought the 'Triumph' trading name in November 1944, creating the Standard Triumph Motor Company a year later. The name Standard was finally dropped in 1963. The photograph on the next page shows the Standard Flying 10 – a replacement for the earlier, less streamlined Standard 10 which began production in 1934. The Flying 10 was introduced in 1937 and produced until the outbreak of war in 1939. A small number of four- door models of the Flying 10 were produced in 1941 for military use.

This photograph (staged as publicity for the West Somerset Railway's annual '40s weekend) features a Flying 10 owned by Robin White alongside the railway's military train.

GROUPS & LINKS

There are owners' clubs for almost every type of historic car as well as generic 'classic car' clubs all across the country. A quick internet search will soon show those nearest to any location. The ones listed are illustrative only and relate to the vehicles depicted in the text.

> **Austin Seven Owners Club**. Dedicated to the preservation of pre-war Austin 7 vehicles, the website has links to regional clubs and their activities. An online shop offers a range of branded products and books while a parts department helps those restoring and maintaining Austin 7s. Website address: austinsevenownersclub.co.uk.

A Standard Flying 10 pauses for directions as a military train passes.

– With permission Robin White

Austin Ten Drivers Club. This club caters for enthusiasts and collectors of the Austin Ten and Twelve models between 1931 and 1939. As well as organising events the Club also offers a parts department to assist in the maintenance of these popular vehicles. Website address: www.austintendriversclub.com

Ford Sidevalve Owners' Club (FSOC). This club covers all Fords produced in the UK between 1932 and 1962. It is a social club with a large network of Regional Organisers who arrange monthly meetings and attend local heritage and classic car events. Offering a club magazine and many other member services the Club is a must for all Ford enthusiasts. Website address: www.fsoc.co.uk

COLLECTIONS

Most collections feature classic vehicles from all ages but there will always be a good representation from the 1930s and 1940s.

National Motor Museum, Beaulieu. In the beautiful setting of Beaulieu's grounds and gardens this collection houses over 280 vehicles. For the the Second World War enthusiast there is also the added bonus of a Secret Army Exhibition recognising Beaulieu's role as a finishing school for the Special Operations Executive (SOE). Details of opening times and special events can be found at www.beaulieu.co.uk/attractions.

British Motor Museum. At Gaydon, Warwickshire, this is the world's largest collection of historic British cars with almost 300 vehicles displayed alongside the story of Britain's motor industry which is explained in a way that will entertain the whole family. Further details from www.britishmotormuseum.co.uk.

Haynes Motor Museum. This is the collection of John Haynes – creator of the Haynes manuals. With activities for the whole family this museum is, fittingly, built on the site of a wartime American munitions dump in Sparkford, Somerset. Still growing, the collection now boasts almost 400 vehicles on display. Further details from www.haynesmotormuseum.com/visit-us.

FURTHER RESEARCH

As with Clubs, the majority of books are devoted to the collection and restoration of a particular type of vehicle. Illustrative examples are included here focusing on the vehicles featured above.

The Original Austin Seven; Rinsey Mills; Herridge & Sons Ltd; 2008; ISBN: 1-9061-3305-0. The book examines the many models of Austin Seven and how they have evolved over the years. Recommended for anyone restoring or maintaining one of these iconic vehicles.

The Austin Seven and Ten; written and published by Brooklands Books Ltd; 2009; ISBN: 1-8552-0880-6. A useful overview of both of these popular cars which jointly dominated the British car market in the pre-war period. Also contains a collection of press articles offering a contemporary perspective on both models.

RE-LIVING BRITAIN IN THE 1940S

TRAINS

Most heritage railways now offer '40s events. The sight and sounds of a steam engine really do help to conjure up a sense of the past and, together with period vehicles, adds a great deal of realism to any scene. Technically, many preserved steam trains are in the wrong livery (which should be wartime black), and the carriages are often restored post-war Mk.1 examples, but this is something worth forgiving for the pleasure they bring.

During wartime the railways were vital to the movement of people, supplies and even livestock around the country. They were also the largest household removal operator prior to the outbreak of war, moving more furniture than any other service. By the start of 1940 all railway assets were focused on the war effort with railway workshops

A military train laden with vehicles and other essential supplies prepares to leave Minehead Station on the West Somerset Railway. – With permission WSR

A United States Army Transportation Corps S160 Class locomotive prepares to haul the military train on the West Somerset Railway. – With permission WSR

being converted to military production and the different railway companies (Southern Railway, London, Midland and Scottish Railway, Great Western Railway and the London and North Eastern Railway) joined together under a single management structure. For a list of heritage railways running '40s events refer to Chapter 13: Events.

Some heritage railways have collections of wartime rolling stock. The West Somerset Railway prides itself on having probably the largest collection of wartime wagons and offers a wartime freight train as part of its '40s commemorations. In 2018 the 'military freight' was headed by a United States Army Transportation Corps S160 Class locomotive. A total of 2,120 of these engines were made to a design by Major J.W.

Marsh of the US Corps of Engineers; 800 were imported to Britain in two batches. The first batch of 400 engines was distributed between the big four railway companies ostensibly for 'running in'. In reality they were used to replace damaged engines and increase the overall capacity of the railway network in the run-up to D-Day. The second batch of 400 engines was stored at the Great Western Railway's Ebbw Junction in readiness to be shipped to Europe.

Among the West Somerset Railway's wartime wagons is number 105493. This Gunpowder van was built in 1924 as part of lot 935. Two types of van, classified as Z2 and Z3, were designed and built between 1913 and 1926, for transporting gunpowder and explosives; 105493 is a Z3 model. When positioned in a train, gunpowder wagons were always shunted into the middle to avoid sparks from the loco or brake van. The roof was painted white to avoid the explosives inside overheating. The sides of the wagon were clearly marked up to indicate hazardous contents. 105493 was in use until the mid–1960s and arrived on the WSR in 1976.

While attending heritage railway 40s events it is always worth checking their rolling stock - there are often many hidden treasures to be revealed!

CHAPTER TWELVE

LIVING WITH THE '40s STYLE

For many, the love of the '40s is a hobby which provides a social opportunity to engage with others several times a year at events all over the country. For those in military groups there are arguably more opportunities to meet because such groups need regular training sessions to ensure that they remain as authentic as possible in their drill, weapons handling and appearance. However, for some the '40s becomes more of a way of life and the line between hobby and 'normal' life becomes less distinct. Some '40s enthusiasts choose to get married in '40s clothing with guests similarly attired, while others embrace the period more fully by reverting to '40s furnishings and utensils in their homes. Some create gardens based on the guidance of the 'Dig for Victory' campaign, while others focus on rescuing Anderson Shelters and re-erecting them in their gardens – often fully equipped with period furniture and accessories.

It is always tempting to imagine what an older property might have looked like at different stages in its life. Very old buildings will have seen multiple changes but properties built in the late nineteenth century or in the housing boom of the inter-war years often retain features from when they were first built, for example fire-places and possibly some art-deco styling. If you are a collector of 1940s furniture and other items, then what better way to display them than by returning the house back to the period either by sacrificing modern conveniences, or at least sensitively hiding them.

Hannah Hall's 40s kitchen clearly evokes the sense of period while remaining functional.
— With permission Hannah Hall

LIVING WITH THE '40S STYLE

Hannah Hall purchased an inter-war house in Nottingham and has set about returning it to its former glory. The idea started when Hannah's grandparents gave her some items of antique furniture and the project has grown from there.

Hannah explains:

> "my biggest fascination with the '40s is the overall aesthetic; the music, the fashion, the furniture; however, I am not ignorant to the fact that this era was one of struggle and I think that that just adds to my fascination. The '40s strike me as the era of 'making-good', living simply and using your initiative, all things that I have been bought up to value as a child of a single-parent, working-class household. And what I love the most is that, in spite of such turmoil, it feels like the people's spirit never died."

In many ways the house is a tribute to Hannah's grandfather who was born in 1936 and whose stories of his early life led to Hannah's fascination with the period. Lisa Knappett also credits her grandparents' influence with her interest in the '40s noting that:

> "I loved their stories from the wartime, one was a Land Girl the other was in the WVS. Both married men in the services – both of my grandads were involved in D-Day. My partner Steve's grandad was an engineer in the RAF so we were always aware of the importance of the '40s."

RE-LIVING BRITAIN IN THE 1940S

Lisa's partner is the proud owner of two classic cars and both of them are immersed in the style and music of the period.

Hannah was able to buy a working 1940s gas cooker from eBay, and piece by piece she has worked on replacing modern furniture and equipment with period counterparts. She explains, 'the theme really started to take off when we did the kitchen in a 1940s style and we

The modern CD collection blends seamlessly with the original fireplace and 40s décor.

— With permission Lisa Knappett

LIVING WITH THE '40S STYLE

loved it so much that we decided we really wanted to go with that theme throughout the house'.

Having finished work on the kitchen, Hannah turned her attention to the rest of the house and began stripping back laminated flooring and carpet to reveal the original wooden floorboards and staircase. Today the floors are stripped and polished, while the stairs have a period 1940s stair carpet runner. Bit by bit other pieces have been added to the different rooms, including a stunning oak wardrobe proudly standing adjacent to the original cast-iron fireplace. Period styled wallpaper and everyday items complete the impression. Lisa and Steve's house is similarly 'full of old furniture or inherited furniture and I collect vintage clothes, hats, bags etc too,' explains Lisa.

Hannah does admit to owning a TV and games consoles, adding, 'I am not somebody who boycotts the modern world. There's lots of things about the modern world that I love, but the past is what really speaks to me. I'm a sucker for nostalgia.' Lisa similarly blends vintage with modern as she explains:

> *"there's not a right or wrong in my mind as we are living today and not actually in the '40s. So, we just enjoy whatever vintage elements we want to have and build them around our modern lives to the best of our ability. It's a way of life and it's who you are!"*

The reaction of others to life in a period styled home could be a challenge, but Hannah explains that:

> *"my friends and family understand that vintage is just who I am and so they are more than used to it by now. Some people think that it's odd when we choose*

> to use older things rather than new (tin openers, mop buckets, weighing scales, wardrobes, phones, drawers etc) but I think that they can appreciate that it's a passion of ours and, because it makes us happy, they understand."

When asked what advice Hannah might have for others wanting to recreate a period home Hannah suggested that the key is:

> "Be patient, unearthing a home's original features takes time, I can't tell you how many hours we've spent stripping door frames and skirting boards! And as far as putting in a 1940s style stair runner, not as easy as you think! But enjoy the process as much as you can. Secondly, charity shops are your new best friend and

A comfortable 1940s sofa and coffee table help to create a period ambience.
— With permission Lisa Knappett

LIVING WITH THE '40S STYLE

really do have the most marvellous pieces at next to no money! Thirdly, if you see a piece that you like – buy it! And finally, it's all about preservation, older things need more love and care but the satisfaction that you get from refurbishing them is really something! In our house, old truly is gold!"

Apart from the electric kettle (still vintage), this kitchen is straight from the 40s from the Belfast sink, to the period cleaning products, and even the carpet beater by the door!

– With permission Trad Casey

Lisa and Steve are similarly accepted by their friends.

> "We attend many vintage events each year and have many friends who share our interests. I set my hair in rollers often. Our friends and family are used to it. When the kids were younger, they would sometimes feel embarrassed but now they are old enough to fully embrace it. We always get lots of compliments when we are out"

…notes Lisa, whose advice to others interested in living '40s is:

> "it's very expensive as a lifestyle if you want to be truly authentic, but follow your dreams and just wear what makes you happy as individuals."

During the 1940s the Anderson Shelter was a common sight in gardens all over the country in areas likely to be targeted by the Luftwaffe bombers. The shelters were named after Sir John Anderson who had been placed in charge of Air Raid Precautions by Prime Minister Neville Chamberlain. Anderson charged engineer William Patterson with designing a cheap, prefabricated shelter which people could site in their gardens. Almost 1 million shelters were produced and distributed within a matter of months, comprising six curved panels bolted together, with flat sheets at either end. At 6ft 6in long by 4ft 6in wide, the Anderson Shelter could accommodate six people and proved to be remarkably efficient when properly dug into the ground. Half buried in the ground, the excavated soil was heaped on top to provide extra blast protection – and also a further 'raised bed' for planting vegetables!

Conditions in the Anderson Shelters were often quite unpleasant. Many were perpetually damp and some actually flooded. Furnishings were basic and limited and few had the luxury of any heating. A contemporary poem, by N.A. Roberts who lived in Southall at the time, published in a newspaper during the war, gives some insight into conditions:

> *"The Siren sounds,*
> *And over the floor*
> *Come a patter of feet*
> *To the shelter door.*
> *We children jump in,*
> *Then follows young Pat;*
> *We jump into bed,*
> *And push out the cat –*
> *Then after a while*
> *In follows our Mum*
> *With her hair done up tight*
> *In a boisterous bun;*
> *She gets into place*
> *With a thump and a thud,*
> *And throws out her shoes,*
> *Which are covered in mud.*
> *Next comes our sister –*
> *Gladys by name –*
> *She's as big as our mother*
> *And comes in the same.*
> *She slides into place,*
> *And we all wait for dad,*

Who sleeps in the middle
Of Mother and Glad.
We all settle down –
And read for a bit –
But sometimes Mother
Will sit up and knit;
Then Dad puts the light out
And we go to sleep.
We've been going down shelter
For many a week."

After the war many shelters were dug up and reused as garden sheds and indeed, surplus shelters were sold by the government for just that purpose. Today, a few remain in their original locations and occasional privately built concrete bunkers still come to light as unsuspecting householders make alterations to their properties.

As years went by these iconic structures were often abandoned as too small and the sections reused to border compost bins and for other uses – many established allotments still contain elements of Anderson Shelters to this day! Recently the Anderson Shelter has seen a resurgence in its popularity and many people are now rescuing decaying and rusting shelters and restoring them as a feature in their gardens. So popular has this become that the hobby has its own Facebook group – unsurprisingly called 'Anderson Shelter in your garden' with almost 2,000 members (www.facebook.com/groups/944044549053735). Because original Anderson Shelters are becoming harder to find, and often require a lot of remedial work to remove rust and corrosion, a company called Tinman Steels Ltd has produced a reproduction shelter to exactly the same specifications as the originals (www.tinmansteelsltd.co.uk).

LIVING WITH THE '40S STYLE

Trad Casey has a 'Tinman' shelter in his garden which is properly sunk into the ground and equipped with essential supplies. It even has a cooking stove to ensure that even the longest air raid can be seen out without too much discomfort. A roll of 'Izal' toilet paper is present to remind people of the older generations of the horrors of wartime, and later, 'waterproof' toilet paper. Toilet paper was not rationed during the war, but not always easily available so cut up pieces of newspaper were often used as an alternative. There are a number of original, government issued information pamphlets giving advice on what to do after a raid and wartime cooking. A small number of first aid items are

Trad Casey mows the lawn outside his 'Tinman' made Anderson shelter.
– With permission Trad Casey

ready for use and the gas mask is securely stored. Even an original 'rat-tail' spanner (provided with the original wartime shelters) is present on the shelf in case any repairs are required.

As the '40s recede further into the mists of history, and those who lived through those turbulent years leave us, the style and music of the period continue to captivate. As we enjoy the spirit of the '40s let us remember that the freedom to do so was won by those who served in any capacity – **'We Shall Remember Them!'**

CHAPTER THIRTEEN
EVENTS

There are many heritage events throughout the country reflecting the growing popularity and interest in this hobby. Some are large scale events, with literally thousands of participants, whereas others are smaller and focused on a town or museum. Increasingly, heritage railways are also staging commemorative events which use the sights and sounds of steam engines to bring another dimension to these events.

No list of events can be exhaustive and dates may vary due to clashes and other factors, and some events may terminate. An up-to-date list of events planned for the current year can be found on Marie and Pete Bainbridge's website **'Love of the '40s'** (loveofthe40s.co.uk) or their Facebook page '**1940s Events & Social Space**' (www.facebook.com/groups/387972647928436). The list below shows annual events and the month in which they traditionally fall by region. All links were correct at the time of writing.

SOUTH-WEST

APRIL

'**Wartime in the Cotswolds**' on the Gloucestershire Warwickshire Railway – www.facebook.com/wartimeinthecotswolds

'**World at War Living History Weekend**' at the Helicopter Museum, Weston Super Mare – www.helicoptermuseum.co.uk/events.htm

JUNE

'**Dig for Victory**' at Ashton Court, Bristol – www.digforvictoryshow.com

'**Saunton D Day**' – www.facebook.com/sauntondday

JULY

'**1940s Festival**' on the South Devon Railway – www.southdevonrailway.co.uk

SEPTEMBER

'**West Somerset Railway Forties Weekend**' – www.facebook.com/groups/113201029316194

'**Avon Valley Railway 1940s Weekend**' – www.avonvalleyrailway.org/events/1940s-weekend

EVENTS

'Bude at War – The Day the Americans Came' – www.facebook.com/BudeAtWar

SOUTH-EAST

MAY

'Sandwich Salutes the '40s' – sandwichevents.org.uk/sandwich-salutes-the-40s

'Tilford a Village at War' – Google search for latest details

JUNE

'Southwick Village D-Day Revival' – www.southwickrevival.co.uk

'1940's Weekend' on the Buckinghamshire Railway – bucksrailcentre.org/section.php/2/1/special-events

'Newport Pagnell & Allies Vintage Wartime Event' – Google for latest details

'Mapledurham at War' – RG4 7TR

'Hever Castle Homefront Weekend' – www.hevercastle.co.uk/whats-on

'War on the Line' – www.watercressline.co.uk

JULY

'Bletchley Park, 1940s Vintage Weekend' –

www.tnmoc.org/events

'War and Peace Revival' is simply the largest '40s event in the nation – warandpeacerevival.com

'Battles for Victory' at Quex Park, Birchington-on-Sea –

www.battlesforvictory.com

'1940s Experience @ Isle of Wight Steam Railway' –

iwsteamrailway.co.uk/events

AUGUST

'Retro Festival' at Newbury – www.retrofestival.co.uk

SEPTEMBER

'1940s Hope and Glory Show' – at Gravesend. Google search for latest dates and details

'Salute to the '40s' at the historic Chatham –

thedockyard.co.uk/whats-on

'Bletchley Park, 1940s Vintage Weekend' –

bletchleypark.org.uk/whats-on

EAST

APRIL

'**Colne Valley at War**' on the Colne Valley Railway – CO9 3DZ

MAY

'**Temple at War**' at Cressing Temple Barns –
www.templeatwar.co.uk

'**Middy in the War Years**' or Mid-Suffolk Light Railway –
www.mslr.org.uk/visit-us/middy-in-the-war-years

'**The Vintage Weekend**' at the Swan Hotel, Lavenham –
theswanatlavenham.co.uk/events

'**1940s Day**' at Bressingham –
www.bressingham.co.uk/events.aspx

JUNE

'**1940s Steam Weekend**' on the Epping Ongar Railway –
www.eorailway.co.uk/events

JULY

'**Festival of the Forties**' at March, Cambs –
www.facebook.com/groups/1489350397775488

RE-LIVING BRITAIN IN THE 1940S

'Mid-Norfolk Railway 1940s Weekend' –

www.mnr.org.uk/events

'Echoes of the Past' at the Rougham Control Tower Aviation Museum, Bury St Edmunds – rctam94th.co.uk

'1940s Event' at the Prickwillow Engine Museum –

www.prickwillowmuseum.com/event-days.html

'Ramsey 1940s Weekend' –

www.facebook.com/groups/115210545172557

AUGUST

'Twinwood' is the ultimate vintage festival for music and dance –

https://twinwoodevents.com

'Echoes of History Show' –

10times.com/military-flying-machines

SEPTEMBER

'The 1940's Weekend' on the North Norfolk Railway –

www.nnrailway.co.uk/special-events

EAST MIDLANDS

MAY

'Great Central Railway 1940s Wartime' –

www.gcrailway.co.uk/wartime

EVENTS

JUNE

'**Retro Festival**' at Newark – www.retrofestival.co.uk

'**Clumber Park 1940's Weekend**' – www.nationaltrust.org.uk/clumber-park

AUGUST

'**Alford 1940s**' – www.facebook.com/alford1940sweekend

'**Harborough at War**' based at Market Harborough Showground – harboroughatwar.co.uk

SEPTEMBER

'**The Victory Show**' is one of the largest '40s events taking place at Foxlands farm, Cosby, Leics. – www.thevictoryshow.co.uk

'**Rufford Abbey 1940s Weekend**' – NG22 9DF

'**Newstead Abbey 1940s Weekend**' – newsteadabbey.org.uk/category/events

OCTOBER

'**'40s Weekend**' at Rushden Transport Museum & Railway – rhts.co.uk

'**Autumn 1940s Weekend**' at the Newark Air Museum – www.newarkairmuseum.org/latest-news

'**Papplewick Pumping Station**' – www.papplewickpumpingstation.org.uk/visit-us.html

WEST MIDLANDS

APRIL

'**Armed Forces & 1940's Weekend**' at Stavely Hall –
www.staveleyhall.co.uk

MAY

'**Ironbridge Gorge WW2**' –
www.ironbridgeww2weekend.co.uk

JUNE

'**Wartime in the Vale**' takes place at Ashdown WWII Camp –
www.ashdowncamp.com/events

'**Black Country Living Museum**' – bclm.com

'**Step Back to the 1940s**' at the Severn Valley Railway –
www.svr.co.uk/whats-on

AUGUST

'**The Second World War Home Front**' at Crich Tramway Museum – www.tramway.co.uk/whatson

SEPTEMBER

'**Wheels of War Weekend & '40s Dance**' at the Crewe Heritage Centre – crewehc.org

EVENTS

WALES

APRIL

'1940s Homefront Weekend' – llangollen-railway.co.uk/events

'Colwyn Bay Forties Festival' – LL29 8DF

MAY

'War Time Wheels' at Caldicot Castle – www.facebook.com/Wartimewheels

JUNE

'Wartime Bridgend' – www.facebook.com/wartimebridgend

JULY

'Vintage for Victory' at the library Gardens, Whitchurch – www.vintageforvictory.co.uk

SEPTEMBER

'Welshpool 1940s Weekend' – welshpool1940sweekend.co.uk

NORTH-WEST

APRIL

'**A Seaside '40s Weekend**' at the North Euston Hotel, Fleetwood – www.northeustonhotel.com/whats-on

MAY

'**East Lancashire Railway 1940s Weekend**' – www.eastlancsrailway.org.uk/events

JULY

'**Ingleton 1940s**' – www.facebook.com/Ingleton1940s

AUGUST

'**Lytham War Weekend**' – www.discoverfylde.co.uk/lytham1940s

'**Yanks are Back in Saddleworth**' – www.facebook.com/groups/416876551672249

'**The Morecombe 1940s Revival**' – m40srev.weebly.com

EVENTS

YORKSHIRE & HUMBERSIDE

MARCH

'WW2 Living History Weekend' at Eden Camp –
www.edencamp.co.uk/events

'WW2 Living History Day – NWW2A' at Eden Camp –
www.edencamp.co.uk/events

APRIL

'WW2 Living History Weekend' at Eden Camp –
www.edencamp.co.uk/events

'York Festival of Vintage' – www.festivalofvintage.co.uk

MAY

'Thorne 1940s Weekend' – DN8 5BE

'Haworth 1940s Weekend' –
www.facebook.com/haworth1940s

JUNE

'Brighouse 1940's Weekend' –
www.brighouse1940sweekend.co.uk

'Queensbury 1940s Event' – BD13 4AJ

RE-LIVING BRITAIN IN THE 1940S

'Bridlington Old Town 1940s Event' –
www.bridlingtonoldtown.com/oldtown–1940s-celebration.php

'Valley Gardens 1940s Day' at Harrogate –
Google search for latest dates and details

JULY

'Appleby 1940s Festival' –
www.facebook.com/applebyhomefront

'Leyburn 1940s' – www.leyburn1940sweekend.org

'The Yorkshire Wartime Experience' –
www.nelz60.moonfruit.com

'Thorpe Camp 1940s Weekend' –
thorpecamp.wixsite.com/1940sweekend

'Woodhall Spa '40s Festival' – woodhall-spa-40s-festival.com

'Meltham Memories' –
www.facebook.com/events/547513193191515

'1940s Weekend' on the Aln Valley Railway –
www.alnvalleyrailway.co.uk

AUGUST

'Baston in the Blitz' – www.facebook.com/Baston.in.the.Blitz

'Salute to the 1940s' at the International Bomber Command Centre
– internationalbcc.co.uk/about-ibcc/news/events/salute-to-the-40s

EVENTS

'**WW2 Living History Weekend**' at Eden Camp –
www.edencamp.co.uk/events/1940s-living-history

'**North Thoresby 1940s Event**' –
www.facebook.com/NorthThoresby1940sEvent

'**1940s Weekend**' on the Lincolnshire Wolds Railway –
lincolnshirewoldsrailway.co.uk

'**Lincoln 1940s Weekend**' – www.visitlincoln.com/whats-on

'**Ayscoughfee Hall 1940s Weekend**' – PE11 2RA

SEPTEMBER

'**Grassington 1940s Weekend**' –
www.grassington1940sweekend.co.uk

'**Crowle and Ealand 1940s Weekend**' –
www.facebook.com/crowleandealand1940s

OCTOBER

'**Pickering 1940s Weekend**' –
www.nymr.co.uk/Pages/Events/Category/events

NORTH-EAST

MAY

'**Blyth Battery goes to war**' – blythbattery.org.uk

JUNE

'**Springwell Village 1940s Weekend**' – www.facebook.com/sv1940 or www.svcv.co.uk/events/1940s-weekend

AUGUST

'**Dig for Victory**' at Beamish Museum – www.beamish.org.uk/whats-on

SCOTLAND

JUNE

'**Keith and Duff Town Railway 1940s Weekend**' – keith-dufftown-railway.co.uk/1940s-weekend

APPENDIX

ACRONYMS USED IN THE TEXT

AAC	Anti-Aircraft Command
ADGB	Air Defence Great Britain
AFS	Auxiliary Fire Service
AOC	Air Officer Commanding
ARP	(Air) Raid Precautions
ATA	Air Transport Auxiliary
ATS	Auxiliary Territorial Service
BD	Battledress
BEF	British Expeditionary Force
CD	Civil Defence
CiC	Commander in Chief
CIGS	Chief of Imperial General Staff
CMP	Corps of Military Police
COSSAC	Chief of Staff to Supreme Allied Commander
DC	Decontamination Parties
ENSA	Entertainments National Service Association
FANY	(First Aid Nursing Yeomanry) Women's Transport Service

FAP	First Aid Posts
FG	Fire Guard
GOC	General Officer Commanding
HAA	Heavy Anti-Aircraft
HR	Heavy Rescue
HSAT	Helmet Steel Airborne Troops
IRA	Irish Republican Army
LDV	Local Defence Volunteers
LMG	Light Machine Gun
LR	Light Rescue
MMG	Medium Machine Gun
MP	Military Police
MVT	Military Vehicle Trust
NFS	National Fire Service
NARPAC	National Air Raid Precautions Animal Committee
NCO	Non-Commissioned Officer
NSDAP	National Socialist German Workers Party (Nazis)
OB	Operational Base
OC	Observer Corps
OP	Operational Patrol
PDSA	People's Dispensary for Sick Animals
PLI	Public Liability Insurance
QAIMNS	Queen Alexandra's Imperial Military Nursing Service
QF	Quick Firing
RA	Royal Artillery
RAF	Royal Air Force
RAMC	Royal Army Medical Corps

ACRONYMS USED IN THE TEXT

RASC	Royal Army Service Corps
REME	Royal Electrical and Mechanical Engineers
RFC	Royal Flying Corps
RM	Royal Marines
RN	Royal Navy
RNAS	Royal Naval Air Service
ROC	Royal Observer Corps
RSC	Royal Signals Corps
RE	Royal Engineers
REME	Royal Electrical and Mechanical Engineers
RSPCA	Royal Society for the Prevention of Cruelty to Animals
SD	Service Dress
SFP	Street/Supplementary Fire Party
SMLE	Short Magazine Lee Enfield
SOE	Special Operations Executive
SP	Stretcher Parties
VC	Victoria Cross
WAAC	Women's Army Auxiliary Corps
WAAF	Women's Auxiliary Air Force
WHD	Woman's Home Defence
WLA	Women's Land Army
WRAC	Women's Royal Army Corps
WRNS	Women's Royal Naval Service
WTC	Women's Timber Corps
WVS	Women's Voluntary Service

WITH THANKS:

A book like this always leans heavily on the willingness of others to share their knowledge and photographs and I am grateful to all who have offered help in any way. Any factual mistakes are mine alone.

My wife Sophie Wichard has been a pillar of strength and support throughout, as ever.

Sincere thanks also go to Joanna Rycroft who undertook the proof reading.